The Oregon Literature Series

General Editor: George Venn
Managing Editor: Ulrich H. Hardt

Volume 4: Oregon Poetry

A project of the Oregon Council of Teachers of English

The Oregon Literature Series

The World Begins Here: An Anthology of Oregon Short Fiction
  Glen A. Love

Many Faces: An Anthology of Oregon Autobiography
  Stephen Dow Beckham

Varieties of Hope: An Anthology of Oregon Prose
  Gordon B. Dodds

From Here We Speak: An Anthology of Oregon Poetry
  Ingrid Wendt & Primus St. John

The Stories We Tell: An Anthology of Oregon Folk Literature
  Suzi Jones & Jarold Ramsey

Talking on Paper: An Anthology of Oregon Letters & Diaries
  Shannon Applegate & Terence O'Donnell

From Here We Speak
An Anthology of Oregon Poetry

Ingrid Wendt & Primus St. John

 Oregon State University Press
Corvallis, Oregon

Dedication

In the name of all Oregon poets
To the living memory of
William Stafford
Cherished mentor and friend
We dedicate this book.

Cover art: Detail from "Southern Exposure" by Jennifer Joyce
Cover design: John Bennett
Text design: Jo Alexander
Permissions: Susanne Shotola
Photographers: Susan Seubert, Ron Finne

The publication of this book is supported in part by a grant from the National Endowment for the Arts in Washington, D.C., a federal agency

The paper in this book meets the guidelines for permanence and durability of the Committee on Production Guidelines for Book Longevity of the Council on Library Resources and the minimum requirements of the American National Standard for Permanence of Paper for Printed Library Materials Z39.48-1984.

Library of Congress Cataloging-in-Publication Data

From here we speak : an anthology of Oregon poetry / Ingrid Wendt, Primus St. John

    p. cm. -- (Oregon literature series : v. 4)

    Includes bibliographic references and index.

    summary : An anthology of Oregon poetry from Native American tribal lyrics to the present.

    ISBN 0-87071-375-2 (cloth : alk. paper). -- ISBN 0-87071-376-0 (pbk: alk. paper)

    1. American poetry--Oregon. 2. Oregon--Poetry. [1. Oregon--Poetry. 2. American poetry--Collections.] I. Wendt, Ingrid. 1944- . II. St. John, Primus, 1939- . III. Series.

    PS571.07F76   1993

    811.008'09795-dc20   93-39979

                                               CIP

                                                 AC

Acknowledgments

Without steady collaboration by many individuals, agencies, and institutions, the *Oregon Literature Series* would never have appeared in print. We wish to recognize those who contributed support, time, and resources here—more or less in the order in which their contributions were received—and knowing that the real evidence of our gratitude lies open before all of them now.

In 1986, the Executive Committee of the Oregon Council of Teachers of English (OCTE) began to discuss the idea of publishing a collection of Oregon literature. We wish to identify the members of that Executive Committee and thank them for their pioneering role: Lauri Crocker, Joe Fitzgibbon, Robert Hamm, Ulrich Hardt, Michelann Ortloff, and Ed Silling. Under then-OCTE President Ulrich Hardt, the Publications Committee was given the goal to further develop the idea of a state-based literary collection.

In 1988-89, the Executive Board of OCTE approved the pilot study by George Venn which became the *Oregon Literature Series*. We would like to recognize the members of that distinguished professional group of teachers by listing them here: Brian Borton, Sister Helena Brand, Suzanne Clark, Darlene Clarridge, Elaine Cockrell, Edna De Haven, Joe Fitzgibbon, Robert Boyt Foster, David Freitag, Debra Gaffney, Tim Gillespie, Irene Golden, Robert Hamm, Ulrich H. Hardt, Martha House, Ilene Kemper, Debbie LaCroix, Bill Mull, Thomas Nash, Debby Norman, Michelann Ortloff, Phyllis Reynolds, Eldene Ridinger, Mei-Ling Shiroishi, Andy Sommer, Daune Spritzer, Kim Stafford, Lana Stanley, Kathy Steward, Paul Suter, Nathaniel Teich, Linda Vanderford, George Venn, Michael Wendt, and Barbara Wolfe. Many members of that board gave many extra hours to reviewing the design, editorial guidelines, rationale, and budgets for that pilot project and other documents.

We would also like to acknowledge the following individuals from Oregon's literary and humanities community who reviewed the pilot proposal, made valuable suggestions, and gave their endorsement in 1988 to the idea of a collection of the best Oregon writing: Richard Lewis, Oregon Council for the Humanities; Brian Booth, Oregon Institute of Literary Arts; Peter Sears, Oregon Arts Commission; Jo Alexander, Oregon State University Press; Bruce Hamilton, Oregon Historical Society. OCTE President in 1988, Tim Gillespie, and Joe Fitzgibbon, OCTE President Elect, also reviewed the pilot proposal and made important contributions not only in these early stages but throughout the project.

When we presented the completed proposal for the *Oregon Literature Series* to the Editorial Board of Oregon State University Press in 1989, they broke with all precedent by signing a guaranteed publication contract and by agreeing to turn over editorial control of the content of the *Oregon Literature Series* to OCTE editors and appointees. We want to thank both press editors, Jeff Grass and Jo Alexander, and these members of that board who voted unanimously in favor of this project: Pat Brandt, Larry Boersma, Richard Maxwell Brown, Bill Denison, Gordon Dodds, Mike Strelow,

Dave Perry, Sandy Ridlington, and the late Marilyn Guin. Without their vote for collaboration and its implicit vote of confidence in us, we would have found it difficult to continue this project.

Our first financial support beyond OCTE was provided by a pilot grant from Eastern Oregon State College, School of Education. Specifically, we wish to thank Deans Jens Robinson, Gerald Young, and James Hottois for their willingness to grant a sabbatical and three years of part-time appointments to George Venn so that this project could be undertaken. At Portland State University, we want to thank Dean Robert Everhart, School of Education, for his steadfast support. He granted Ulrich Hardt a sabbatical to help launch the project, and he continued that support throughout the four years of the project. At Portland State University, we also want to acknowledge Interim Provost Robert Frank and Provost Michael Reardon for the faith they showed in the project by assigning graduate assistant Susanne Shotola to help us.

When we drafted our "Call for Editors" in 1989, we received helpful critiques from Kim Stafford, Edwin Bingham, Paul Suter, Sister Helena Brand, Edna DeHaven, Daune Spritzer, Lana Stanley, Michelann Ortloff, as well as other members of the OCTE Executive Board. When it was time to mail that "Call for Editors" to all Oregon libraries, newspapers, and other regional and national media, Lana Stanley assisted us. When it was time to select Volume Editors, these Publications Committee members assisted us: Robert Hamm, Marti House, Ilene Kemper, Debbie LaCroix, Mei-Ling Shiroishi, Michael Wendt, and Linda Vanderford. We'd like to thank them for the many hours they gave to evaluating the applications of 130 highly qualified individuals from Oregon and across the U.S. who applied for or were nominated for editorships.

When we needed to verify that these anthologies would, indeed, be both needed and used in the public schools, Portland State University School of Business Administration faculty member Bruce Stern gave us important assistance in designing a survey instrument which demonstrated a clear demand for the *Oregon Literature Series* in Oregon schools and homes. When we needed public relations expertise during editorial appointments, Pat Scott in the Portland State University Public Relations Office provided it.

When we needed legal advice, Leonard DuBoff and his firm of Warren, Allan, King, and O'Hara were more than helpful in contributing their contractual expertise.

As the project began to take a clear and definite shape in 1989, we received formal endorsements from these individuals whose confidence in the project made it possible to continue in spite of meager funding: Wes Doak, Oregon State Librarian, and Director, Center for the Book; Brian Booth, Director of Oregon Institute of Literary Arts; Kim Stafford, Director of the Northwest Writing Institute at Lewis and Clark College; Jennifer Hagloch, President of the Oregon Museums Association; Richard Lewis, Executive Director, Oregon Council for the Humanities; Joanne Cowling, President of the Eastern Oregon Library Association; Leslie Tuomi, Executive Director of the Oregon Arts Commission; Peter Sears, Oregon Arts Commission; Michael K. Gaston, President, Oregon Library Association; John Erickson, State Superintendent of Public Instruction; Carolyn Meeker, Chair, Oregon Arts Commission; Carolyn Lott, Chair,

National Council of Teachers of English (NCTE) Committee on Affiliates; Shirley Haley-James, President-Elect of NCTE; the late William Stafford, Oregon's past poet laureate; and Terry Melton, Director of the Western States Arts Foundation.

Essential financial support after 1989 came first from a generous allocation from the OCTE Executive Board. Later, we received modest one-time contributions from the Oregon Center for the Book and the Jackson Foundation. We would also like to state that this project was made possible—in part—by two minor grants from the Oregon Arts Commission.

Our sustaining patrons in the final four years (1990-94) of the project have been five; each of them contributed amounts in five figures so that the *Oregon Literature Series* could be completed in a timely and professional manner:

(1) the OCTE Executive Board, who sustained and underwrote us when regional foundations failed us;

(2) the Oregon Council for the Humanities, an affiliate of the National Endowment for the Humanities, which made and honored an exemplary three-year commitment ably administered by Robert Keeler;

(3) the National Endowment for the Arts, Literature Program, which assisted us at a time when we had been sent begging by all but one of the private foundations in Oregon;

(4) Portland State University, which granted multi-year support for graduate assistant Susanne Shotola to help with the many details of the publication of this six-volume series;

(5) Oregon State University Press, where Jo Alexander and Jeff Grass contributed the vital tasks agreed to in 1989—designing, printing, and distributing these volumes. OSU Press set a national precedent by becoming the first university press in the United States to publish a multi-volume, comprehensive collection of a state's literature in the same state where the university press is located.

When we came to recommending graphics and cover designs for the *Oregon Literature Series* in 1992, we welcomed the generous and expert advice of three of Oregon's most knowledgeable art historians: Ron Crosier, Portland Public Schools; Gordon Gilkey, Curator, Portland Art Museum; and Nancy Lindburg, arts consultant and former staff member of the Oregon Arts Commission. Some of the works they recommended were selected by them from the slide inventory in Oregon's Percent for Art in Public Places Program. Other works were chosen from the Gordon and Vivian Gilkey Collection of Prints and Drawings at the Oregon Art Institute, and from the Institute's collection of photographs. Petroglyph images were provided by James L. Hansen from sites flooded by The Dalles dam. In addition to those three individuals, we were also fortunate to attract the services of John Bennett, book designer and publisher at Gardyloo Press in Corvallis, who collaborated on all features of the graphic design, and created covers for these volumes.

No literary project of this magnitude can be accomplished without skillful and reliable staff. The General and Managing Editors would like to express their profound appreciation to Susanne Shotola and Barbara Wiegele—both of Portland State University—for their patient, professional, and timely attention to thousands of pages of details during the past four years: keeping accurate records, handling all permissions and finances, doing all the copying, typing, and mailing. We thanked them during the project and here we want to thank them again. Thank you, too, to Gayle Stevenson, editorial assistant at OSU Press, for many hours of patient labor on this project.

Unfortunately, this naming of our benefactors will be incomplete. We cannot list here all of those writers, families, and institutions who waived permissions fees, those innumerable librarians, archivists, storytellers, and historians who have safeguarded many of these pieces of writing for more than 100 years, those many who sent us notes of encouragement, those members of the public press who considered this project worthy of coverage. What we can say, however, is that every contribution moved us one page closer to the volume you now hold in your hands. Those others who failed us when we needed them most—they may eat—well?—cake?

Finally, George Venn would like to thank his wife Elizabeth who has tolerated great financial sacrifice for four years and who has begun to wonder about this tough, miserly Oregon muse her husband seems to have been serving at the expense of his art and her budget. Also, Ulrich Hardt would like to thank his wife, Eleanor, for her insights and interest in this project as Social Studies Specialist for Portland Public Schools, and for being more patient than could have been expected and tolerant of being alone many evenings and weekends while he was occupied with editorial responsibilities.

Ulrich Hardt, Managing Editor
Portland State University
Portland and Stuttgart

George Venn, General Editor
Grande Ronde Valley, Oregon
September 1992

Editors' Preface and Acknowledgments

For a listing of the criteria guiding our decisions, we direct the reader to George Venn's General Introduction (page ix), where he lists nine guidelines for the *Oregon Literature Series* given to all editors by the Oregon Council of Teachers of English. Given the nature of this particular volume, we added two more: that we include Oregon poets of national and international reputation and stature, and that we represent poets who have made significant contributions to the life of Oregon letters.

To find these poems we began by going to the library—to previous anthologies and to the work of scholars before us—for material by poets no longer living. For living poets, we began by sending letters of invitation to those whose work we knew and admired as well as to poets recommended to us by our Advisory Board and other respected colleagues. Shortly thereafter, fearing oversights, and purposely seeking new and still-unheralded poets, we opened submissions by announcing our project in *Poets and Writers* and the *AWP Chronicle*, two nationally distributed newsletters, in the newsletter of the Oregon Arts Commission, through regional arts councils, and in major Oregon newspapers.

With well over three thousand submissions to consider, as well as a gold mine of historical riches to unearth, a clear division of labor became necessary. Parts I to IV of the book, poets born before 1930, would be researched and compiled by Wendt; responsibility for Part V of the book, poets born after 1930, would be assumed by St. John. While both editors read everything under consideration and offered each other suggestions, each editor made final decisions and prepared introductions, headnotes, and bibliography for the agreed-upon part or parts of the book.

After more than three years of careful and continuous labor, and despite the inadvertent oversights we trust others to discover, we present this anthology with pride and with thanks for the privilege of having been its editors.

In finding and in choosing the selections for this book, we have been helped by many people. They include friends, colleagues, librarians, museum curators, regional arts councils, Oregon citizens, and the contributors to this book, who have shared information and given us their enthusiastic support.

The Oregon State Library, Special Collections librarians James Fox, Fraser Cocks, and Bernie McTigue, and many reference librarians at the University of Oregon, Elizabeth Bickford at the Oregon State Historical Society, as well as librarians in Astoria, Port Orford, Grant County, and Coquille (Oregon), Caldwell (Idaho), and Bellingham (Washington), went out of their way to help us. Peter Sears and Vincent Dunn of the Oregon Arts Commission, and the coordinators of regional arts councils throughout the state, helped put out the call for manuscripts. Others also helped in the search, especially Lynda Jasso, Joanne Mulcahey, Centro Cultural (Cornelius), Marjorie Edens, Sara Jameson, Andrea Lerner, Ann Koppy of the Coos Historical Society, Jack Bennett, Elizabeth Woody, Vincent Dunn, William Hotchkiss, Judith Shears, Tom Fertè, and Nan Hammond. The late William Stafford not only suggested names, but provided some photos. Relatives of poets also were of help to us, including Miriam Ostroff, Eldridge Huffman, Anna Smith, Virginia Corning, and Catherine Evenson. We wish to thank them all.

A special acknowledgment of indebtedness is due to certain scholars whose previous anthologies and recent pioneering studies in Oregon history and literature have been invaluable to us. These include Alfred Powers, Ruth McBride Powers, Edwin (Bing) Bingham, Glen Love, Stephen Beckham, George Venn, Michael Strelow, Anita Helle, Tim Barnes, and Karen Reyes. Prior scholarship in Native American literature by Dell Hymes, Brian Swann, and Jarold Ramsey has provided material otherwise inaccessible to us, and we thank these authors also for the great amount of time they spent in correspondence with us, offering suggestions, corrections, and advice.

We also wish to thank the advisory editors for this volume (David Axelrod, Linda Christensen, Margarita Donnelly, Barbara Drake, Lawson Inada, Karen Keltz, and William Sweet), as well as our co-editors in the *Oregon Literature Series*—especially Glen Love, Shannon Applegate, Jarold Ramsey, and Stephen Beckham— for helping us in the complex selection process and for suggesting new works. Thanks, too, to Ulrich Hardt, for his masterful organizational abilities, his stabilizing presence, and his constant balance, and to George Venn—not only for his conscientous involvement with every stage of this book, for his help in finding selections, and his feedback regarding the book's organization—but also for his patience and good humor at all times.

Other special people helped with research and secretarial duties and greatly lessened our collective loads. Margot Peralta served as a tireless researcher and typist at Portland State University. Denise Wallace spent endless hours in the University of Oregon library tracking down biographic and bibliographic details, as did Martina Salisbury, who also helped proofread and "log in" over three hundred manuscripts. Susanne Shotola, of Portland State University, has throughout this project been at the hub of all correspondence and business matters. Andrea Skufca and Gandalf Nightingale aided in research and typing of bio-bibliographic information. And the office staff of the English Department of the University of Oregon was most generous with time, advice, and the use of office machines for printing the manuscript draft of this work. We cannot thank them enough.

Finally, we wish to offer a note of special gratitude to our families—Ralph and Martina Salisbury, May and Laura St. John, and Gandalf Nightingale—who aided and encouraged us in many daily ways, who lived with our absences, grumblings, deadlines, and crises, as well as with our joys, as we worked for over three years to complete this book.

Ingrid Wendt, Eugene, Oregon
Primus St. John, Portland, Oregon

Contents

Part II. Tales Half Told: Nineteenth-Century Oregon Poems

Part III. Leaving the Myths: Poems in Transition

Part IV. Pioneers on Aesthetics: Poems by Early Oregon Modernists

Introduction to Part V by Primus St. John 155

Part V. Contemporary Voices: Arriving and Leaving Here—1960-1991

General Introduction

The idea for the *Oregon Literature Series*, six anthologies of the best Oregon writing, was first proposed to the Oregon Council of Teachers of English (OCTE) in 1988. At that time, OCTE decided to depart from the conventional state literary anthology—a monolithic tome put together by a few academic volunteers and generally intended for libraries and adult readers. Instead, OCTE decided to create six shorter, genre-based anthologies: prose, poetry, autobiography, folk literature, letters and diaries, and short fiction. OCTE would publish a public "Call for Editors," and the most qualified individuals would be hired for their expertise and treated professionally—honoraria, expenses, research assistance, travel, etc. The anthologies would be intended as classroom/reference texts for students and teachers, and as introductory readers for the general public. Books would be designed to be easily held, carried, and read.

Numerous arguments were raised against this innovative proposal—most of them signaling Oregon's 150-year status as a literary colony. *No one had ever done this before. Oregon's literature was non-existent. There wasn't much writing of merit. Most scholars and critics have ignored Oregon literature—even in the best histories of Western literature. There's no literary history of Oregon. It will take years to find this work. In Oregon, literature has the least financial support of all the major arts. We had no publisher. It might rain.*

Nevertheless, in 1989, Ulrich Hardt and I were appointed by OCTE to complete the *Oregon Literature Series*. The work began when we signed a publication contract with Oregon State University Press, our first and most important professional collaborator. Next, from a pool of 130 applicants, OCTE chose these editors to discover Oregon's literary heritage: Shannon Applegate, Stephen Dow Beckham, Gordon B. Dodds, Primus St. John, Suzi Jones, Glen A. Love, Terence O'Donnell, Jarold Ramsey, and Ingrid Wendt. Appointed in August 1990, those individuals began the search for Oregon writing that eventually spread beyond every corner of the state—from ranch houses to university archives, from oral storytellers in longhouses to Chinese miners' letters in museums, from Desdemona Sands to Burns. Some editors traveled thousands of miles. Others corresponded with hundreds of authors. Most read thousands of pages. Poets, historians, folklorists, critics, scholars, teachers, and editors—they all benefited from and shared their research expertise. Even though honoraria were small, editors gave generously of their time. While the editors looked for Oregon writing, Ulrich Hardt and I sought out and received endorsements from many major cultural and arts organizations. Financial support was like rain in the time of drought, but we attracted a few wise, faithful, and generous patrons, as the Acknowledgments record.

Once the editors had discovered this vast, unstudied, and unknown body of writing, they assembled their manuscripts by using the following guidelines—guidelines that required them to choose writing—in its broadest sense—that might reveal the Oregon experience to both students and the public:

1. The volume must include a representative sample of the best Oregon writing from all periods, regions, occupations, genders, genres and sub-genres, ethnic, religious, political, and cultural backgrounds.

2. Oregon birth should not be used as a single criterion for inclusion. Oregon residence is important, but no arbitrary length of stay is required for a writer to be included.

3. Works about experience in Oregon are preferred, but editors are not limited to that criterion alone.

4. "Oregon" will be defined by its changing historical boundaries—Native American tribal territories, Spanish, Russian, British, U.S. Territory, statehood.

5. One or more translations and original from non-English languages should be included when appropriate to show that linguistic multiplicity has always been a part of Oregon.

6. Controversial subjects such as sexism and racism should not be avoided. Multiple versions of events, people, and places should be included when available.

7. Length of works must vary; limit the number of snippets when possible. Meet the need for diversity in reading, from complex to simple.

8. New, unknown, or unpublished work should be included.

9. Works will be edited for clarity but not necessarily for correctness. Editors may invent titles, delete text, and select text as appropriate and with appropriate notation.

Once assembled in draft, most of these manuscripts were two to three times longer than could be published by Oregon State University Press; therefore much fine writing had to be omitted, which all editors and our publisher regret. After being reduced to the requisite size, the manuscripts passed through two separate reviews: first, a different Advisory Board for each volume read and rated all selections; second, the Editorial Board composed of all fellow editors of the *Oregon Literature Series* read, responded, and eventually voted to adopt the manuscript for publication. At all stages, both Ulrich Hardt and I worked closely with editors in many ways: readers, critics, fundraisers, administrators, arbitrators, secretaries, grant writers, researchers, coordinators, pollsters.

Now, we hope that these books will create for Oregon literature a legitimate place in Oregon schools and communities, where the best texts that celebrate, invent, evaluate, and illuminate the Oregon condition have been invisible for too long. Here, for the first time, students will have books that actually include writing by Oregonians; teachers can find original, whole, local, and authentic texts from all regions, periods, and peoples in the state; librarians will be able to recommend the best reading to their patrons; the new reader and the general reader can find answers to the question that has haunted this project like a colonial ghost: "Who are Oregon's writers, anyway?"

Let it be known that an Oregon literary canon is forming—rich, diverse, compelling. Here we give this sample of it to you. Let your love of reading and writing endure.

George Venn, General Editor
Grande Ronde Valley, Oregon, September 1992

Introduction to Parts I–IV
From Here We Speak

This state called Oregon always has been, and promises always to be, a place of celebrated beginnings. Long before Lewis and Clark sent back reports from this far corner of the United States, over forty different tribal nations (with more than twenty-five language groups) proclaimed this land as the center of the world. For hundreds of years, these first Oregonians had been maintaining a rich oral tradition of myths and legends, songs and invocations, that celebrated the origins of all of earth's creatures and taught how to live in harmony with the land in its endless cycles of rebirth and renewal.

For the mostly Euro-American settlers of Oregon, this land between the Pacific Ocean and the Snake River, between the Columbia River and the Siskiyou Mountains, represented a beginning, not of the world, but of a new way of life. Poetry about the westward expansion echoes with a heightened sense of what has gone into making up the characteristically American psyche. Out here, somewhere, was Paradise, waiting to be found and owned. Possibilities here seemed as endless as the belief in endless resources, or the desire to leave back East a host of social and personal ills.

From Here We Speak is an attempt to provide a historically arranged sampling of poetry from the earliest transcriptions of tribal lyrics, through successive generations of pioneers and their descendants, into the present day. "The frontiers," said Thoreau, "are not east or west, north or south, but wherever a man [or woman] fronts a fact."[1] With this idea in mind, we can see that the poetry of the state of Oregon is not merely a record of historical and geographical images, but also of changes, over time, in our social condition, and of the many kinds of frontiers there have been. From the Nez Perce "Morning Song" of thanks for being alive yet another day, through Ursula Le Guin's sombre association of the eruption of Mount St. Helens with a potential nuclear winter, we see in Oregon poetry a tremendous range of responses to ever-changing circumstances, compressed into a span of little more than one hundred and fifty years.

With literally thousands of poems, by scores of poets, to choose from (apart from the tribal materials, of which little is to be found), the principles guiding selections were several. First priority went, always, to poems of quality: poems judged excellent by standards of their time; poems which are still valuable today. Next came a whole range of questions. How was the poet regarded by audiences of the day? Was there a balance of subject and style? And was the subject representative of an important social or historical reality? (Part II has, for example, one shipwreck poem, one poem about farming, one covered wagon poem, and so on.) How important was length of residence in Oregon, when other compelling facts came into play? (Edwin Markham left the state at age 6, but he was later named Oregon's Poet Laureate. Mary Barnard has lived most of her life in Vancouver, Washington; but Reed College, in Portland, was where she launched her writing career.) There were issues of balance: of gender, age group, profession, religion, as well as of geographic region. Attempts were also made at ethnic representation. (History tells us that Hispanics, Asians, African Americans, and other minority groups were present in early Oregon, but, unfortunately, little poetry could be found to demonstrate this fact.)

Throughout my search for poems representative of important aspects of Oregon society and of the time in which the poems were written, I was making another search: for poems *unlike* the "typical" verse of the day. Were there any rebels or risk takers? Who were the (deliberate or accidental) mavericks of each literary period who moved that period forward, and who continue to surprise and delight us? While searching for poems on the Oregon landscape, or events in Oregon's history, I was also looking for poems that showed an awareness of the world outside the boundaries of the state. Happily, my search was more than amply rewarded. Sadly, many worthy poems, by such notable poets as O.C. Applegate, Senator Edwin Baker, and Governor George Curry, as well as poems on important topics like the Civil and the Spanish-American wars, had to be left out for reasons of space.

Most challenging of all my editorial goals was the search for representative Native American oral literature, nearly all of which was lost along with the lives of most indigenous people in the second half of the last century. Thanks to the efforts, however, of several nineteenth- and early twentieth-century anthropologists, with the tremendous help of a few remaining native speakers, we are able to read a sampling of the lyrics of at least eleven different tribal groups, collected from widely scattered enthnographic texts. Thanks to devoted scholars living today, we are able to read re-translations that give us a sense of the dignity and artistry involved in the original creations.

After the challenges of search and selection there was the added challenge of how to present oral literature on the printed page. None of the lyrics and songs in Part I was ever intended to be written down and used outside its original ceremonial setting. Nor was any piece meant to be read and evaluated according to contemporary "literary" standards. The ways in which tribal lyrics were spoken or sung profoundly affected their meanings. How could this book reproduce the dancing that often went with the words? How could printed words capture the beat of the drum or the sounds of other musical instruments, played while the words were once being sung? Furthermore, how could merely printed texts convey the complexities in seemingly simple phrases? Just as the words "burning bush" bring a whole complex story to mind for people raised in the Judeo-Christian tradition, so, too, many words in Native American lyrics have stories behind them. Readers not familiar with these stories might think the lyrics are simpler than they really are. As scholar and translator Brian Swann explains, Native songs were almost always short because the people already knew "so much."[2] Readers today do not know what the original audiences knew.

Some of the songs in Part I are secular. The Kalapuya game song and the Klamath songs of satire and social comment were intended to entertain and to encourage correct behavior. The Modoc lullaby and the Coos love song were meant to communicate personal feelings. Most of the songs, however, were sacred. The songs of prophecy and of healing, the songs to make things happen, the incantations, the exorcisms and spirit power songs were parts of religious ceremonies. Their words were often supernaturally given, in dreams or visions. Some, like the spirit-power songs, were personal property, to be shared with the group only on rare ceremonial occasions. Others, such as "When It Storms in Winter," were community property, to be passed along through generations, without giving credit to the original authors. Every song was a way for the singer to participate in something bigger than the self—to enter into an "intimate connection between right acting and right singing."[3]

Although it is risky to take sacred songs out of context, the importance of sharing some of this wonderfully rich oral literature makes the risk worth taking. Many of the tribal lyrics are referred to as songs, because they usually were sung or chanted, rather than spoken. Various words were often repeated like refrains. Still other lyrics are rearrangements of prose narratives—myths, for example, or legends—that originally did not look like poems at all, but have recently been seen as such by Professor Dell Hymes and other scholars working in the exciting new field of ethnopoetics. By breaking the old prose paragraphs into poetic lines, Hymes and other writers are allowing today's readers to see the organizing principles in such traditional narratives as "A Tualatin Shaman Named Cimxin," and to appreciate their stylistic sophistication.

Some lyrics are printed both in English and in their own original language. Some presentations let the reader compare modern versions with the first translations made by early anthropologists. Some lyrics appear in more than one modern translation. Still other translations (or verse adaptations) do not follow original texts word for word but fill in or add phrases and images, making up for the unspoken contexts in which the songs first appeared. To emphasize that they are truly "translations," these pieces have been grouped together at the end of Part I.

Except for this first section (where all lyrics were part of the oral tradition, with few authors or fixed dates available), the poems in Parts I-IV are arranged chronologically, by authors' dates of birth. In addition to providing a practical form of organization, this method allows readers to see some striking differences, as well as the expected similarities, among poets of roughly the same age. It also permits grouping the poems into three main stylistic and thematic sections. "Tales Half Told: Early Oregon Poems" contains poems written mainly between 1838 and 1900. "Leaving the Myths: Poems in Transition" presents poems that appeared roughly between 1900 and 1940, paving the way for the generations of poets included in Part IV, "Pioneers on Aesthetics: Early Oregon Modernists."

The first recorded Oregon poem, by missionary Anna Maria Pittman Lee, was written in 1838. It illustrates one of several somewhat two-dimensional (or "Half Told") modes of early Oregon poems—modes that changed very little until around the turn of the century. Literary historian Herbert Nelson has identified four main kinds of poetry written during this time, and Part II includes representative samplings of each kind: 1) lyrics lauding Oregon ("Beautiful Willamette," for example); 2) romantic tales in verse (melancholy death in battle, tales of shipwrecks or other kinds of disasters), often with a moral attached; 3) sentimental lyrics on such topics as love, death, friendship, religious belief, and homes left behind; and 4) topical verse on such "questions of the day" as temperance, or on significant current events.[4]

Much of this poetry came to public attention through pioneer newspapers and journals of the mid to late 1800s, as well as through the publication of books by single authors. Much of it, in keeping with literary fashions of the day, was full of learned and even classical allusions. Considered a sign of intellectual accomplishment and refinement, writing poetry was an amazingly popular activity in the 1800s, and newspaper and magazine editors published poetry not only as filler material but as proof of their own sophistication.

Yet early Oregon poets led lives that, for the most part, were far from "literary": lives of teaching or householding, farming or sailing; lives spent converting the Indians, or in garrisoning forts to protect the settlers from Indian attacks. Perhaps, we might speculate, writing poetry was one way of "fronting" the facts of a wilderness almost too large to comprehend. Perhaps it was a way to deal with the many kinds of losses almost all pioneers faced, or of making something permanent and noble in the face of so much change. The anonymous "To the Oregon Emigrants of 1846," Frances Fuller Victor's "Do You Hear the Women Praying?", and much of the other early poetry had an overt message. Like pioneer quilts which were beautiful and also kept one warm, early Oregon poems were meant to be of use: to encourage, to persuade, to immortalize, and (like "Ace Carey and the Bear") to entertain.

By today's standards much of the language of these early poems seems stilted and two dimensional. It seems to lack the specific details that might distinguish the Willamette, for example, from any other river on the continent. Today's readers might also find the language somewhat flowery—even overdone. Yet we can sympathize with these early settlers in their struggles to describe a new and overwhelming landscape—trying to describe wonders the eye could hardly believe. They may have felt such wonders could never be captured in the language of everyday use. Wouldn't a loftier language be called for—something grand enough to equal the grandeur of nature?

We can also see, as in "The Oregon Farmer's Song," how fronting the fact of a new landscape often meant recreating (as Hildegarde Flanner says) "little by little, the exterior world in the image of old truths and convictions" brought from the East.[5] How could the land not always be here for the taking? Shouldn't everyone get a piece of the pie? Won't honest hard work bring eternal success? Why introduce a new way of looking at things?

With most poets voicing the popular and "expected" sentiments of the day, there were also poets of protest. There were voices questioning, as well as upholding, the status quo. Poet Elizabeth Markham, for example, demonstrated an early feminist awareness long before the suffrage movement provided a support network. Poets Margaret Jewett Bailey and Robert Starkey protested the treatment of Indians by the Whites, at a time when the generally accepted thing to do was to convert Indians to Christianity, along with taking their lands. Poet Joaquin Miller, whose poetry often glorified pioneer life, began to see that some of the old stories really were secular "myths" settlers thought they could live by. Some of these "myths" were beginning to fail. Maybe these stories were only "half told." The two poems of Miller included here were chosen because they do *not* fit the mold of convention. Rather, they are forecasters of the change that was to occur in Oregon poetry, as it did elsewhere around the United States, at the turn of the century.

Part III, "Leaving the Myths: Poems in Transition," contains many poems that illustrate this change. Despite the persistent Romanticism of such popular poets as Valentine Brown, for the first time in the history of Oregon poetry we see a substantial number of poets challenging the dominant social value of conquest and exploitation (both of the environment and the native people in it). More three dimensional, almost defiant in tone, these poems begin to present the realities of human experience in all of its forms, even if that means exposing the crude or unpleasant.

Beginning with "The Old Emigrant Road," which puts the "romance" of the wagon train firmly in the past, the poems in this section "front" new kinds of facts. They show that wandering and rootlessness sometimes lead to despair. Ada Hastings Hedges, for example, speaks for those Oregon-born pioneers from the crowded western valleys who headed back across the mountains, to the "promised lands" of the desert, and the toll this took on their lives. Poets such as C.E.S. Wood, John Reed, Charles Oluf Olsen, Edwin Markham, Haralambos Kambouris, and the Japanese immigrants of Hood River, all refuse to echo the comfortable, capitalist myth of the "happy, humble worker," presenting, instead, working class realities in a clear light. New, too, are the challenges made by Wood and Mary Carolyn Davies to the taken-for-granted glories of war and the taken-for-granted institution of marriage. Women's voices, especially those of Ada Hastings Hedges, Mary Carolyn Davies, Hazel Hall, and Frances Holmstrom, are among the first to present alternative visions of human connection and continuity rooted in traditionally female values.

The literary period 1900-1930 brought other kinds of changes. For the first time in Oregon literature, we see a substantial number of authors who regarded poetry as more than an avocation: it was a calling, a career. Growing numbers of Oregon poets were winning prestigious national awards. And it became possible for a few poets of the time to earn a living by writing, especially when they published in such nationally popular magazines as the *Saturday Evening Post*, and filled in the income from poetry with other kinds of journalism.

More significantly, the period represented in Part III was the beginning of a kind of "literary Renaissance" that was to come to full bloom in the 1930s. During this period of intense activity (mostly in the Willamette Valley), writers often came together, both socially and professionally, to work on publishing projects, to establish new literary journals, and to debate aesthetics. Poets debated the distinction between popular "verse" and "poetry" as an artform, knowing full well that what "sells" is not always what's "good," and they began to redefine and to set new literary standards for themselves as Northwesterners.

Change comes slowly, and not all poets of this or later periods were equally affected by the New Realism. Nor were many poets yet able to write convincingly of the Oregon landscape. "I wonder, Ethel Fuller," Ben Hur Lampman is known to have said, "who among us will be the one to do justice to our own out-of-doors." Fuller's reply: "Probably no one of the present generation of poets; we are still too busy climbing our mountains and exploring our hinterlands; we are too close to our natural marvels for a 'subliminal' perspective."[6] Whatever the reason, it isn't until the work of such poets as Paul Tracy, H.L. Davis, Howard McKinley Corning, Jeanne McGahey, Mary Barnard, and others in Part IV that we begin to see the Oregon landscape in all its uniqueness.

This section, titled "Pioneers on Aesthetics" after one of Paul Tracy's poems, contains work published for the most part after 1930 by poets consciously committed to artistic change and individuality of style. These poets continue the trend set by writers before them to favor of the rhythms of everyday speech over the conventions of traditional meter and rhyme, and to favor the vernacular over abstract, flowery language. Poets of Part IV carry forward, as Karen Reyes has said, "a new awareness of contemporary events, realistically treated, and written in language more reflective of the speech patterns of American English."[7] Or, as poet Paul Tracy asserts, "You poets keep singing of smoothness/And the beautiful cadence of living: . . . Life to me is a series of yanks and jerks."

Is it possible to characterize and label the types of poetry written by the great number of poets in Part IV, many of whom are still living and writing today? Or is it possible that what begins to emerge is a tremendous variety of visions, resulting in part from an increased mobility among poets? In this section we see poets moving into and out of the state and the country, poets studying their craft at colleges and universities, and poets teaching in academia. We see poets whose occupations range from forest lookout to lumberjack, from blacksmith to strawberry picker, from homemaker to plumber. We see these modern poets as inheriting the comforts won by earlier Oregon settlers, yet being sobered by the Great Depression of the 1930s and by two world wars. Some poets fought in those wars; others resisted on grounds of conscience. What, if anything besides chronology, brings the work of these poets together? Is there anything about the body of Oregon poetry of this time which distinguishes it from that written in other regions of the country?

Pioneers not only "on aesthetics," modern Oregon poets possess a new alertness to the places where they have chosen to live. Whether speaking of specifically human concerns, or of the environment, most poets in Part IV use a variety of images, references, allusions, and figures of speech that show that the land is never far from mind. In the poems of H.L. Davis and Clara Hoff, of James Stevens and Courtland Matthews, of Jeanne McGahey and Madeline DeFrees, of William Stafford and Willis Eberman, of Vi Gale and John Haislip, of Beverly Partridge and Gary Snyder, among others in this section, we see a loyalty and an attentiveness to the land—to our human connection with it. If anything about the body of Oregon poetry distinguishes it from that of other regions of the country, perhaps we can see it in the ways the poets in Part IV assert their connection to the land, and in how they reject, as George Venn has said, society's obsession with an exclusively human world.[8]

Many poets in Part IV not only observe and describe their connection to the natural world. They also explore ways to live in harmony with that environment. Their poems ask: How are we at home here? Their answers are as different from each other as the poets themselves, yet their mutual quest foreshadows the words of poet John Daniel, in his recent book *The Trail Home*: "It is not a matter of owning the land, or of working the land, but of learning to hold the land in mind, to begin gropingly . . . to imagine ourselves as part of it." "Home," says Daniel, "is not the place we were born, or that perfect somewhere else we used to dream of, but the place where we are—the place . . . we learn to see and listen for and come to know as part of our lives."[9]

Poems in Part IV also ask: How do we heal the wounds—to society and to the environment—that have been made in getting us where we are? They suggest that the very qualities which have made America strong have also had negative counterparts. Whether the American quest has been for personal freedom or for wealth, for beauty or for power, perhaps the American emphases on competition, on conquest and on control have created a society which is out of balance, a society which throws the world out of balance. Our ability to survive as a planet is called into question. Inheriting countless problems along with the fruits of their ancestors' labors, left with no unifying vision or shared mythology to bind them, the poets in Part IV are beginning to make concrete the fact the world, as they know it, will not last forever unless we learn how to become better custodians for future generations. "The earth is ours to destroy/ or love once again," says Willis Eberman, in his poem "Elk." "We must decide very soon which it will be."

Perhaps, with all of the North American continent charted, with most of the wilderness tamed, the pioneer sense of "rugged individualism" has become a fronting of new social realities and a reexamination of the myths that have driven our society. Poets such as Lawrence Pratt and Verne Bright, Mary Barnard, and Willis Eberman, hint at "endings" to some of those "beginnings" described by poets a hundred years before. Poets such as William Everson, Phyllis McGinley, Ralph Salisbury, James B. Hall, Shizue Iwatsuki, and Ursula Le Guin explode the myths of the glamours of war and of nature's upheavals. They, and other poets in Part IV, bring us personal accounts that show how individuals, with their individual human lives, are affected by events that otherwise could be too big and impersonal to comprehend.

Alone sometimes in their perceptions, as artists often must be, the poets in Part IV continue the pioneer quest—but this time for meaning, and for new ways to imagine themselves active participants in the global community. Determined to see and to speak clearly, these regional poets at the end of the trail come together in their search for ways to connect "right action and right singing." In the words of William Stafford:

> They call it regional, this relevance—
> the deepest place we have: in this pool forms
> the model of our land, a lonely one,
> responsive to the wind. Everything we own
> has brought us here: from here we speak.[10]

Ingrid Wendt
Eugene, Oregon, September 1992

1. This quotation was used as the epigraph on the title page of all issues of H.G. Merriam's literary journal *The Frontier* (Missoula, Montana, 1920-1939).

2. Brian Swann, *Song of the Sky: Versions of Native American Songs and Poems* (Ashuelot, New Hampshire: Four Zoas Night House, Ltd., 1985), p. 6.

3. Swann, *Ibid.*, p. 2.

4. Herbert Nelson, *The Literary Impulse in Pioneer Oregon* (Corvallis, Oregon: Oregon State College Press, 1948), pp. 70-76.

5. Hildegarde Flanner, "A California Problem," *The Saturday Review of Literature*, May 24, 1930.

6. Ethel Romig Fuller, "Who and How Good Are the Poets?" the *Sunday Oregonian* (November 19, 1933), Mag. p. 3.

7. Karen Reyes, *Finding a New Voice: The Oregon Writing Community Between the World Wars* (Portland, Oregon: Portland State University Master's Thesis, 1986), p. 41.

8. George Venn, "Continuity in Northwest Literature," *Marking the Magic Circle* (Corvallis, Oregon: Oregon State University Press, 1987), pp. 84-109.

9. John Daniel, "The Trail Home," *The Trail Home* (New York: Pantheon, 1992) pp. 203-213.

10. William Stafford, "Lake Chelan." *Stories That Could Be True* (New York: Harper & Row, Publishers, 1977), p. 84.

Alsea

The Alsea lived along the central Oregon coast. Eclipses of both the sun and the moon were seen as supernatural and sometimes frightening events to many native peoples. This Alsea ritual poem offers explanations for the moon's disappearance. It also offers reassurance by telling the people what they can do to bring the moon back. William Smith dictated this exorcism, as well as the "Thunderstorm Exorcism," on the Siletz Reservation, in northwestern Oregon, in 1910.

Moon Eclipse Exorcism

come out come out come out
the moon has been killed

> who kills the moon? crow
> who often kills the moon? eagle
> who usually kills the moon? chicken hawk
> who also kills the moon? owl
> in their numbers they assemble
> for moonkilling

come out, throw sticks at your houses
come out, turn your buckets over
spill out all the water don't let it turn
bloody yellow
from the wounding and death
of the moon

o what will become of the world, the moon
never dies without cause
only when a rich man is about to be killed
is the moon murdered

look all around the world, dance, throw your sticks, help out,
look at the moon,

> *dark as it is now, even if it disappears*

it will come back, think of nothing
I'm going back into the house

> and the others went back

> *Narrated by William Smith, Alsea*
> *Adaptation by Armand Schwerner*
> ❦

Like many native peoples, the Alsea believed the proper words and actions could influence natural phenomena. In this poem, their chant takes the form of a challenge to Lightning and Thunder (rare events on the Oregon coast). It also takes care not to offend the sky, saying the sky is not to be blamed for the actions of Thunder.

Thunderstorm Exorcism
The people would shout at Lightning
> *Look sharp, jump back, my friend*
> *You can't hide behind me, my friend*
Then the Thunder would roar,
the people would yell at him
> *Look sharp, jump back, my friend*
> *You can't come in here, my friend*
Then someone would go outside and dance
and beat the house with sticks and soon
all the people would be outside dancing
and while Lightning and Thunder were leaving
one man would sing all around the house
> *The sky does not always act like this*
> *The Thunder only comes sometimes*
> *The sky is not doing anything bad*
> *It goes right on, this world*

Narrated by William Smith, Alsea
Adaptation by Jarold Ramsey

It is interesting to see the choices made by contemporary poets as they retranslate native literature for readers of today. Here is the original narrative translation, first published in 1920 by Leo Frachtenberg:

Whenever (the thunder) began to roar loud, the people would usually shout, and would keep on saying, "Do you take good care of yourselves!" Whenever it would lighten, it would seem just like fire. Then (the lightning) would be shouted at, "Dodge thyself, my friend! Thou shalt not put thyself right behind (me), my friend!" Then again the noise (of the thunder) would roar. It would be said to him there, "Dodge thyself, my friend!" Then some of the people would go out. Whenever it lightened, it would almost rend the house (in two). Then the house would be hit with sticks, while all the people would be dancing outside in a body. Whenever the house was hit with sticks (the people would say), "Do you pour out your water; all of you shall pour out your water; you shall also upturn all your buckets." Whenever it lightened, the house would seem to crack. One man would be talking all the time while the elements acted thus: "(It) is nothing; (it is) just the thunder. Never (will any harm) befall the world."

Nez Perce

Many Native American peoples had religious ceremonies appropriate to different times of the day, to the changing of seasons, and to other natural phenomena. Little is known about the source or the uses of this Nez Perce song, first recorded and translated in prose in 1907 by Herbert Spinden, but it seems to be part of a practice common to many tribes of greeting the dawn in an aubade of thanksgiving for the renewed blessing of being alive.

Morning Song

The herald rides all around the camp and sings—
    It is morning!
    It is morning!
    I wonder if everyone is up.
    We are all alive, be thankful!
    Rise up! Look sharp! Go see
    to the horses, maybe the wolves have killed one.
    The children are alive, be thankful!
    And you, older men
    and you, older women
    in other camps your friends are still living,
    maybe, but elsewhere some are sick
    this morning, and therefore their friends are sad
    and therefore the children are sad.
    Here, it is morning!

Anonymous, Nez Perce
Versification by Jarold Ramsey

Like many Native American peoples of the Northwest, the Nez Perce believed that each individual had a personal guardian spirit, usually an animal, who could offer counsel or protection, or simply help connect the individual to the world of the spirits. Typically, these guardian spirits were revealed to young people through dreams, vision quests, or in mystic experiences. In the tradition of the Nez Perce, who lived in an area extending from northeastern Oregon into central Idaho, the knowledge of this guardian spirit was kept private for a long time and was revealed only in the annual Guardian Spirit Dance, where each dancer wore a costume according to the nature of his vision. (See also "Songs of the Clackamas.")

According to Spinden, the first vision below was sung by a man whose sacred name was Silu-we-haikt, which means "Eyes-Around-the-Neck." His vision revealed Coyote returning from successful warfare, with a trophy that seems to belong more to the world of myth than of actual events. Nothing is recorded about the speakers of the other two songs, also belonging to individual persons. Nez Perce guardian spirit songs could be inherited and thereby pass into a generally known tribal literature.

Three Guardian Spirit Songs of Mad Coyote

1.
Ravening Coyote comes,
red hands, red mouth,
necklace of eye-balls!

2.
Mad Coyote
madly sings,
then the west wind roars!

3.
Day break finds me,
eastern day break finds me
the meaning of that song:
with blood-stained mouth,
comes mad Coyote!

Narrated by Silu-we-haikt, and Anonymous, Nez Perce
Translated by Herbert J. Spinden

Nehalem Tillamook

Mrs. Clara (Oskalowis) Pearson (born ca. 1873), one of the last remaining Nehalem Tillamook native speakers, dictated these songs, which are part of the myth "Ahecks Leads a War Party," to Elizabeth Jacobs in 1934. Mrs. Pearson, who lived in Garibaldi, on the northwest Oregon coast, stated that she heard them, along with other myths and tales, from her parents every winter until she was nearly forty years old. (See "Songs of the Clackamas" and "Three Guardian Spirit Songs of Mad Coyote.")

Spirit-Power Songs

Bear:

Ah, I can reach
right to the sky.
With my paw I
can feel that sky.

Beaver:

I build dams,
I build dams.
I build and watch
the pond lilies grow.

Elk:

Although it may be buried
far beneath the earth,
with my feet I dig it out
as I travel in the woods.

Rabbit:

Even though he is a rich person
I can take his power from him.
Even though he is very rich
I can make him weak.
That is what I am able to do!

Narrated by Clara Pearson, Nehalem Tillamook
Translated by Elizabeth Jacobs
❦

Clackamas

The Clackamas, like many Native Oregonians, learned from their dreams or visions which birds or animals were to be their personal guardian spirits. In these dreams, the animals would sing. Their words would then become the personal songs of the dreamers and would be sung only in private, when speaking to or calling upon these guardians. (See also "Three Guardian-Spirit Songs of Mad Coyote.")

With the Clackamas people, who lived near Portland, the words described the animal's appearance and habits, never its supernatural strength. Often the creature selected one or two distinctive characteristics of him- or herself, as in Owl's song. The mournful Bear woman grieves for her dead child by redirecting pain into anger at the ripe, edible, and tempting salmonberries which were falling on her and which, she decided, were dropping deliberately on her. Coon, taking care of Panther's orphaned son, feeds the baby with marrow spread on a burl and sings the lullaby below.

These songs were dictated or sung in the Clackamas dialect of the Chinook language by Mrs. Victoria (Williams) Howard, a Clackamas storyteller (1865-1930) who lived in West Linn. They were recorded by Melville Jacobs in 1929 and 1930. When they were sung in their original tribal setting, they were repeated over and over, often building in intensity and speed, as part of a ritual dance.

Lyrics

Owl Shaman's Spirit-Power Song

This is how his little bill goes—it is noisy.
My legs are covered with feathers.
My eyes are yellow-green.

Bear Woman's Mourning Song

Keep away! salmonberries!
My child is dead! salmonberries!

Coon's Lullaby to Panther's Baby Boy

The tiny nipples, the tiny nipples,
they make him grow, they make him grow.
My brother's son! my brother's son!

Narrated by Victoria Howard, Clackamas
Translated by Melville Jacobs

Takelma

The Takelma lived in southern Oregon's Rogue River Valley. They used hornwood sticks, made from the hardwood of a bush and shaped like a horn, for digging camas roots, one of the staples of the Takelma diet. The sifting-pan, used to sift acorn meal, was made of basketry. Because women used these implements, it is quite likely the Takelma believed the wind was female. Wilámxa Pass, also called "Alwilamxadis," refers to a mountain. Frances Johnson dictated this poem to Edward Sapir at the Siletz Reservation, Oregon, in 1906.

When It Storms in Winter

If a great wind comes,
   why then

        "Go past us! Your hornwood stick,
        "Go past us with it!
        "Go past the mountain with your sifting-pan!
        "Go past Wilámxa with your hornwood stick!
        "Do not come here with it,
        "Do not come here.
        "Perhaps with their feet your children
        "Touch the bones of the dead"—
            that is what was done to it.

A friend of my mother's had told her,
   "When a great wind comes,
  "Do that to it."

        Narrated by Frances Johnson, Takelma
        Retranslation by Dell Hymes

It is interesting to compare Hymes's version with Sapir's earlier translation:

When It Storms in Winter

When a great wind arrives, thereupon

   "Pass thou away from here. With thy digging-stick
   Pass thou away from here.
   Beyond the mountain pass thou with thy sifting basket-pan,
   Beyond the Wilámxa Pass thou with thy digging-stick.
   Come thou not hither with it.
   Come thou not hither!
   Thy children dead people's bones
   Perchance with their feet do touch,"

just that was said to her. A friend of my mother's told her,
"Should a great wind arrive, that shall you say to it."

The Takelma, the Kalapuya, and many other native people used to shout greetings to the rising new moon. This Takelma medicine formula was dictated by Frances Johnson to Edward Sapir at Siletz Reservation, Oregon, in 1906. According to Sapir, the word "Bo" was probably intended to frighten away the frogs and lizards that eat up the moon.

When the New Moon Appears

When the moon rises,
  it is shouted to:
"I shall be blessed,
          I shall go ahead
Even if people say of me,
      'Would he were dead,'
        I shall do just as you,
          I shall still rise.
Even if all kinds of things devour you,
      Frogs eat you,
        Everything,
            Snakes with hands,
Even if those eat you,
      Yet I shall still rise,
        I shall do just as you from this time on.
          Bo . . . !"

Narrated by Frances Johnson, Takelma
Retranslation by Dell Hymes

In the native Takelma language, the oral poem was phonetically transcribed like this:

Pixal pa•t' epètha', skelewàltan "Taphòithe•, tèhi k'yàkhte•.
ʔìsiʔ yap'a, 'Amati lohòyʔ!' néxikiʔ, ma yᵃ• naʔnàthe•, hawiʔ
pa•téphte•. ʔìsiʔ khai kwala hèʔnɛ he•nakwàspikhnaʔ laphám
kaíspikhnaʔ, khai kwala, laskùm i•u•xkwát, ʔisiʔ ka gaíspikhnaʔ,
kasiʔ hawi ba•t'epètham. Ma yà• naʔnàthe• tè•xa. Po . . . ."

Frances Johnson also served as an informant for John Peabody Harrington of the Smithsonian Institution. She provided extensive ethnographical data.

Kalapuya

Gossip among native peoples sometimes found its way into tales passed on for generations. In this poem, we see how a man from another tribe, dressed as a woman, became the source of much speculation. John Hudson, speaking the Santiam dialect of the Kalapuya Indians of Oregon's Willamette Valley, reported the facts of *what* took place and rumors of *why* it happened: Coyote (a favorite supernatural character in Oregon Indian legend and myth) was giving Shimxim special "medicine power" by changing him into a woman. Contrary to what we've learned from Hollywood, Native American women, as well as men, often had the power of shamans.

Hymes's version retains the original teller's custom, important in Kalapuya and other Indian traditions, of making clear the narrator's relation to what has been said: whether or not he speaks from first- or secondhand knowledge. Notice how the speaker does not claim to know for sure whether the shaman actually took a husband.

Hymes's arrangement also illuminates something linguists call "evidential." The speaker is saying two things: "this is the tradition" and "this is *my relation* to knowledge of the tradition." Such thorough explanation, typical of the care given to stories by most native speakers, involves the repetition of "people said" and "they say"—giving structure and order to the spoken words much as poets do when they give form to their written ones.

A Tualatin Shaman Named Shimxin

A long time ago there was one,
        I saw that one myself.

People said,
        "He is a man, they say, that one,
        "Even though he wears a dress.
        "He always ties his hair just like a woman.
        "He always acts the way women do.
        "He always goes around with women."

They would say,
        "He's a man,
        "But he's become one of the women.
        "He isn't a woman.
        "They say his power told him,
            'Become one of the women.
            'Always wear your dress just like women.
            'Do it all the time.'"

They said,
        "They say his power is Coyote.
        "Coyote told him,
            'That's what you're to be.
            'You'll be a shaman.'"

He was a great shaman.
That's what he was when I saw him myself.

They said,
        "At one time, they say, he had one young fellow.
        "They say it was his husband."
I didn't see that myself.
That's what people said.

That's all I know about it.

Narrated and translated by John B. Hudson, Kalapuya
Verse adaptation by Dell Hymes

Here is a different, much shorter, adaptation of the text.

The Shaman Cimxin of the Tualatins

In a dream
Cimxin, the boy,
met the transformer,
master of metamorphosis.

Coyote gave him a dress,
a handsome young husband,
and becoming woman,
boy became shaman.

Narrated and translated by John B. Hudson, Kalapuya
Verse adaptation by John Gogol

It is interesting to note that Gogol's version takes the original text as a report of fact. Important points can be expressed in a few lines!

John B. ("Moses") Hudson (1868-1954), was an important Santiam Kalapuya informant who worked with Melville Jacobs from 1928-1936. His voice was recorded in April, 1935, on Ediphone wax cylinders speaking in the Santiam Kalapuya dialect. He and his wife Madeline Hattie (Sands) (1897-1955) had fourteen children, six of whom died in infancy.

Klamath

The Klamath people had many kinds of tribal lyrics. Incantations often were sung as part of doctoring ceremonies to drive away a particular disease. Each song was sung many times by a conjurer, then repeated perhaps a dozen times by a chorus of listeners. The animals mentioned are being sent out by the conjurer to find the whereabouts of the personified disease; whatever the conjurer sings about the animals is what he sees them doing on their errand. Winds, which are often compared with the spread of disease, are frequently seen in these songs as blowing upon some animal or object which has been sent out by the conjurer.

These incantations, or shamanic songs, in use on the Williamson River in south central Oregon, were dictated in 1877 by Mary, a young student of the Klamath Agency boarding school. Minnie Froben assisted in translating them for ethnographer Albert Gatschet, who wrote down over fifty of them.

Incantations

Song of the Wind

Who, I wonder, is blowing out of my mouth?
The disease is emanating from my mouth.

Song of the Skunk

In the north wind I dance around,
tail spread, festive and gay.

Song of the Black Mouse

Through what do I pass with my paws?
My paws glide over the hair of the disease.

Song of the Blind Girl

In the fog I am straying blind,
All over the earth I am wandering.

Narrated by Mary, Klamath
Translated by Minnie Froben and Albert Gatschet

Contrary to popular belief, Native American oral literature contained far more than myths, legends, or references to the supernatural. Like literatures everywhere around the world, the traditions of indigenous Oregonians also included chants and songs about everyday people in their everyday lives.

In the universal tradition of satire, the songs below comment on specific individuals who have in some way broken with tribal customs or standards of behavior, such as flaunting the bright woodpecker scalps used for ornamenting tools, or acting in ways that seemed to jostle social norms.

Songs of Satire and Social Criticism

Showing-Off Song

He dresses in a borrowed woodpecker-blanket
and trails it along on the ground.

Song of False Boasting

Where is he, the alleged wealthy man?
She has entered the house of a poorly dressed husband.

Song of Gluttony

A young woman from Klamath Marsh
is swallowing, swallowing.

Song of the Long-Legged Person

You always strangely stride on
on your long legs.
The crane's progeny,
you walk strangely long-legged.

Narrated by Minnie Froben, Chief Johnson, and Anonymous, Klamath
Translated by Minnie Froben and Albert Gatschet

The Klamath songs below, as well as the Songs of Satire and Social Criticism, were dictated in 1877 by Minnie Froben, Chief Johnson, and others in the Klamath Lake dialect, to ethnographer Albert Gatschet. Froben, who was 17 at the time, was born near the Williamson River to a full-blood Klamath woman and a French settler. She was the assistant to the matron of the boarding school for native children at the Klamath Agency, and assisted Gatschet in his study of tribal songs, the names and uses of edible and medicinal roots and plants, and the Klamath language, customs, and family relationships. These and many other puberty songs include lines on courting, womanhood, feelings of love or disappointment in love, marriage fees paid to parents, marrying, quarrels, and other aspects of married life.

Cooing and Wooing Songs

Courting Song

Very much I covet you for a husband,
For in times to come you will live in affluence.

Courting Song

She: And when will you pay me for a wedding gift?
He: A canoe I'll give for you half filled with water.

Taunt

He spends much money on women
thinking to obtain them easily.

Young Woman to Lover

Why did you become estranged, estranged?
By running in neighbors' houses estranged, estranged?

Accusation

Just now you affirmed that hairless you were,
But the women say, that hairy you are.

Playful Courting Song

Girls: Young man, I will not love you,
      for you run around with no blanket on.
      I do not desire such a husband.
Boys: And I do not like a frog-shaped woman with swollen eyes.

Narrated by Minnie Froben, Chief Johnson, and Anonymous, Klamath
Translated by Minnie Froben and Albert Gatschet

Coos

Unlike poems in the European-American literary tradition, the poems of most Native Americans were not meant to be written or even to be told apart from the myths and stories in which they were often included. There was no one author to such myths and stories, and each speaker retold it in his or her own personal style and created a personal variation of the title. The myth below, retold in 1933 in the Hanis dialect of the Coos Indians of the southern Oregon coast, explains why bats fly only at night. It also seems to suggest a warning to human beings: make up your mind whose side you are on!

 Annie Peterson (ca. 1858- ca. 1944) learned this and dozens of other tales as a child, listening to the older people of the Yachats Reservation as they went root and camas digging, berrying, hunting, drying salmon, or camping during traveling. Before the reservation period, myths were told only in the winter time. Children were expected to repeat, word for word, each phrase or sentence, until they got it right, so adults would not say children "got it mixed up and 'lied' when they told it."

Dr. Melville Jacobs was one of several late nineteenth- and early twentieth-century anthropologists to record the language, customs, and oral literature of the few remaining native language speakers of only a handful of Oregon tribes. Annie Peterson, one of Jacobs's most valuable resources, contributed numerous narrative texts of ethnologic importance.

The Walkers (Animals) and Winged Things (Birds) Fought

The people were going to fight, on the one hand the winged things, on the other the walker things, (and) all sorts of small walker things. All the winged things came to fight, all sorts of winged things. Then they commenced fighting, a long long time they fought.

Now the bats, half winged thing and half walker thing, (they) fought on both sides, and they bore information to both sides. They did not remain fighting on one side, because they were half walker thing and half winged thing. They did not remain on one side, but fought on both sides. That is why they do not go around in the daytime, because this is what they were told, "You must not go around, because the winged things will kill you, and because the walker things will kill you too." Today now they never go around in daytime. They hide. That is why their heart aches, and this is the way they cry,

> *Why did I do that?*
> *I fought on both sides.*
> *Now I cannot go round in daytime at all.*
> *Indeed I feel so sad at heart,*
> *Because I cannot go about in daytime.*

Narrated by Annie Miner Peterson, Coos
Translated by Melville Jacobs
❧

The following lyrics also were dictated to anthropologist Melville Jacobs in 1933 by Annie Miner Peterson. They were composed, however, by her niece, Lottie (Jackson) Evanoff, a full-blood Coos and daughter of Doloose (Chief Jackson). Peterson's voice, singing this song, can be heard on wax cylinder No. 14579 in the Jacobs Collection of the University of Washington, Seattle.

Lottie Evanoff

My Sweetheart

My sweetheart,
Poor thing.
He just stays away
Because my parents do not want him.
But I love him.
I wish he were near here,
I wish he were here,
So that he could hold me in his arms.

Composed by Lottie (Jackson) Evanoff, Coos
Narrated by Annie Miner Peterson, Coos
Translated by Melville Jacobs

Modoc

The cradle song below, in the universal tradition of lullabies, reassures the infant that all is right with the world. Day follows night, as usual. Animals (as in the American folksong "All the Pretty Little Horses") are behaving just as they should. "Look, don't worry," the song seems to say. "Robin is looking for ants in the cedar tree, just as it always does, first thing in the morning."

Also in the universal tradition of lullabies, the Modoc cradle song includes some sounds that have no meaning—nonsense syllables, such as an adult often makes when playing or speaking with an infant. According to Albert Gatschet, who first translated this song in 1894, the *p's'w'p* sound is the song that robins sing to their young (and sometimes also to their grandmothers!).

Cradle Song

Early in the morning robin will eat ants,
Early, early will it pick at the cedar tree,
Early in the morning it chatters, *"Tchiwi'p, tchiwi'p,*
    Tchĭ tch, tsĭ ts, tchĭ tch."

Una'sh pa'tak kimā'dsh p's'w'p,
una'sh pa'tak kimā'dsh wi'sxak,
una'sh, una'sh p's'w'p, p 's 'w 'p.
    tchĭ 'ts, p's'w'p, tsĭ 'ts.

Anonymous, Modoc
Translated by Albert Gatschet
Adaptation by Katherine Berry Judson
❦

Northern Paiute

Throughout recorded history, people around the world have passed down to us a wide variety of stories about the creation of the world and of the creatures who live in it. The poem below, a retranslation of one such creation myth, places Coyote in a leadership position among other animals, and describes how different animals came to live where they do.

Throughout the Oregon country, Coyote was perhaps the most important mythological animal figure, and tales about his exploits, tricks, and examples—both good and bad—can be found in the oral literature of nearly every tribe. As Jarold Ramsey has pointed out, sometimes Coyote is a Transformer, or hero: the engineer of the Columbia River, the inventor of salmon fishing and its rites. Other times he is a selfish, foolish, or outrageous rogue, who sets a moral example for the people of what *not* to do.

In the following tale, not only animals but inanimate objects—the ground and the rocks—have voices. And, although Coyote is boss, he demonstrates a sense of fairness in granting everyone's wishes.

Charlie Washo, of the Great Basin Northern Paiute Indians, who lived in south central Oregon, narrated the above tale to Isabel Kelly in 1938.

How the Animals Found Their Places

In the old time Coyote was boss.
Coyote said, "Bear, you better stay in the mountains."
Deer said, "I want to go live in the mountains too!"
Sucker said, "I want some water."
Duck said he wanted water too.
Swan said, "Look at me, I am growing pretty now;
see, I am white all over."
Bear pounded the ground.
"Ground," he said, "who is talking about me?"
Ground said, "Indian talks pretty mean,"
so Bear went out and bit him.
"I want to stay here in the rocks,"
said Mountain Sheep.
"I like to feel the ground," Rock said,
"I like to stay here in one place and not move."
Sagebrush said he felt the same way.
This is Coyote's story.

Narrated by Charlie Washo, Northern Paiute
Verse adaptation by Jarold Ramsey
❦

The translator of the following text, W.L. Marsden, was a medical doctor who practiced for 22 years in Burns, Oregon. He devoted himself to learning the language, myths, and tales of the Northern Paiutes in that area. Among the many invaluable notes he published is the Paiute explanation of the cause of thunderstorms.

The Thunder Badger

Thunder Badger lives up in the sky,
he is striped like any badger.
When the earth dries up it makes him angry,
he wants the earth to be moist.
Then he puts his head down and digs like a badger,
then the clouds come up in a flurry,
then the loud earth-cursing comes, the thunder,
then the rain comes down all over.

Anonymous, Northern Paiute
Translated by W.L. Marsden
Verse adaptation by Jarold Ramsey

A phonetic transcription of the original Northern Paiute oral text is as follows:

1. Usu niniaba sakwaiina ka oka tapi pasape oka kai osogokaku osogokakukwesi oka pa pasape.

2. Usu niniaba paumaba pabi'i kumiba pidakwabatu tibiwagayu.

3. Husiabagayu usu niniaba mataiti hunakwatnizu tabe 'ada paumaba temataiti usu niniaba.

4. Tihiwisi tugupa'atu anuna otnohu ka kumiakina yaisi paumakina oka tipe nasagwai'ikukina niniabakina tukwukwitsikina seda enikina.

5. Usu tibitsi huna semezu motohawoyua ibitu hupodotu.

6. Usuta'a sikwi huna uniyuhu.

7. Usu niniaba mataiti oka tipe pasape kai pizapi tehuwina ku atsimapanana.

8. Otnohu ka tugupa'atu anudzakwi ka paumabituna yaisi ka kumiakina.

Clackamas

Children around the world have always enjoyed making up their own games and repeating chant-like verses as part of the fun. "Girls' Game" shows that Native American children also had their imaginative games, with their own made-up rules, which included both rewards and friendly insults.

The verse below, originally spoken as a prose memoir, was passed along in the Chinook Jargon to Mrs. Victoria Howard (a Clackamas Indian) by her mother. It was dictated by Mrs. Howard, also in Chinook Jargon, to Melville Jacobs in 1930, near Oregon City, Oregon.

The Chinook Jargon was a trade language used among many northwest tribes and the first white traders, trappers, and settlers. Mrs. Howard, in addition to speaking Chinook Jargon and English, was also one of the last three surviving speakers of the Clackamas dialect of the original Chinook language. The Clackamas Indians originally lived in a large area ranging from the east banks of the Willamette River, south of Portland, Oregon, to the Cascade Mountains.

Girls' Game

Let every girl go gather flowers
from marsh and meadow, hill and headland,
let one girl stand as *it*
to be draped with flowers
until it is a tree in blossom standing there
and all the others dancing quiet in a ring.
Then let her tease her friends around the ring

> Come now, look at me.
> You, your mouth is surely puckered
> You, your eyes belong to Owl
> You, your mouth is like a sturgeon's
> You, your breasts are toadstools

When someone giggles in the ring
then let her go and take her turn
as *it*, the flowering girl.

Narrated by Victoria Howard, Clackamas Chinook
Translated by John B. Hudson
Verse adaptation by Jarold Ramsey

Kalapuya

The famous photographer Edward S. Curtis, when studying the ways of the Nez Perce of eastern Oregon, remarked that almost every tribe in the Northwest had a tradition that before the first whites appeared, a dreamer (or a wandering person of another tribe) prophesied "the coming of a new race with wonderful implements." It is unlikely that Curtis ever read the following Kalapuya prophecy, dictated sometime between 1928 and 1936 by John Hudson, who spoke the Santiam dialect of the Kalapuya of Oregon's Willamette Valley; but its presence bears witness to the tradition Curtis identified.

A Kalapuya Prophecy

In the old time, by the forks of the Santiam,
a Kalapuya man lay down in an alder-grove
and dreamed his farthest dream. When he woke in the night
he told the people, "This earth beneath us
was all black, all black in my dream!"
No man could say what it meant,
that dream of our greening earth.
We forgot. But then the white men came,
those iron farmers, and we saw them plow up the ground,
the camas meadow, the little prairies by the Santiam,
and we knew we would enter their dream
of the earth plowed black forever.

Narrated by John B. Hudson, Kalapuya
Translation by John B. Hudson
Verse adaptation by Jarold Ramsey

Several of today's poets and scholars have begun to modernize original native texts, while staying as close as possible to the content and intention of the original. It is interesting to compare Jarold Ramsey's verse adaptation above to John Hudson's original narrative recorded by anthropologist Melville Jacobs:

> Long ago the people used to say that one great shaman in his dream had seen all the land black in his dream. That is what he told the people. "This earth was all black (in my dream)." He saw it in a dream at night. (1) Just what that was likely to be he did not know. And then (later on) the rest of the people saw the whites plough up the ground. Now then they said, "That must have been what it was that the shaman saw long ago in his sleep."

Both versions of this text lament the Kalapuya's loss of the land to the white settlers. As noted by scholar Dell Hymes, this kind of loss is continuous with English nature poetry of several centuries, and one that early farmers might also sense, "not because of farms, but because of cities, highways, sprawl." The poems are also about power: the great spirit power that enabled the Kalapuya dreamer to foresee the coming of the whites; and the loss of power to prevent this from happening.

Anna Maria Pittman Lee

Born in New York City, and educated at Miss Hall's School, Troy, New York, Anna Maria Pittman Lee (1803-1838) came by ship to Oregon as a missionary in May of 1837 and two months later married Jason Lee, the leader of the Methodist Mission at Fort Vancouver. History accords her several firsts: the first white bride in Oregon Territory, the mother of the first white child born in Oregon, the first white woman to die in Oregon, and the first Oregon poet. Like much writing of the time, her work was usually written for special occasions (she wrote a poem accepting her husband's proposal of marriage) and generally in the conventional language of piety. The following poem, one of nine that have been preserved, was written before her husband's departure in March 1838, for the East to seek much-needed funding for the mission. Her baby, born in June, lived only two days. Anna Lee died the day after. Jason Lee returned to the mission in 1840, bringing a new wife with him.

Must My Dear Companion Leave Me?

Must my dear companion leave me,
    Sad and lonely here to dwell?
If tis duty thus that calls thee,
    Shall I keep thee? no; farewell!
Though my heart aches
    As I bid thee thus farewell.

Go then, loved one, God go with thee
    To protect and save from harm:—
Though thou dost remove far from me
    Thou art safe beneath His arm.
        Go in peace then,
Let thy soul feel no alarm.

Go, thy Savior will go with thee,
    All thy footsteps to attend;
Though you may feel anxious for me,
Thine and mine He will defend;
    Fear not husband,
God thy Father is, and Friend.

Go and seek for fellow laborers;
    Tell them that the field is white;
God will show them gracious favors
    While they teach the sons of night.
        Bid them hasten
Here to bring the gospel light.

Though thy journey may seem dreary
   While removed from her you love;
Though you often may be weary,
   Look for comfort from above.
     God will bless you,
And your journey prosperous prove.

Farewell husband! while you leave me
   Tears of sorrow oft will flow;
Day and night will I pray for thee
   While through dangers you may go.
     Oh remember
Her who loves you much. Adieu.

Anonymous

"To the Oregon Emigrants of 1846," published in Oregon City's weekly newspaper, the *Oregon Spectator*, is but one of a number of verses addressed to the major immigrations of 1843, 1845, and 1846. Laudatory of Oregon, in an attempt to encourage newcomers, its clichéd sentiments combine nostalgia for the old with an attempt to dignify human effort through the use of an elevated language most readers thought inseparable from lofty ideals. The preface to the poem, printed by the editors of the *Oregon Spectator*, reads as follows:

> We cheerfully insert the following anonymous poetical effusion communicated to us, believing it speaks the sentiments of hundreds of our old settlers who are anxiously awaiting the arrival of their friends and relatives, in order that they may have the extreme pleasure of congratulating and introducing them to their newly made homes.

To the Oregon Emigrants of 1846

   Welcome! ye freeborn yeomen of the soil,
Right welcome are you to our new made home;
   Here ends your weary pilgrimage and toil,
You've reached the goal, and need no longer roam.
   O'er dreary wastes, and sterile sands,
O'er mountain crag, through torrents mad'ning roar
   You've toiled undaunted in courageous bands,
To seek a home, on this far distant shore.
   Here waits ye then, ye tillers of the land,
The verdant prairie and prolific field,
   Rich forest dells, where giant cedars stand,

Shading fresh treasures yet to be revealed.
  The cunning artisan of every trade,
The learned professions, and the man of wealth,
  Will for his journey here, be soon repaid
With ample competence, and blooming health.
  Unlike the bee, that daily roams the bower,
Culling the nectar from each blushing stem,
  Forsakes the rose, to taste some brighter flower,
But finds that none are quite as sweet as them
  You leave the crowded towns and worn out fields,
Of *old* Columbia for our virgin soil.
  Here industry, a richer harvest yields;
In *new* Columbia, health repays your toil.
  Come seize the plough, the awl, the axe, the spade,
The pond'rous sledge, or what so e'er you please,
  And soon your labour will be well repaid,
With showers of plenty in the lap of ease.
  Then here united let us firmly be,
And when Columbia shall extend her laws,
  We'll hoist the stars and stripes of Liberty,
From Old Atlantic, to Pacific's shores.

Anonymous ("T")

In 1847, when this poem appeared in the *Oregon Spectator,* most of Oregon's pioneer population—explorers, trappers, traders, missionaries, and settlers—was made up of single young men. Many took Indian wives. Others, such as the missionary Jason Lee, wrote back home that "A greater favour could not be bestowed upon this country, than to send to it pious, industrious, intelligent females." And females were sent. But for some, such as the poet who signed the following poem only with the initial "T," the state of bachelorhood was worth maintaining, despite peer pressures to marry. Worth noting here also is the poet's whimsical tone and use of word-play: a style of poetry equally popular, in its time, as the rhapsodic verses praising landscapes and the pioneer effort.

The Bachelor's Decision
Yes—yes, I'll lead a single life,
(A married man is lost;)
For the *dearer* that a wife may be
the more that wife will *cost!*

Ye meddling matchmakers may try,
To wheedle me 'tis true;
But though I'll never *match* your choice,
I'll be a *match* for you.

Myself to you I'll never lend
To fret, and sigh and groan,
For though I am a *single* man,
I'll prove I'm not a *loan*.

I've sought all Oregon through and through,
'Mong dames of each degree;
I've seen a hundred pretty *maids*,
But not one *made* for me.

A Bachelor! my friends may laugh,
No Benedict they'll find me:
Free as the *air* I'll live and die,
And leave no *heir* behind me.

Elizabeth Markham

Elizabeth Winchell Markham (1805-1891) was born in New York, lived several years in Ohio and Michigan, and crossed the plains, pregnant, in 1847, with her husband Samuel and their five children. The trip was not a smooth one; on September 15, Elizabeth Markham refused to go on, and set one of her husband's wagons on fire, burning off the cover and some goods. Historians disagree as to the fate of the marriage; but whether Samuel Markham died or divorced his wife, she moved from Oregon City, with her three youngest children, to a farm at Suisun, California, and married a John Whitcraft in 1859. He left her in 1862, and they divorced 10 years later. Mother of the poet Edwin Markham (her seventh and last child), Elizabeth Markham frequently contributed poems to the *Oregon Spectator*, and a collection of twelve of them were published in book form after her death. "Her verse," said her son Edwin, "celebrated all the local affairs, such as the arrival of ships, the deaths of pioneers, the flight of strange birds." Different, however, from most of her work, the following poem—which seems to echo popular sentiments about "the weaker sex"—is in reality one of the earliest feminist poems in the history of American literature. First published in June of 1848, it may even be a response to "The Bachelor's Decision," published a few months before.

A Contrast on Matrimony

1. The man must lead a happy life,
2.   Free from matrimonial chains,
3. Who is directed by a wife
4.   Is sure to suffer for his pains.

1. Adam could find no solid peace,
2.   When Eve was given for a mate,
3. Until he saw a woman's face
4.   Adam was in a happy state.

1. In all the female face, appear
2   Hypocrisy, deceit and pride;
3. Truth, darling of a heart sincere,
4.   Ne'er known in woman to reside.

1. What tongue is able to unfold
2.   The falsehoods that in woman dwell;
3. The worth in woman we behold,
4   Is almost imperceptible.

1. Cursed be the foolish man, I say,
2.   Who changes from his singleness;
3. Who will not yield to woman's sway
4.   Is sure of perfect blessedness.

To advocate the ladies' cause, you will read the first and third, and second and fourth lines together.

Margaret Jewett Bailey

Margaret Jewett Bailey (1812-1882) was one of Oregon's most important writers of the 1850s. She came to Oregon in 1837 from Saugus, Massachusetts, with a Jason Lee missionary party and worked with the Indians until 1839, when she married Dr. William J. Bailey and moved with him to a farm near French Prairie. The marriage was unhappy; she obtained a divorce in 1854 and married twice after that. She died in Seattle at the age of 70, as Margaret J. Crane. A regular contributor of poetry and prose to the *Oregon Spectator,* and the author of a women's column for that paper, she published a long, autobiographical novel in 1854, just two years after the appearance of Harriet Beecher Stowe's *Uncle Tom's Cabin.* Like Stowe's novel, Bailey's *The Grains* is a novel of social protest containing criticisms of Jason Lee and the mission community, of the mission's failure to convert the Indians, of the sexual double standard as it discriminates against women, and of woman's lot in marriage. The following poem, from the "diary" of the novel's main character, Ruth Rover, expresses a critical view of the white man's right to tame the "savages."

We Call Them Savage

We call them savage—O be just;
Their outraged feelings scan
A voice comes forth, 'tis from the dust—
The savage was a man!
Think you he loved not? Who stood by,
And in his toils took part?
Woman was there to bless his eye—
The savage had a heart!
Think you he prayed not? When on high
He heard the thunders roll,
What bade him look beyond the sky?
The savage had a soul!

Alas! for them—their day is o'er,
Their fires are out from shore to shore;
No more for them the wild deer bounds;
The plow is on their hunting grounds;
The pale man's axe rings through their woods
The pale man's sail skims o'er their floods.
      Their pleasant springs are dry;
Their children—look—by power oppressed,
Beyond the mountains of the west,
      Their children go to die.

His heraldry is but a broken bow,
His history but a tale of misery and woe,
His very name must be a blank.

John Minto

John Minto (1822-1915) began his working life as a miner: first, at age eight, in his home town of Wylam, England; and then, from 1840-43, in Pennsylvania. Coming to Oregon in 1844, he worked first as a logger and then began raising sheep, specializing in pure-bred Merinos. A state representative from 1862-64, secretary of the State Agricultural Society (1867-69), and secretary of the state board of horticulture (1895-98), Minto was editor of the *Willamette Farmer* (1867) and president of the Oregon Pioneer Association (1890), wrote extensively on all aspects of farm life and local history, and contributed many articles to agricultural periodicals and the *Oregon Historical Quarterly*. He also surveyed the Minto and Santiam passes in the Oregon Cascades, married, and was the father of eight children. The following poem, written in 1861 and sung for the first Oregon state fair (which he helped organize), reflects a time in which American small business and farming interests had begun to hold their own against the giant monopolies—most notably the Hudson's Bay Company, which (in Minto's words) "in 1835 had a complete monopoly over the trade and even the livestock of Oregon."

The Oregon Farmer's Song

Ye farmer friends of Oregon—respected brethren of the plow,
Waver not, but labor on; your Country's hopes are all on you.
"You have your homes upon her breast," you have your liberty and laws;
Your own right hands must do the rest; then, forward! in your Country's cause.

To shear the sheep, the steer to feed, and for your pleasure or your gain,
To rear and tame the high-bred steed and bring him subject to the rein;
To prune the tree, to plow the land, and duly, as the seasons come,
Scatter the seed with liberal hand, and bring the bounteous harvest home.

To stand for justice, truth, and right, against oppression, fraud, and wrong,
And by your power, your legal right, succor the weak against the strong;
The seeds of knowledge deeply plant, restrain ambition, pride, and greed;
See that all labor, and none want of Labor's fruits, to help their need.

These are your duties: and the gain, which you'll receive as your reward,
Will be your own and your Country's fame, and every honest man's regard.
Then, friends and brothers, labor on to bring our State up with the best,
And make our much-loved Oregon the brightest star in all the West.

Henry H. Baldwin

Contrary to popular belief, not all transplanted Europeans traveled the Oregon Trail. Born in Bandon, County Cork, Ireland, Henry Hewiat Baldwin (1823-1911) participated in one of the first events leading to the settlement of Coos Bay: the wrecking of the three-master transport schooner *Captain Lincoln* on January 2, 1852, just north of the Coos Bay bar. All 35 members of "C" troop, 1st U.S. dragoons (to which Baldwin belonged) and the crew of ten survived. They built a temporary settlement on the beach, were aided and fed by the local Cowan Indians, and three months later succeeded in struggling overland to their original destination, Port Orford, where there was a military settlement. Baldwin continued to Eugene City, where he enlisted in the First Oregon Volunteer Cavalry and was mustered out at Vancouver. He spent the last 27 years of his life on a ranch in the Upper Coquille Valley. The following poem is perhaps the first in a long line of Oregon poems dealing with the power as well as the majesty of the sea: a compelling natural force in the lives of countless Oregonians even today.

The Wreck

Come all you hungry soldiers who live on pork and beans,
With lots of dam'd hard scouting and deuced slender means;
Come listen to my shipwreck tale, a deep and dismal one,
Which happened thirty-five dragoons, close to the wild Cowan.
A Captain and a Colonel, a Major and General too,
All council'd with each other, a vile and cunning crew,
All council'd with each other the Rhino for to make,
To fill their breeches' pockets, and government coffers rake,
Saying, the *Captain Lincoln*'s laden and ready for to sail,
We'll send some 8th dragoons on board, they'll help her in a gale;
We'll send some 8th dragoons on board and stow them in the hold,
Like Paddy's pigs to market sent in an Irish packet bold.
The plan being laid these brave dragoons were straightway marched on board,
Who quickly fixed themselves below, where "pork and beans" were stored.
A favoring tide, we anchor weighed, for Port Orford she was bound,
To land her "pork and living stock" from thence, to Puget Sound.
In time we reached the Golden Gates, the wind blowing fresh and fair,
When to the pumps six drag's were put, for this we did not care,
As hard work, soldiering was our drill for now full three long year.
Right merrily all plied the brake, for naught we knew to fear.
The winds Sou'west, our old doomed bark rode on right gallantly,
But Oh! through stem and weather side the daylight we could see;
The break increasing, pumps were manned by twice their former force;
Still on the old craft pitched and rolled; but held her compass course.

In morning of the thirty-first, the last of the old year,
It filled all hands with joy, for each knew the port was near.
Alas! how short is human bliss, the wind commenced to blow,
Which forced our poor, short-handed crew, all canvass safely stow.
The sailors hove the vessel to, the soldiers worked at pumps,
Our doctor and his brother Luff betook themselves to bunks,
Because they happened higher clay and wore the golden lace,
While many gallant hearts, for days, stared hunger in the face.
For three long days and dismal nights the tempest blew its best;
The water broke into our hold, the pumpers saw no rest.
At length the angry seas grew calm, the howling storm grew still,
When a balmy, soft and gentle breeze did our snow white canvass fill.
At five a. m., "Great God! she's struck," the morning of the third;
Then fore and aft and either side were roaring breakers heard.
Again she struck with giant force, the mad waves leaped her deck,
Another giant, partly blow, "then _Lincoln_ lay a wreck."
"A stitch in time and nine are saved," is a proverb old and true,
For her open sides and half pay'd seams lay plainly to the view;
So, if things were done in ship shape style, the schooner caulked abaft,
"Young Lockwood might have saved his goods, and Uncle Sam a craft."
So now, I've told my shipwreck tale, an unvarnished one of truth,
I'll bid good bye, as I am dry, and fill my aching tooth
"With a humper of good brandy, my sorrows for to drown.
I'm bound to keep my spirits up by pouring spirits down."
When next I go on board a ship the briny deep to roam,
Oh! may it be, when I am free, bound for dear island's home
And should I think in after years, of what I once had been,
I'll drown it, with all other cares, in a bowl of good potheen.

Frances Fuller Victor

One of the most important literary figures in nineteenth-century Oregon, Frances Fuller Victor (1826-1902) published her first book of poems, co-authored with her sister Metta, when both were still in their teens. Born in Rome, New York, Frances and her naval engineer husband moved in 1863 to San Francisco, and to Oregon in 1865, where she began writing some of the earliest local color stories and poems of Oregon. In 1875, after her husband's drowning in the sinking of an ocean steamship, Victor worked 15 years as staff writer for H.H. Bancroft, writing the histories of Oregon (for which he took most of the credit) and contributing other sections of his *History of the Pacific States*. For a while forced to earn a living selling toiletries door to door in Salem, Victor later found other literary assignments, among them a $1500 commission from the Oregon legislature to write the history of the Indian wars. The poem which follows, published in her 1877 book of stories and poems, was read before the Women's Prayer League of Portland, on May 27, 1874, and is representative of many similar calls for social justice in the poetry of the time.

Do You Hear the Women Praying?

Do you hear the women praying, oh my brothers?
　Do you hear what words they say ?
These, this free-born nation's wives and mothers,
　Bowing, where you proudly stand, to pray!
Can you coldly look upon their faces,
　Pale, sad faces, seamed with frequent tears;
See their hands uplifted in their places—
　Hands that toiled for all your boyhood's years?

Can you see your wives and daughters pleading
　In the dust you spurn beneath your feet,
Baring hearts for years in secret bleeding,
　To the scoffs and jestings of the street?
Can you hear, and yet not heed the crying
　Of the children perishing for bread?
Born in fear, not love, and daily dying,
　Cursed of God, they think, but cursed of *you* instead?

Do you hear the women praying, oh my brothers?
　Hear the oft-repeated burden of their prayer—
Hear them asking for one boon above all others
　Not for vengeance on the wrongs they have to bear;

But imploring, as their Lord did, " God forgive them,
  For they know not what they do;"
Strike the sin, but spare the sinners—save them—
  Meaning, oh ye men and brothers, *you* !

For your heels have ground the women's faces;
  You have coined their blood and tears for gold;
Have betrayed their kisses and embraces—
  Returned their love with curses twentyfold;
Made the wife's crown one of thorns and not of honor,
  Made her motherhood a pain and dread;
Heaped life's toil unrecompensed upon her;
  Laid her sons upon her bosom, dead!

Do you hear the women praying, oh my brothers?
  Have you not one word to say?
Will a *just* God be as gentle as these mothers,
  If you dare to say them nay?
Oh, ye men, God waits for *you* to answer
  The prayers that to him rise,
He waits to know if *you* are just ere *He* is—
  There your deliverance lies!

Rise and assert the manhood of this nation,
  Its courage, honor, might—
Wipe off the dust of our humiliation—
  Dare nobly to do right!
Shall women plead from out the dust forever?
  Will you not work, men, if you cannot pray?
Hold up the suppliant hands with your endeavor,
  And seize the world's salvation while you may.

Yes, from the eastern to the western ocean,
  The sound of prayer is heard;
And in our hearts great billows of emotion
  At every breath are stirred.
From mountain tops of prayer down to sin's valley
  The voice of women sounds the cry, " Come up!"
O, men and brothers, heed that cry, and rally—
  Help us to dash to earth the deadly cup!

❧

Henry H. Woodward

Henry H. Woodward (1826-1915), the "poet of the Umpqua," was born in Scarborough, England, left home for the sea at the age of nine, and was a sailor until arriving in Oregon in 1850. After joining Company C and fighting in the Rogue Indian War, Woodward lived from 1857 to 1867 on the South Fork of the Coquille River and then moved to Roseburg, where he worked as store clerk, deputy tax assessor, and book agent. In 1867, his first two-part collection of poems, *The Pioneer's Offering*, brought mixed reactions among its readers. Reviews and editorials in the *Oregonian* panned the work, but, as Ruth McBride Powers remarks, the poems "inspired many other pioneers to enliven their solitude with poetic effort." Woodward, a bachelor all his life, traveled to England in 1875, where a second book of poems was published. His third collection, *Lyrics of the Umpqua*, from which the following poem is taken, ranges in topic from religion, the geology of Douglas County, and various social ills, to numerous elegies for comrades fallen during the Indian campaigns.

The Homeless Girl

I wander to and fro, and on charity depend
No one to guide my youth or no brother to defend.
Weary at mind, and sick at heart, I trudge from door to door,
O God! it is a pitiful sight to be so very poor!

The rich folks can have joys which to me are e'er denied;
I've sat at their door-step many times and sadly I have cried.
From ladies I've met with kindness as oft their love is sure,
Yet it is very hard for me so young to be so very poor.

Sometimes hard-visaged folks will give me a stony-hearted stare,
For such a one as me they say that they've naught to spare.
All their scoffs and insults I have always to endure,
Because, forsooth, they all know I am so very poor.

The school-girls are sometimes good, for kindly do they give
A portion or their luncheon so that I might live;
Gentle are their manners, and their hearts feel very sore
To think that one of their own sex should be so very poor.

At nights, too, when I've no money to pay for a humble bed,
I lay me down to rest with a hard stone 'neath my head.
Before morning's light I rise, for the vans make such a roar,
That causes but little sleep for one who is so very poor.

And often I'm awaken'd by rough orders to "move on"
By a man that is warmly clad, and as fine as any *Don*,

Whilst I am in rags and tatters I'm taken by this boor,
To the nearest City Jail because I am so very poor.

I'm tried before a magistrate, and then to prison sent,
When by this harsh sentence my very brain seems rent;
This mandate of the law sends me reeling to the floor;
Crying, "O my God, have mercy on all the suffering poor!"

Samuel A. Clarke

Pioneer journalist and historian, Samuel Asahel Clarke (1827-1909) was born on a Cuban sugar plantation, raised in South Carolina and New York, and came to Oregon in 1850. He operated a sawmill in Portland and within a few months had circulated a petition which resulted in getting Portland incorporated as a city. In the following years he joined the gold rush to the Umpqua, married Harriet T. Buckingham (with whom he had four children), bought a land claim near Salem, joined another unsuccessful gold rush (to Baker County), returned to Salem as its first county clerk, and then spent three years as a railroad executive. He is best known, however, for his editorial positions on the *Oregonian*, the Salem *Statesman*, and the *Willamette Farmer*, and as librarian of the General Land Office in Washington, D.C. (1898-1908), where he wrote his famous *Pioneer Days of Oregon History*. Throughout these years Clarke also wrote poetry. His book of six long poems, *Sounds by the Western Sea*, published in 1872, is one of Northwest literature's earliest attempts to recognize and try to preserve in verse form the legends of the vanishing first Oregonians. A slightly revised version of the 566-line "Legend of the Cascades" was reprinted two years later in *Harper's New Monthly Magazine*. An excerpt of this version appears below. See *The World Begins Here* (*Oregon Literature Series* Short Fiction volume) for a Native American version and *The Bridge of the Gods* by Frederick H. Balch for an early Oregon novel in which this same story appears.

from Legend of the Cascades

Back in the early days of all the Siwash men were few;
Before they dwelt in all the land as far as falls the dew
The snowy peaks that north and south now rise to summits grand
Stood here the river's flow beside, and watched it near at hand.
The Spirit of the Storms kept one, and when his robe he shook,
The roar that swept the clouds along was heard to far Chinook:

His was the snowy peak, far south, whose name with you is Hood;
Mount Adams, whiter than the snow, across the river stood:
'Twas there the spirit dwelt whose fires flash from the mountain's shroud
In lightning strokes that signal when shall peal the stormy cloud—
Dread spirits, born of gloomy power, whose anger sometimes woke
In jealous wrath, and then would flash the lightning's fiery stroke;
Then thunder with its muffled roll would answer peal to peal,
And fires would light the mountain-side, like blows of flint on steel.
Far-reaching then, from mount to mount, in one broad native span,
A rock-hewn arch or bridge was thrown, 'neath which the river ran,
And with its flow the light canoe went down the tranquil stream,
While underneath the darkling arch the river gave no gleam.
    * * *

And here was held high carnival when many tribes were met,
For festival and worship joined. The legend lingers yet
That, circled on the river's arch, the tribes looked on—each one—
While fairest maids laid sacrifice upon the altar stone.
Rude flames leaped up from mossy logs high piled the arch along,
And by their glare the aged priest doled out his chanted song.
His child, the priestess of the arch, of Indian maids most fair,
On altar steps, with hands outstretched, and with wide-flowing hair,
As one entranced by vision stood, all statue-like and still—
A bronze ideal votaress who knew no self or will.
    * * *

The bravest of the braves loved Mentonee, who fed the sacred flame,
And hoping to deserve her love, they sought for fields of fame;
And when they launched the light canoe, or swept the lowland plain,
Or scaled to heights of summer snow, they hoped her love to gain.
And one there was, of noblest deeds and of a chieftain's line,
Who loved fair Mentonee from far, and worshiped at her shrine.
He uttered never word of love; he wooed no other maid;
But, voiceless, at her vestal feet gifts from the chase he laid.
No voice to thought gave utterance his soul's one deep desire;
He watched and worshiped as afar she fed her altar's fire.
Vigils by night would guard her lodge if danger hovered nigh,
And his the truest arm that e'er let feathered arrow fly.
    * * *

As, standing by the altar's glow, we list the priest's low song,
The genii of the snowy mounts go gliding through the throng.
Her voice keeps time-beat with the flames that claim her sacrifice.
With mystic presence by her side the spirits seek device

To win from her a word, a look. Now summer lightnings flash;
Now through the gloom of nearer hills we hear the thunder crash;
Then rising into forms of shade, these jealous spirits grow
To giant height on either hand, and fiercer flashes glow.
Her rite has ended; yet she stands there, statue-like and still,
Unheeding all the demon strife—no thought of coming ill.
On one hand darts the living fire, on other hand a cloud,
And answering back the bolts of flame, the thunder peals aloud.
Amid the gleamings of the fire a flame-wrapped form is seen,
And robed in shadows of the cloud is shape of angry mien.

They strove, and 'neath their earthquake tread tall pines and cliff shores shook;
The lofty forests prostrate fell. The awe-struck tribes forsook
The quivering arch, whose mighty span rocked o'er the wondering tide,
Till every beating heart thereon with fear seemed petrified—
Save two, and one had ceased to beat: her form was reft of life.
Even as she worshiped she had died—slain in the demon strife.
Nor died she there alone: nor hellish strife nor earthquake shock
Spoke fear to Tamalis' great love to drive him from that rock.

Fire answered fire from mountain high, cloud answered peal to cloud.
The great arch hung in space a while, and then it tottering bowed;
And as it fell the gleamings high of sacrificial flame
Lit up the maid's imploring form, that stood in death the same—
Her head uplift, her arm upraised, and her beseeching eye
Went down to meet the whelming wave fixed on the night's deep sky.

And he, so mute of love in life, whose heart such silence kept,
Stood by, and clasped the lifeless form as downwardly they swept.

Robert Starkey

Born in New York state, Robert Starkey (1830-1925) fought in the Mexican War before arriving, via San Francisco, in Coos Bay in 1862 with his Mexican wife Rosita Diaz. The author of many eulogies in the *Coos Bay Times*, as well as acrostics, he worked on the staff of the *Coquille Herald* and wrote the article on "Climate of Coos and Curry Counties" for Orvile Dodge's 1898 history volume. For many years he contributed verse to numerous county newspapers, either anonymously or under the pen name "Le Garçon," and in 1880 the Coos Bay New Printing House published his collection *Sparks of Poetic Fire*. In poems such as "The Coal Miner's Evening Chime," "The Office Seeker," and "Lines on the Chinese Question," Starkey showed an enlightened awareness of working-class realities. The following poem openly criticizes United States government policy and bureaucracy in taking the Curry and Coos Indians to the Siletz Reservation.

A Specimen

Our Indian Civil Service is not good,
    'T has cost a mint of treasure—lakes of blood
And all for what? To feed some idle knaves
    Who cheat the nation and also, the braves,
Whilst the much plundered "Lo" in vain contends,
    Not one to aid him, none his rights defend.
In January, Eighteen Sixty-eight,
    At the Siletz, in this the Sun-set State
'Twas cold; and yet, not colder than the man
    That was in charge when that cold snap began.
Psalms he would sing, and shout, "The Lord be thankit,"
    Then cheat the "Diggers" out of half a blanket.
And when the Indians loudly did implore
    He'd talk Chinook, and in that jargon swore,
    Were they to "memeloos" they'd get no more.
If one requested it, he'd get a pass,
    Then he could go to work or go to grass—
Returning, buy his own from out the store,
    The goods that his "Great Father" sent before.
Of mathematics, books were there the pride,
    'Twas healthy, too, no Indians ever died.
Dead or alive, the Indians' shoes and flannels
    Poured money in his purse from sundry channels.
A school was kept where everything went merry,
    And squibs writ to the papers for "School Jerry."

Belle W. Cooke

Susan Isabella Walker (1835-1919) was born in Connecticut. At age 17 she crossed the plains with her widowed mother and her Baptist uncle, Rev. George C. Chandler, founder and first president of McMinnville College (now Linfield College). Married to Joseph Cooke the following summer (at the Portland home of Samuel A. Clarke), and the mother of six children, Belle Cooke nevertheless maintained an active professional life as a teacher and poet—teaching at Willamette University, at a country school in Clackamas County, and at a private school in her home in Salem. The first woman clerk in the Oregon legislature, and a correspondent for the *Oregonian*, Cooke was a friend and supporter of Abigail Scott Duniway (publisher of the *New Northwest*, a journal of political and social dissent, especially in regard to the woman's suffrage movement), of Frances Fuller Victor, and of both Minnie Myrtle and Joaquin Miller. "Snow Birds" is one of several short poems near the end of her first volume of poems, *Tears and Victory*, which also contains a very long narrative poem of the same title: a response to the United States Civil War from the point of view of the women left behind. Her second book of poems was burned in manuscript form in the San Francisco earthquake and fire of 1902.

Snow Birds

A little one saw the white doves sailing
Afar in the sunny sky,
And she said, " Come down to me, little white specks,
Why are you there so high?"
"They are birds," said Mamma, "swiftly flying,

And cannot hear you call,
Sometime they may come and settle near
Then you can count them all!"

The clouds were gray, as the days grew colder,
And the birds were seen no more,
And the snow-flakes came in multitudes down
Close by the little one's door.
She stood and watched them a while intently.
Then earnestly did she call,
"The little white birds are come, Mamma,
But I never can count them all."

Joaquin Miller

One of the most colorful figures in Oregon literary history, Cincinnatus Hiner Miller (1837-1913) was born in Indiana, the son of a Quaker schoolmaster. After he crossed the plains with his family in 1852, and they settled in the Willamette Valley close to Eugene, he left home at age 15 to mine gold in northern California. He lived for a time with the Indians along the McCloud River near Mount Shasta. In 1857 he fought the Pit River Indians; married an Indian girl (who bore him one daughter, Cali Shasta); returned to Eugene City; and attended Columbia College. He later taught school, studied and practiced law; rode pony express from Florence, Oregon, via Walla Walla, Washington, to the Idaho gold mines; edited the Eugene *Democratic Register*; married Minnie Myrtle Dyer (in 1862); and planted orchards near Canyon City. Eight years and three children later, he left home for San Francisco and London to pursue a career as a poet. Taking his name from the Mexican bandit Joaquin Murietta, Miller soon became known as "The Bard of the Sierras" and "The Byron of Oregon." The publication in Portland of his first books, *Specimens* and *Joaquin et al.*, and in London of *Pacific Poems, Songs of the Sierras*, and the prose work *Life Among the Modocs*—as well as his flamboyant lifestyle and frontiersman style of dress—brought him fame almost overnight and even the attention of European royalty. For many years he traveled in America, Europe, and Asia, worked as a newspaper correspondent in the Klondike and in the Boxer War in China, and published many more books of poems and prose. His third marriage, to hotel heiress Abigail Leland, lasted from 1878-1883. In 1887 he purchased a 75-acre estate near Oakland, California, where he lived off and on until his death. "Exodus for Oregon," below, is one of the best of countless nineteenth-century poems on this popular theme. "Pace Implora," on the other hand, in its regretful retrospection, is remarkable in the context of Miller's life and provides a rare glimpse into another aspect of the poet's character and work.

Exodus for Oregon

A tale half told and hardly understood;
The talk of bearded men that chanced to meet,
That lean'd on long quaint rifles in the wood,
That look'd in fellow faces, spoke discreet
And low, as half in doubt and in defeat
Of hope; a tale it was of lands of gold
That lay below the sun. Wild-wing'd and fleet
It spread among the swift Missouri's bold
Unbridled men, and reach'd to where Ohio roll'd.

Then long chain'd lines of yoked and patient steers;
Then long white trains that pointed to the west,
Beyond the savage west; the hopes and fears

Of blunt, untutor'd men, who hardly guess'd
Their course; the brave and silent women, dress'd
In homely spun attire, the boys in bands,
The cheery babes that laugh'd at all, and bless'd
The doubting hearts, with laughing lifted hands! . . .
What exodus for far untraversed lands!

The Plains! The shouting drivers at the wheel;
The crash of leather whips; the crush and roll
Of wheels; the groan of yokes and grinding steel
And iron chain, and lo! at last the whole
Vast line, that reach'd as if to touch the goal,
Began to stretch and stream away and wind
Toward the west, as if with one control;
Then hope loom'd fair, and home lay far behind;
Before, the boundless plain, and fiercest of their kind.

At first the way lay green and fresh as seas
And far away as any reach of wave;
The sunny streams went by in belt of trees;
And here and there the tassell'd tawny brave
Swept by on horse, look'd back, stretch'd forth and gave
A yell of warn, and then did wheel and rein
Awhile, and point away, dark-brow'd and grave,
Into the far and dim and distant plain
With signs and prophecies, and then plunged on again.

Some hills at last began to lift and break;
Some streams began to fail of wood and tide,
The somber plain began betime to take
A hue of weary brown, and wild and wide
It stretch'd its naked breast on every side.
A babe was heard at last to cry for bread
Amid the deserts; cattle low'd and died,
And dying men went by with broken tread,
And left a long black serpent line of wreck and dead.

Strange hunger'd birds, black-wing'd and still as death,
And crown'd of red with hooked beaks, flew low
And close about, till we could touch their breath—
Strange unnamed birds, that seem'd to come and go
In circles now, and now direct and slow,
Continual, yet never touch the earth;
Slim foxes slid and shuttled to and fro

At times across the dusty weary dearth
Of life, look'd back, then sank like crickets in a hearth.

Then dust arose, a long dim line like smoke
From out of riven earth. The wheels went groaning by,
Ten thousand feet in harness and in yoke,
They tore the ways of ashen alkali,
And desert winds blew sudden, swift and dry.
The dust! it sat upon and fill'd the train!
It seem'd to fret and fill the very sky.
Lo! dust upon the beasts, the tent, the plain,
And dust, alas! on breasts that rose not up again.

They sat in desolation and in dust
By dried-up desert streams; the mother's hands
Hid all her bended face; the cattle thrust
Their tongues and faintly call'd across the lands.
The babes, that knew not what this way through sands
Could mean, did ask if it would end today . . .
The panting wolves slid by, red-eyed, in bands
To pools beyond. The men look'd far away,
And, silent, saw that all a boundless desert lay.

They rose by night; they struggled on and on
As thin and still as ghosts; then here and there
Beside the dusty way before the dawn,
Men silent laid them down in their despair,
And died. But woman! Woman, frail as fair!
May man have strength to give to you your due;
You falter'd not, nor murmur'd anywhere,
You held your babes, held to your course, and you
Bore on through burning hell your double burdens through.

Men stood at last, the decimated few,
Above a land of running streams, and they?
They push'd aside the boughs, and peering through
Beheld afar the cool, refreshing bay;
Then some did curse, and some bend hands to pray;
But some look'd back upon the desert, wide
And desolate with death, then all the day
They mourned. But one, with nothing left beside
His dog to love, crept down among the ferns and died.

❧

Pace Implora

Better it were to sit still by the sea,
Loving somebody and satisfied
Better it were to grow babies on the knee,
To anchor you down for all your days,
Than wander and wander in all these ways,
Land forgotten and love denied.

Better sit still where born, I say,
Wed one sweet woman and love her well,
Laugh with your neighbors, live in their way
Be it ever so simple. The humbler the home,
The nobler indeed, to bear your part.
Love and be loved with all your heart,
Drink sweet waters and dream in a spell,
Share your delights and divide your tears,
Love and be loved in the old east way,
Ere men knew madness and came to roam
From the west to the east and the whole world wide;
When they lived where their fathers lived and died—
Lived and so loved for a thousand years.

Better it were for the world, I say—
Better, indeed, for a man's own good—
That he should sit down where he was born,
Be it a land of sands or of oil and corn,
Valley of poppies or bleak northland,
White sea border or great black wood,
Or bleak white winter or bland sweet May,
Or city of smoke or plain of the sun,
Than wander the world as I have done,
Breaking the heart into bits of clay,
And leaving it scattered on every hand.

Minnie Myrtle Miller

Minnie Myrtle Miller (1845-1883), the "Poetess of the Coquille," had chosen her own pen name and was publishing poems in Oregon periodicals long before meeting and marrying (four days later) "the Byron of Oregon." Born Theresa Dyer, she came to Oregon with her family in 1859, settling with them on a farm on the Sixes River near Coos Bay. Her verses printed in the Eugene *Democratic Register* caught the attention of editor Joaquin Miller, who wooed her first through correspondence and then by riding horseback to Curry County to meet her. In 1864, with a new baby, the Millers settled in Canyon City, a new mining camp in Eastern Oregon. Following the birth of their third child, and Joaquin Miller's departure, Minnie Myrtle Miller supported herself and her children with the help of her mother and friends such as Belle Cooke and Ella Higginson, as well as by sewing, writing poetry and articles for the *New Northwest*, and lecturing in Oregon and California, where the subject of the Millers' broken marriage was of great public interest and aroused the public claim that she was at least as good a poet as her husband, if not the better poet of the two. Divorcing her husband in 1870, Minnie Myrtle Miller made her loss the subject of much of her poetry. "Have Mercy" was printed in 1871 in the *New Northwest*. A second marriage in the early 1870s lasted only a short time. Destitute and in ill health, Minnie Myrtle Miller died in New York City, where she had traveled, too late, to seek medical attention and the financial aid of her first husband.

Have Mercy

Since *one* had been unkind to me,
    I cannot bear that others are kind!
Hush all the sweet voices of sympathy!
    Let me walk in my loneliness groping blind!

Since *one* has been untrue to me,
    Let others all be false—and then
I can hold the world a faithless world,
    And not my darling the worst of men!

My spirit is strong in slight and scorn;
    Help me not down through the intricate street;
Since one has chosen to scatter the thorns,
    Let them press into my sensitive feet.

Men, who are pitiful oaks of the world,
    Lend not your vigor to weakness of mine
Since *one* has bidden me stand alone,
    I am no longer a clinging vine.

Women, with tears and with tender pride,
    Bravely cheering and counseling wise,

Know ye not if ye did but chide
    That I would laugh with my scornful eyes?

I hastened away from the dim, old sea,
    And I fled from the wailing haunts of old,
For they chilled my heart with a mystery
    That my spirit could never to me unfold.

Stars that once I did deem divine,
    Claiming a sisterhood in your songs,
Light your beams for another shrine—
    My spirit to dusky silence belongs.

I can bear the world with its cold deceit;
    I can smile in its dark face covered with sneers—
But touch me not loving or speak to me sweet
    Or my heart will sink with its weight of tears!

Anonymous

Published anonymously in the *New Northwest*, Oregon's only woman's suffrage journal of the nineteenth century, as well as an important literary paper, "Drunk for a Week" appeared in 1871, when both woman's suffrage and temperance were controversial journalistic and literary subjects. Many such pieces were written by the indefatigable editor Abigail Scott Duniway (1834-1915), who may or may not be the author of the following poem. A champion of women's rights, Duniway came to Oregon from Illinois in 1852, married a young farmer of Clackamas County at 19, and at age 25 published her first novel, *Captain Gray's Company*. After her husband was crippled in an accident, Duniway supported him and their six children by teaching school and operating a millinery store. Already active in the suffrage movement, Duniway bought a printing plant in Portland and started the *New Northwest* the same year (1871) that she escorted Susan B. Anthony on a speaking tour of Oregon and Washington. Although women were not granted the right to vote until 1920, Duniway and her co-workers achieved a landmark (although brief) victory in Oregon in 1880, when the state legislature passed a constitutional amendment to give women the vote. It was defeated in 1884 by a 2 to 1 popular (male) vote.

Drunk for a Week

"Tom!" and the tones of the master's voice
    Came sharp to the listening ear;
"Where is the woman who does this work?"
    Said Tom, with a shrug, "I fear
She's had to give it up. She was ghostly white
    When she left the office at six last night."

"Well, scratch her name from off of the books;
  Get somebody in that's well.
These women are always in trouble, I think;
  And Tom—about Timothy Snell:
When he gets over that last week's spree
  And comes to his senses, send him to me.

"It's a week to-day since he's shown his face,
  But he's got his oats to sow;
And I'll give him a hint on the evil of drink,
  And let the whole thing go,
Tim's a good fellow—he'll steady at last;
  Who wants young men to grow old too fast?"

So "drunk for a week" is a young man's joke,
  And sick for a day is a sin;
The woman who faints is sent out to the dogs,
  While the fellow who drinks is kept in.
And why? Oh! that is a riddle confessed;
  The answer I'd give, but it's never been guessed.

Willis White

Willis White (1846-1939) was known, at the time of his death, as the oldest Mason in the world in continuous membership. He was born in Maine, attended school until age 18, worked in the tanning trade until age 24, and settled, in 1871, on the Rogue River. After twelve years of working at lumbering and other jobs, White began a career of homesteading and ranching, eventually owning and operating some of the most valuable ranches in southern Oregon. Married in 1882 to Margaret Curry, with whom he had six children, White served two terms as Curry County assessor and twelve years as deputy sheriff. Moving to Port Orford in 1912, where he owned one-third of the townsite, White was active in civic affairs until his death. Little is known of his life as a poet, but one may suppose that he, like many of his generation, wrote poems for entertainment and to commemorate colorful local events. An Oregon version of the typically American tall tale, "Ace Carey and the Bear" describes a famous pioneer event that occurred in 1870 in Ellensburg, Curry County. The poem's allusion to Greek mythology in stanza five shows that both poet and audience wanted to be thought of as educated and refined, despite their primitive circumstances.

Ace Carey and the Bear

You have heard this story though strange tis true as well,
And not one fancy painted like I've heard others tell,
But really a true story a fact I will declare and emphasize with firmness,
Ace Carey rode a bear.

This happened down in Curry a part of this fair state,
Which now seems forging to the front a coming out though late,
Like a blossom on the sweetest rose, but really I declare,
I quite forgot my story—Ace Carey rode a bear.

Ace went and set a bear trap beneath a spreading oak,
Trouble then was brewing for Bruin—this was no joke,
And to a limb suspended he placed a bill of fare,
I think he called it "Marwich Bearmeat," and Acey caught a bear.

He caught it by a hind leg—well up and thus secure.
He went and called a neighbor to have a witness sure.
The neighbors came and saw him throw a rope that landed fair
Around the neck of Bruin; to this tree he snubbed the bear.

Horatious at the bridge is naught, Thermopylae is tame,
This ursine ride of terror entitles greater fame.
Ace stood there like a Spartan, erect, serenely fair,
Then bowing to his audience he calmly rode the bear.

Bear *with* me just a moment, my story has been told,
There was no tragic end, to this I should mere unfold,
Ace rode this one for pleasure, next time he'll ride a pair,
The hall of fame should claim the name of Ace who rides a bear.

Samuel L. Simpson

Perhaps the best-loved nineteenth-century Oregon poet, Samuel Leonidas Simpson (1846-1899), the "Burns of Oregon," arrived at fame at age 22, when his poem "Beautiful Willamette" was published in the Albany *Democrat*. Called by Joaquin Miller "the most musical poem written on the Pacific Coast," "Beautiful Willamette," or "*Ad Willametam*," as Simpson originally titled it, was reprinted by several Oregon papers, by leading California papers, and by some eastern papers as well. Born in Missouri, and brought to Oregon as an infant of six months, Simpson grew up in Polk and Marion counties, worked for a while in his father's store at Fort Yamhill, near the Grande Ronde Indian Reservation (where he was given a copy of Lord Byron's poetry by General Sheridan), and graduated from Willamette University in 1865. In 1868 he married Julia Humphrey (with whom he had two children) and began to practice law in Albany. He quit the bar in 1870 to begin a career as newspaper editor of various journals—the *Corvallis Gazette*, the *Oregon State Journal*, and papers in Salem, Astoria, and Portland. By the age of 30, however, he had become a quiet alcoholic, unable, until the time of his death, to work steadily at any one thing. He did continue, however, to publish poems from time to time, and a collection of all of his poems was published by colleagues and friends ten years after his death. All but unknown today, possibly less interesting or accomplished than some of Simpson's later work, "Beautiful Willamette" is included here for its historical significance, as well as an example of the kind of pastoral poetry so popular with readers of the time.

Beautiful Willamette

From the Cascades' frozen gorges,
    Leaping like a child at play,
Winding, widening through the valley,
    Bright Willamette glides away:
        Onward ever,
        Lovely river,
    Softly calling to the sea;
        Time that scars us,
        Maims and mars us,
    Leaves no track or trace on thee!

Spring's green witchery is weaving
    Braid and border for thy side;
Grace forever haunts thy journey,
    Beauty dimples on thy tide.
Through the purple gates of morning,
    Now thy roseate ripples dance;

Golden, then, when day departing,
    On thy waters trails his lance;
        Waltzing, flashing,
        Tinkling, plashing,
    Limpid, volatile and free—
        Always hurried
        To be buried
    In the bitter, moon-mad sea.

In thy crystal deeps, inverted,
    Swings a picture of the sky,
Like those wavering hopes of Aidenn
    Dimly in our dreams that lie:
Clouded often, drowned in turmoil,
    Faint and lovely, far away—
Wreathing sunshine on the morrow,
    Breathing fragrance round today.
        Love could wander
        Here, and ponder—
    Hither poetry would dream:
        Life's old questions,
        Sad suggestions,
    "Whence and whither?" throng thy stream.

On the roaring waste of ocean,
    Soon thy scattered waves shall toss:
'Mid the surges' rhythmic thunder
    Shall thy silver tongues be lost.
Oh, thy glimmering rush of gladness
    Mocks this turbid life of mine,
Racing to the wild Forever,
    Down the sloping paths of time—
        Onward ever,
        Lovely river,
    Softly calling to the sea;
        Time that scars us,
        Maims and mars us,
    Leaves no track or trace on thee!

Carrie Blake Morgan

Elder sister of the more popular poet Ella Higginson, Carrie Blake (Rhoads) Morgan (ca. 1850-?) wrote fewer but intellectually more complex poems, then collected and published her poems in *The Path of Gold* (1900), a volume she dedicated to Ella. Born in Kansas, the 12-year-old Carrie helped her mother drive the two-seated carriage that took them and infant Ella alongside the family's covered wagon westward to Oregon, where the Rhoads family lived in La Grande, in the Grande Ronde Valley, Oregon City, Portland, and on a Willamette Valley farm. Little is recorded of Carrie Blake Morgan's adult life, except that she married and lived for a time in Portland, contributed to magazines, moved to Bellingham, Washington (then called New Whatcom), and died before her sister. Humanistic in subject and theme, many of Morgan's poems in *The Path of Gold* foreshadow twentieth-century modernism's challenges to the status quo. Like the old emigrant road in her poem, Morgan's work stands as a fine example of this transitional period in Oregon poetry, where the ways of the past are no longer in use, though their influence haunts today.

The Old Emigrant Road

Aged and desolate, grizzled and still,
It creeps in slow curves round the base of the hill;
Of its once busy traffic is left little trace,
Not a hoof-print or wheel-track is fresh on its face.

Rank brambles encroach on its poor ragged edge,
And boulders crash down from the mountainside ledge;
The elements join to efface the dim trail,
The torrents of springtime, the winter's fierce gale;

Yet, with pioneer sturdiness, patient and still,
It lingers and clings round the base of the hill;
Outlasting its usefulness, furrowed and gray,
Gaunt phantom of Yesterday, haunting To-day.

❧

Faith

Faith shuts his eyes and says, "I know! I know!"
Because his weakling heart would have it so.

❧

Sam Wata

Dr. Sam Wata (birth and death dates unknown) was about 80 years old when he dictated the following myth, in 1930, to anthropologist Isabel Kelly, who was collecting tales from three different bands of the Northern Paiute. Wata was a member of the Beatty (Oregon) band known as the *Go'y'atikad*, or Freshwater Crab Eaters (a post-reservation name)—originally from Summer and Silver lakes, Oregon, where they were known as *Duhu'tcyatikad*, or Deer Eaters. Wata, a former chief and shaman of the Silver Lake band, was unwilling to give traditional tales but did contribute the following creation myth. Different from traditional tribal literature, this is a personal synthesis, incorporating some old elements, but connecting the old with personal observations. Aware that "traditions and traditional ways of speaking have continued to be used to address situations brought about by the coming of Whites," scholar Dell Hymes has arranged Wata's words (originally translated by Susie Archie) into poetry form, so that today's readers may more easily see the formal elements in this traditional speech.

The Beginning of the Earth

One time this was all water but just one little island.
>That is what we are living on now.
Old Man Chocktoot was living on top of this mountain.
>He was living right on top of this mountain.
In all directions the land was lower than this mountain.
>It was burning under the earth.
Numuzoho was under there,
>and he kept on eating people.

The Star was coming.
When that Star came
>it went up into the sky,
>>and stayed there.
When that Star went up,
>he said:
>>"That is too bad.
>>"I pity my people.
>>"We left them without anything to eat.
>>"They are going to starve."
This Star gave us deer,
>and antelope,
>>and elk,
>>>and all kinds of game.

They had Sun for a god.
When the Sun came up,
>he told his people:
>>"Don't worry,

come to me.
"I'll help you.
"Don't worry,
        be happy all your life.
"You will come to me."

The Sun and the Stars came with the Water.
   They had the Water for a home.
The Indian doctor saw them coming.
   He let his people know they were coming.
There were many of them.
The little springs of water are the places from which the silver money comes.
   It comes from the Sun shining on the water.

The first white man came to this land
   and saw that silver
      but he lost himself
         and didn't get to it.
Finally white people found this place
   and they came this way looking for the silver.
Those white men brought cattle,
   sheep,
      pigs,
         and horses.
Before they came,
   there were no horses in this land.

The Sun told his people,
   "Deer belong to you.
   "They are for you to eat."
These white men don't know
   who put the deer and other animals in this land.

I think it is all right for me to kill deer,
   but the white men say they will arrest me.
Whenever I see cattle or sheep,
   I know they don't belong to me,
      I wouldn't kill them.
I feel like going out and killing deer,
   but I am afraid.
      I am getting too old.
Maybe the white people don't know about the beginning of this earth.

Edwin Markham

Chosen Oregon Poet Laureate in 1921 by a unanimous vote of the Oregon Authors' Club, Edwin Markham (1852-1940) was born in Oregon City. The seventh child of pioneer poet Elizabeth Markham, Charles Edward Anson Markham grew up on a farm in northern California, where he plowed a neighbor's fields the summer he was thirteen in order to buy poems by Tennyson, William Cullen Bryant, and Thomas Moore. It was the poems of Byron, however, that started Markham writing, as they had started Sam Simpson and Joaquin Miller before him. Literary success came later in Markham's life. His first poem was published when he was 28; and it was only after the poet worked many years as teacher, principal, and superintendent of schools that "The Man with the Hoe," based on a painting by Millet, catapulted him to fame at 47. With his wife Anna and their only son, Virgil, the poet moved to Staten Island, New York, where he continued to write and publish numerous books of poems, contributed to leading journals, including *Poetry* magazine (Chicago), and founded the Poetry Society of America. Occasionally dismissed by critics as too imitative and sentimental for modern tastes, Markham nevertheless was such an immensely popular poet that friends rented Carnegie Hall for his 80th birthday, and 35 nations sent representatives. Known today mainly for his two most widely anthologized poems, "Lincoln" and "The Man with the Hoe," Edwin Markham contributed a poetry of concern for the working classes at a time when most poets still preferred to rhapsodize the picturesque. "I am by nature an idealist," Markham once remarked, "but . . . nothing but stern realism can express the awful tragedy of life."

The Man with the Hoe

God made him in His own image
In the image of God He made him.
—GENESIS

Bowed by the weight of centuries he leans
Upon his hoe and gazes at the ground,
The emptiness of ages in his face,
And on his back the burden of the world.
Who made him dead to rapture and despair,
A thing that grieves not and never hopes,
Stolid and stunned, a brother to the ox?
Who loosened and let down this brutal jaw?
Whose was the hand that slanted back this brow?
Whose breath blew out the light within this brain?

Is this the Thing the Lord God made and gave
To have dominion over sea and land;
To trace the stars and search the heavens for power;
To feel the passion of Eternity?
Is this the dream He dreamed who shaped the suns
And marked their ways upon the ancient deep?
Down all the caverns of Hell to their last gulf
There is no shape more terrible than this—
More tongued with censure of the world's blind greed—
More packt with danger to the universe.

What gulfs between him and the seraphim!
Slave of the wheel of labor, what to him
Are Plato and the swing of Pleiades?
What the long reaches of the peaks of song,
The rift of dawn, the reddening of the rose?
Through this dread shape the suffering ages look;
Time's tragedy is in that aching stoop;
Through this dread shape humanity betrayed,
Plundered, profaned and disinherited,
Cries protest to the Powers that made the world,
A protest that is also prophecy.

O masters, lords and rulers in all lands,
Is this the handiwork you give to God,
This monstrous thing distorted and soul-quencht?
How will you ever straighten up this shape;
Touch it again with immortality;
Give back the upward looking and the light;
Rebuild in it the music and the dream;
Make right the immemorial infamies,
Perfidious wrongs, immedicable woes?

O masters, lords and rulers in all lands,
How will the future reckon with this Man?
How answer his brute question in that hour
When whirlwinds of rebellion shake all shores?
How will it be with kingdoms and with kings—
With those who shaped him to the thing he is—
When this dumb Terror shall rise to judge the world,
After the silence of the centuries?

C.E.S. Wood

Another Oregon poet to further the advance of New Realism in literature, and one of the first to employ the technique of free verse, Charles Erskine Scott Wood (1852-1944) was a controversial public figure, nonconformist both in his writing and in his personal life. Born in Pennsylvania, Wood graduated from West Point and from Columbia University, spent ten years in the army, fought in the Indian campaigns, and moved to Portland, where he practiced corporate law until 1919. Well known as a speaker and tireless campaigner for progressive causes, a self-declared anarchist, devoted to a wide range of humanitarian principles, Wood was a frequent contributor of poems, stories, essays, and literary and art criticism to the *Pacific Monthly*, the leading literary magazine of the Pacific Northwest. He was married twice: first to Nannie Smith; later to feminist leader and poet Sara Bard Field, with whom he retired to Los Gatos, California, where their home became a gathering place for artists and writers, including Robinson Jeffers, Ansel Adams, John Steinbeck, and Yehudi Menuhin. Wood was the author of several books of poems and prose, the most famous of which remains his book-length *Poet in the Desert*, first published in 1915 but revised throughout his lifetime. The selections published here are from the 1918 version reprinted after his death by Sara Bard Field.

First Snow

The cows are bawling in the mountains.
The snowflakes fall.
They are leaving the pools and pebbled fountains.
Troubled, they bawl.
They are winding down the mountain's shoulders
Through the open pines,
The wild-rose thickets, and the granite boulders
In broken lines.
Each calf trots close beside its mother
And so they go,
Bawling and calling to one another
About the snow.

from **The Poet in the Desert**
XLII

How rich is our palace of Light.
Not only the overarching skies,
The wide-spreading sea
And the engirdling mountains,
The Desert and towering clouds;
But the carefully painted wildcat,
The striped skunk, the spotted fawn,
Kittens and puppies,
All soft, helpless young things,
Butterflies, winged-flowers,
And hummingbirds, jewels of the air,
Green beetles, with emerald backs;
Coral ladybugs, enameled with black spots,
Carefully touched by the artist.
The pigeon's neck, the pheasant's breast;
The jaybird's wing; the blackbird's back;
The royal spreading peacock;
A baby's foot,
Pink as the shells which have caught the dye
Of sunset;
Corals and seaweeds,
Fishes fantastic,
Which swam through a rainbow;
Steaming, new-ploughed fields and the dark loam of the forest;
Leaves, blossoms, flowers, skies and cobwebs,
The illimitable Evening and Morning,
And, also, the illimitable diamonds
Which the sparkling fingers of the Frost
Hang upon wintry boughs.
The Universe as much within a frost-crystal
As in the constellations which cover the night
With their patterns.

from **LI**

Suddenly, as a dry prairie fired by lightning,
A conflagration roars to the horizon,
Hate falls upon the peoples.
They run about killing each other,
Not knowing why.

Whose are the fingers slipped through
The collars of the dogs of war,
Ready to release them;
Baying: "War. War. War?"
Do the peasants who plough the kindly fields
Declare war against each other,
Or laborers, after their toil,
Sit in cottages, planning battle?
Do miners hasten from the dark
Communion of the ages
To slaughter their brothers?
Or the Titans of the forges
Plot murder against their fellows?
Who is it orders this hate;
This carefully arranged murder?
Whose is the quarrel?
Whose the profit?
Answer—Whose the profit?
For profit maketh war.
The herd slavishly keeps step
To the time set by their Rulers
And crowd up the slaughter chute
To the butcher's knife;
Fooled by wiles of the Masters,
They enter the dark cave
Whence is no return:
Neither baby-fingers, nor lovers' cheeks;
Neither sun, nor moon, nor the ripple of waters;
Neither seeing, nor hearing;
Nor thought, nor laughter any more.

William Hartless

Although descendants of the various Kalapuyan (western Willamette Valley) tribes still live in Oregon, none today speaks any of the original dialects of that nation. In 1914, William Hartless (1855-1920), the last living Kalapuyan to speak the Mary's River (Pinefu) dialect, assisted anthropologist Leo J. Frachtenberg of Columbia University in recording some of the history of his people. Little is known of the life of William Hartless, who was raised in the traditional Native American ways before the reservation period of the 1860s. Catholic Church records show he was confirmed by the priest at the mission church at the Grande Ronde Reservation in 1880 and married Christine Petit in 1884. Of their seven children, two were still living in 1900. In addition to providing extensive information about the ways of his people and dictating numerous legends and myths, Hartless spoke frankly and deeply to Frachtenberg of his own personal impressions. Discovering formal speech patterns in Hartless's words, contemporary scholar Dell Hymes, one of America's most respected figures in the field of ethnopoetics, has retranslated Hartless's original narrative into the following poem.

I Am the Only One Now

I am the only one now
     I've been left alone,
          all my people have died.

The only one now,
     I stay on.

I being dead,
     my tribe will indeed be gone.

My country—
     I am Kalapuya,
          at Corvallis my country,
               the Indian people name my country 'Pinefu'—
                    my tribe.

So I now am indeed the last,
     I in my country.

Ella Higginson

Younger sister of the poet Carrie Blake Morgan, Ella Rhoads Higginson (1862-1940) crossed the plains from Kansas as an infant and lived with her family in La Grande, in the Grande Ronde Valley, in Oregon City, in Portland, and on a farm in the Willamette Valley. Her first poem was published in the Oregon City *Enterprise* when she was fourteen. She began working on that newspaper at age sixteen, learning to set type, and taking responsibility for the editorial page. In 1885 she married Russell Higginson, and three years later they moved to Bellingham, where she became Washington's poet laureate and where she lived until her death. She was a prolific writer of both poetry and fiction, as well as a newspaper columnist, choosing Oregon and Washington as her subject matter throughout her life. More than fifty composers are said to have created musical settings for her poems, the most famous of which was "Four-Leaf Clover," the official song of the National Federation of Women's Clubs. Her poem "Hate," originally titled "Cleopatra," different from most of her poems, explores a negative feeling—something not generally done at the time—from the point of view of a historical character. A challenge, also, to standard ways of thought, and reminiscent of poet Emily Dickinson, "God's Creed," in its complete version, shows Oregon poetry becoming more specific in its use of local images, unique to the Pacific Northwest, and less imitative of the generic pastoral verse so much in vogue at the time.

Ella Higginson age 10

Hate

If hate be unforgivable,
    Then must I unforgiven be,
For I shall hate one woman, Lord,
    For all eternity.

Forgiven or not, I hate her so
    That did she, burnt with fever, lie,
I'd spill the ice-cup that she craved
    And laugh to see her die.

Yea, Lord, yea, Lord—I hate her so
    That, were she sent to deepest hell,
I'd pray the awful fires might do
    Their part slow—slow—and well.

from **God's Creed**

Forgive me that I hear thy creeds
　　Unawed and unafraid;
They are too small for one whose ears
　　Have heard God's organ played;
Who in wide, noble solitudes,
　　In simple faith has prayed.

Forgive me that I cannot kneel
　　And worship in this pew,
For I have knelt in western dawns,
　　When the stars were large and few,
And the only fonts God gave me were
　　The deep leaves filled with dew.

And so it is I worship best
　　With only the soft air
About me, and the sun's warm gold
　　Upon my brow and hair;
For then my very heart and soul
　　Mount upward in swift prayer.

My church has been a yellow space
　　Ceiled over with blue heaven,
My pew upon a noble hill
　　Where the fir-trees were seven,
And the stars upon their slender tops
　　Were tapers lit at even.

My knees have known no cushions rich,
　　But the soft, emerald sod;
My aisles have been the forest paths
　　Lined with the crimson-rod;
My choir, the birds and winds and waves—
　　My only pastor, God.

Valentine Brown

Born in Portland, Oregon, Valentine Brown, Jr. (1862-1926) began writing in the 1880s and published his first book of poems in 1900. He had a paper route at age 11 and became a flyboy at the *Bee* office press and printer's devil on the East Portland *Vindicator*. He was educated at Bishop Scott Academy and for three years worked his way around the world as a sailor. After several years as a railway mail clerk and real estate dealer, he graduated from the University of Oregon law school, married Jennie Ham, had three children, and spent the rest of his life as an attorney and poet. He wrote nearly 1,000 pages of poetry, all of which he typeset himself into five books. Many of Brown's poems carry on the tradition established by such earlier poets as Samuel A. Clarke: to record in poetry some of the Native Oregonian's legends and myths, as well as the efforts of the earlier settlers to describe the grandeur of the Oregon landscape. In "The Chinook Wind," Brown goes beyond earlier generic verse by referring to Oregon landscape and events. (Other texts about the Chinook wind are listed in the suggested readings at the end of this book.)

The Chinook Wind

In the spring I awaken from ocean's dominions,
In a mist I arise o'er the wave beaten height;
With the storm for my talons and cloud for my pinions,
To the snows I will look for my far away flight.

I will sweep on the passes, and shout to the fountains,
They will drink of my wrath and in torrents will flow;
I will mock at the trees on the forest clad mountains,
Which are waving their impotent arms in their woe.

I will race on the river that rolls in the ocean,
And winnow the rain with the lash of a flail;
As the boatman beholds me in angry commotion,
He will turn to the shore and condemn me a gale.

But my goal is the hills where the snowdrifts are hiding,
And my foe is the winter which cuts with a blast;
As the bleak icy canyons my pinions are guiding,
I will strike with my talons and winter has passed.

Though the torrents shall flow, and the forests are sighing,
And the mariner pales when I rise from the sea,
With the bearers of gladness I ever am vieing;
I will bring a green mantle for hillside and lea.

Then the breath of my wings will repose on the bowers,
And the blossoms will smile in the sunshine of spring;
As the valleys are feeling the warmth of my showers,
I dissolve in the joy of the carols I bring.

Katsuko and Tamu: Issei Poets of Hood River

Often overlooked in the history of Oregon is the fact that many early settlers came not across the Rocky Mountains but across the Pacific. In 1904 the first Issei (first-generation Japanese) immigrants arrived in Hood River, Oregon, and began to clear an area for farming 30 miles from north to south and 8 miles from east to west, as well as an area near Cascade Locks, 19 miles down the Columbia River. In 1905 more than six hundred Japanese settlers were making farmlands of forests with hand tools, supporting themselves meanwhile by working as laborers on other farms and in sawmills, enduring tremendous hardships—adding to their lands slowly and patiently over many years, until they could be self sustaining. The following poems are taken from a chapter on Hood River agriculture in the book *Issei*, a more than 1,000-page compilation of historical articles, letters, diaries, statements, and poems by hundreds of Issei in the Pacific Northwest. Specific biographical information is unavailable about either poet. Whatever their particular pasts, their words speak for the experiences of many. The brevity and the precise language of these traditional haiku, as well as their honest portrayal of painful experience, make them seem much more modern than most poems written by other Oregon poets of the time.

Spades in the dark soil.
Spirit of the pioneers
Burning on the earth.

Katsuko

Alien hardships
Made bearable by the hope
I hold for my children.

Katsuko

Ripening autumn,
And within, secretly held,
Old times and sad tales.

Tamu

Translated by Shinichiro Nakamura and Jean S. Gerard

Bert Huffman

Bertram Wilson Huffman (1870-1954) was born in a log cabin on one of the first farms in the Grande Ronde Valley and raised on a ranch in Pyle's Canyon, 5 miles east of Union, on the Old Oregon Trail. His boyhood was spent riding the range, breaking horses, and trailing cattle. To continue his upper-grade schooling, he swept the offices and hallways at Union's Booth Hotel in return for room and board. At age 15 his poems were being published in Union County newspapers. Leaving home at age 19, marrying Ella Green at age 20, Huffman worked a variety of jobs—as typesetter, at sawmills, as editor of the *La Grande Journal*, as a railroad engineer, and as managing editor of Pendleton's *East Oregonian*—all the while contributing articles, poems, and letters to the *Oregon Scout* and other papers, earning the respect of other writers around the state, including Joaquin Miller, who publicly praised Huffman's poem on Sacajawea. In 1908 he bought a farm in Alberta, Canada, where he lived the rest of his life, continuing to write both poetry and prize-winning short stories. His "Umatilla County Statistics," with its catalog of place-names, shows Huffman as a poet of wit whose verse exhibits a strong regional pride as well as a colorful folk idiom.

Umatilla County Statistics

Freewater grows the strawberry,
      Two crops in the selfsame year;
Athena yields the golden corn
      That equals the Kansan ear;
The fleece grows heavy at Pilot Rock,
      Alfalfa at Hudson Bay,
And the spuds of Weston mountain
      Are big as a bale of hay.
No spot on earth beats Helix
      For wheat weighing sixty-five;
And the swarming herds of Butter Creek
      Are thick as bees in a hive!
Fair Milton's smiling vineyards,
      The sweetest draughts distil,
While smiles and dollars grow on the trees
      At Adams, under the hill!
Prim Weston's crop of schoolma'ams
      Is fairest in forty states,
But for a yield of rabbit hides
      Old Echo "skins" her mates.

Charles Oluf Olsen

Charles Oluf Olsen (1872-1959) was one of the first poets, along with his contemporaries Laurence Pratt, Paul Tracy, James Stevens, and H.L. Davis, to bring the realities of the laboring classes into Oregon literature. Born in Lyngby, Denmark, Olsen came to America at age 16, settling in Oregon in 1899. An ironworks laborer, cook, salesman, lumberjack, and (for 10 years) a blacksmith, Olsen turned to writing when he couldn't find a blacksmith job in Portland. In 1922 he married Elizabeth Thompson, a teacher and poet, and from then on he wrote feature articles for the *Morning Oregonian*, technical articles for lumber journals, fiction, and poetry, and was active in Portland literary circles. Called "the best of all the Northwestern bards" by writer James Stevens, Olsen edited a poetry section of the *Morning Oregonian* and presented a special Oregon poets section in the June 1926 *American Mercury*. Olsen's own poems were published in many leading journals of the 1920s and 1930s, including *Poetry* (Chicago) and *Measure*. His partially completed history of Milwaukie, Oregon, written during the Oregon Writers' Project for the Works Progress Administration (WPA), can be found in the Multnomah County Public Library.

Zero Hour in the Factory

There's hissing and panting of steam
And a throbbing everywhere,
As I hang for a breath of air
Over a dusty window-sill
Out of a room that is never still
From whir of wheel and thump of press.

The whole thing seems so meaningless . . .
Below me on the railroad track
An engine tries to move a train,
But groans and coughs and pulls in vain,
The hot smoke spouting from its stack.

There seems no sense to life at all—
Work and heat and smoke and sound . . .

I am one of the sparks that pour
From a belching stack, to glow and soar
For a moment, only to die and fall,
A cinder-speck on the sooty ground.

Frances Holmstrom

Frances Johnson Holmstrom (1881-1956), painter as well as poet, was born in Michigan and, before she was 16, studied two years at the Cleveland School of Art. Moving with her family to Oregon, she taught in a rural school, married Charles Holmstrom, had four children, lived in logging camps where her husband was an engineer, and later settled on a dairy and berry farm near McKinley. In addition to developing a new form of art using myrtlewood plaques and oil paint, Frances Holmstrom began publishing poems in the early 1920s in such journals as *Forum, Sunset*, and *Ladies' Home Journal.* One of her poems was entered in the Congressional Record via Senator Wayne Morse, and she was the author of three books of poems. "The Shearers," below, first appeared in the special June 1926 Oregon poets issue of *American Mercury*, and, with "The High Lead Tree," shows Holmstrom as one of the first poets in Oregon's literary history to express a concern for our limited environmental resources. Different in subject matter, "Values" is also a poem ahead of its time. Aware that women's traditional work is generally not considered as valuable as "high art," Holmstrom (like Fuller, in a following piece) challenges common assumptions and redefines "values" for herself.

Values

Within me somewhere, lies a poem, dead.
I glimpsed it; it was lovely where it lay.
Its soul of light, its flesh of words unsaid,
Were more than beauty, they were ecstasy,
But it is cold, its hour of birth gone by,
With no more tribute than an unsighed sigh.

Against my arm a little boy leans; he
Is four years old; he has a round white head.
He is much more than merely words are, so
Because of him I let the poem go
And made a little gingham shirt, instead.

The High Lead Tree

I am a Judas, yet as firm I stand,
As close Earth holds my roots within her hand,
As when I was her kingliest son, and stood
Shoulders and head above my brotherhood.

My brothers' trunks upon the hillside lie,
And, I, who live, envy the ones who die,
For I am slave. Steel woven cables bind
My living body, torn, dismembered, blind,
To the betrayal of my forest kind.

For such as I there is no day, no dark.
No circling seasons wind within my bark
Their secret record, like a silken thread.
My live heart pulses in a body dead.
Not log I am, not bough, no longer tree.
I am a thing that men have made of me.

They shout below, the heavy fetters thrum.
The singing cable winds about the drum.
The donkeys shriek, the timber-fallers cry
Warning! the forests take the ax and die,
While I stand high in nakedness, and swing,
Above the carnage and the clamoring,
My brothers' flesh down to the marketing.

The Shearers

Shorn are the sheep that are mountains, huddled against each other,
Looking askance and bewildered, each at his naked brother.
The Titan flocks of the mountains, that ruled the plains in peace,
Have bowed to the shears of the shearer, have yielded the golden fleece.

That which was down upon them ere breath touched the shearer's lips
Shall rise in his cloud-hung towers, shall rock in his masted ships.
But when the cities are leveled, and the great hulks rot in the sun,
They shall ask again of the mountains, and learn that the shearing is done.

Ethel Romig Fuller

Oregon Poet Laureate from 1957 until the time of her death, Ethel Romig Fuller (1883-1965) climbed Mount Hood when she was 26, three years after coming to Oregon from her home state of Michigan. "From that day on," she said, "I had to write about the Northwest." Published extensively throughout the United States and around the world in magazines, school textbooks, and anthologies, Ethel Romig Fuller was one of Oregon's most energetic literary figures, a great friend to writers throughout the state, and a voice of encouragement to countless younger poets. Editor of the Portland *Oregonian*'s weekly poetry section for more than 25 years, she also wrote the foreword to Henry Harrison's influential *Oregon Poets* anthology of 1935, was a member of Verseweavers, a Portland literary organization, and published three volumes of her own poetry. The following poems, in both free and traditional forms, show Fuller, like many poets of her generation, beginning to ignore "the decorous" in both language and subject, as well as sometimes challenging popular sex-role stereotypes.

These Are the Strong

Not rushing, sudden water,
Not wild and bitter wind,
Not a body hanging
For the black deed he has sinned;

Not streams of molten lava,
Not showers of meteors,
Not tidal waves or thunder,
Not famine and not wars

Can prevail against the birthing
Of a baby or a song—
These are the strong, my brothers,
These are the strong.

Fireweed

It follows on the heels of carnage;
It revels in ashes. It thrives on the hot ashes of pine needles
And fir cones; on the stilled laughter of larches.
It inhales smoke with impunity and exhales magenta flame.
It sears new wounds; it congeals on the edges of old wounds.
It distils a strange pungency from pitch-globules,
(Melted rosin is the death-sweat of burning trees)
It sacks ghost-honey for conspiring bees.

It ignores the decorous black of burnt-over hills and shouts
Ribald chanteys in the charnel house.
It dances in the deserted abodes of wild creatures;
At the dried sources of mountain brooks, on the grave of a forest.
Fireweed . . . .

Ada Hastings Hedges

Ada May Hastings Hedges (1884-1980) was born in Illinois, educated
at a teachers' college in that state, married a Chicago physician, and
moved with him to eastern Oregon around 1915. For eight years he
worked as a railroad physician and she taught high school in Juntura
(Malheur County)—a setting that was to become the chief subject of her
1930 book, *Desert Poems*. An author of short fiction as well as poetry,
published in American and English magazines, Hedges moved to Portland
where, after the death of her husband in 1935, she became active in the
veterans' rights movement and was supervising editor of 54 writers
employed by the Works Progress Administration to write the *Oregon State Guide*. She
last taught in the 1960s at Warner Pacific College. She lived and wrote until the age of
96, when she received her last literary prize—an honorable mention in the annual Ben
Hur Lampman poetry contest. The following selections from *Desert Poems*, written in
traditional sonnet form (a literary fashion of the time), seem contemporary even today
in their feminist outlook and in their forceful and realistic appraisal of the rigors of
eastern Oregon life in the early part of this century, so different from the experiences
of settlers west of the Cascades. "The desert region," she once said, "fascinated me
always, and still does. I found it full of mystery and beauty in its own bleak fashion,
with a certain collective consciousness, strangely haunting and baffling. . . ."

from **The Desert Wife**
III

They had their dreams of green alfalfa fields
With thriving growths to cut—and lusty clover,
Of yellow acres and their yellow yields
To fill their granaries and brim them over.
Seasons would follow—summer follow spring
As orderly as in a gentler place;
By sowing and by reaping they might bring
Time to a desert that had known but space.
They would diminish with their poplar trees
Horizons that were too remote and vast,
Surround the house and garden, and from these
Bar out primeval loneliness at last . . .

She must have trees against the hill, she said,
That frowned unbearably upon her head.

X

If roads were passable they drove to town,
Her high adventure once or twice a year;
(To climb the rocky summit and then down
Made miles too many when his time was dear).
A store, a church, a barn with empty stalls,
A dozen houses in this oasis,
With families sheltered by their drunken walls,
Made it for her a fair metropolis.
But more than talk of women she had craved,
Than piles of bright prints on the shelves—far more—
She loved a battered lilac that had braved
The desert drought and grew beside a door—
The dusty scent that quickened in her breast
Something she thought had perished with the rest.

XII

They grew more passive with the meagre years,
Upon their lips and hearts the desert lay
The silence that had throbbed upon their ears—
And after all there was not much to say.
Disheartened neighbors vanished one by one,
A hill grave claimed the last child of the four,
She watched the sagebrush billow in the sun,
A lonelier exile on a lonelier shore.
Then life so long a tread of weariness
Waned suddenly, perhaps to her surprise,
And one blue-aproned, faded woman less
Stared from a door with hunger in her eyes . . .
And he surrendered what faith he had kept
To an empty kitchen and a hearth unswept.

Neighbor

She of the wild blood and the truant feet
That spurned dull paths, is now a prisoner
Within her four low walls. Her will was sweet
But homely needs have made a slave of her.
The brilliant golden plumage has been shed,
The restless hands that scorned a pan or seam
Are stained from serving him she chose, instead
Of many passing through her shoddy dream.
What man of them would think that love could tame
A wanton thus; that from the garish lights
Should bloom one shaded lamp; or that the blaze
Of dying fires should kindle this hearth's flame;
That from the feverish chaos of old nights
Should blossom forth these white and ordered days?

Silent Juniper

Yes, I am lonely . . . but I know a tree
That stands alone upon a grey hill's crest,
The reach about it empty as the sea,
The waste winds bitter from the east and west.
To this dark tree the seasons come and go
But bring no white bloom nor a burning leaf—
By its grim foliage you would never know
That sometimes, passionate and mute and brief,
The spring is at its heart. And once betrayed
By wings too eager or a flight too long,
A bright bird came to rest within its shade,
And turned the morning golden with his song . . .
Songs live in fairer trees from sun to sun—
The silent juniper remembers one.

Hazel Hall

One of Oregon's most celebrated poets of the first half of the century, Hazel Hall (1886-1924) spent most of her life confined to her Portland home. Unable to walk after a bout with scarlet fever and a fall when she was 12, Hall took in needlework to support herself and, when her eyesight began to fail, she turned to poetry as a way to earn extra income. Born in St. Paul, Minnesota, she came as a young girl to Portland with her parents. Her formal education ended with the fifth grade, but she read a great deal and was familiar with the works of most American and British writers of the time. Her first poem appeared in the *Boston Transcript* when she was 30 years old, and she was one of the first of several Oregon poets to be published in the prestigious *Poetry* magazine of Chicago. Numerous magazine and anthology publications followed, several prizes, including the Young Poets' Prize from *Poetry* and the *Contemporary Verse* award for 1921; and Hall's portrait was hung over the mantel of the "Poet's Corner" of Portland's J.K. Gill's bookstore—a cozy nook designed as a gathering place for literati of the day. Two books of poems were published before her sudden death from illness; a third book was published posthumously. Recognition continued to come: Harold G. Merriam, editor of *The Frontier*, dedicated his 1931 anthology *Northwest Verse* in her memory; Viola Price Franklin edited a 1939 memorial volume, *A Tribute to Hazel Hall;* and, in 1987, the Oregon Institute of Literary Art established an annual Oregon Book Award for Poetry in her name. Hall's poetry, written usually in metrical, rhymed forms, and occasionally in free verse, often deals with her experience as an invalid, her observations of the people passing by her window, and her awareness of various kinds of grief in the world.

Monograms

I am monogramming
Seven dozen napkins,
With tablecloths to match,
For a bride.

Ninety-one times my needle shall trace
The leaf-like scrolls that interlace
Each other; up the padded side
Of the monogram my eye shall guide
For ninety-one days where the stitches run;
And every day one more is done.

She is tall and fair,
She will be married
In June. . . .

The linen is fine as satin is fine;
Its shining coolness flaunts design

Of death-white poppies, trailing ferns
Rioting richly from Grecian urns.

Ghost flowers,
Cold, cold . . .

All these patterned splendours fade
Before the crest my hands have made;
In the lifeless flax my stitches cry
With life my hands may not put by.

June . . .
Real flowers,
Moist and warm to touch,
Like flesh . . .

And by and by with all the rest
Of intimate things in her bridal-chest,
Gentle muslins and secret lace,
Something of mine will have a place;
Caught in these scrolls and filigrees
There will be that which no eye sees,
The bulk of a season's smothered wonder,
My ninety-one days stitched under and under.

They will be decking an altar
With white roses,
And lacing an aisle
With white ribbon. . . .

Measurements

Stitches running up a seam
Are not like feet beside a stream,
And the thread that swishes after
Is not at all like echoed laughter.
Yet stitches are as quick as feet,
Leaping from a rocky pleat
To seams that slip like marshy ground;
And thread-swish has a hollow sound.

Stitches that have a seam to sew
Must not forget the way they go,
While feet that find the cool earth sweet
Have forgotten they are feet,

And a laugher cares not why
His echoes have a haunted cry.
So stitches running up a seam
Are not like feet beside a stream,
And the thread that swishes after
Is not at all like echoed laughter.

Inheritance

Over and over again I lose myself in sorrow;
Whatever I have borne I bear again tenfold.
The death of sorrow is a sleep; a newer sorrow
Wakes into name from ashes of the old.

They said that sorrow died and that a sorrow buried
Made your mind a dear place like a grave with grass,
Where you might rest yourself as in a willow's shadow,
And cold and clean, might feel the long world pass.

But sorrow does not die, sorrow only gathers
Weight about itself—a clay that bakes to stone.
When your own share of sorrow has worn itself to slumber
Then every woman's sorrow is your own.

Ben Hur Lampman

Oregon's first official poet laureate, from 1951 until his death, Ben Hur Lampman (1886-1954) was born in Wisconsin, moved to North Dakota, where he started newspaper work in his father's print shop at age 11, became a journeyman printer in his early teens, and established and edited the Michigan City *Arena* at age 19. The following year he married Lena McEwen Sheldon, and, in 1912, the Lampmans, with their three children, moved to Gold Hill, Oregon, where Ben Hur Lampman published and edited the Gold Hill *News* and fished the Rogue River. He began working as a police reporter and feature editor for the *Oregonian* in 1916. In 1939 he was appointed associate editor. First serialized in the *Oregonian* in 1926, his collection of poems and editorial articles, *How Could I Be Forgetting?*, appeared as a book in 1933. Subsequent books included poems and short stories, nature writings, and a novel. *Reader's Digest* reprinted his famous *Oregonian* editorial "Where to Bury a Dog" (also read on a national radio program), and two of his stories were included in the 1943 and 1945 O. Henry Memorial prize volumes. While Oregon's Poet Laureate, Lampman received the Freedom Foundation certificate of merit "for outstanding achievement in bringing about a better understanding of the American way of life."

How Could I Be Forgetting?

Often I try to remember fragments of things,
As how many days has November, and names of kings,
And measures for corn and barley, and hay in the stack—
But always they will elude me and won't come back.
That which I learn for tomorrow is quite forgotten today,
As a mist that meets a breeze and is driven away.
How strange I should remember, for many and many a June,
The lilt and the running laughter of an old tune.

When I open a book to follow the way a scholar should,
Fleet as a glancing swallow my heart is off to the wood;
The lines are dim before me and have no meaning, while
I stand in a lane by the river, at the end of a country mile.
There is wind on the water, and a sprinkle of dancing rain,
And I am so glad within me that the joy of it hurts like pain—
I have closed the book without knowing what it is all about,
But well, so well, I remember the glint of a leaping trout.

So I have given it over, and am minded not to try
Ever again to recover such matters as when and why,
And how many days has November, and names of kings,
And any number of other very important things.
It seems I must be content with trivial memories, quite
Like one I have of the stars on a windless winter night,
Or one of a golden wave on an acre I'd sown to grain—
And how could I be forgetting the whisper that heralds rain?

The best of a sorry bargain—yet in my heart I am glad,
For I have kept each picture that I have ever had—
I've but to dream for a moment, and so in a moment to be
Dazed with a wind from ocean and filled with a sight of the sea;
But to reflect for a moment, and then to stand in the rain,
Silver rain by the river, where the bright trout leap again;
For I could never remember the rules that are found in books—
But how could I be forgetting the way that a sunset looks?

Under a dark sky sweeping three gulls are driven by—
Given into my keeping till the day that I come to die;
The sheen of a mallard's feather, a blackened tree on a hill,
And a whitened weave of waters where the stream will not be still;
All spider-webs at seven, when they are heavy with dew,
And cold and bright with fires, burning in white and in blue;
Trumpets ringing above me—I cannot remember a sum—
But how could I be forgetting the way the wild geese come?

John Reed

The only Oregon author and poet to be buried in Red Square in Moscow, John Silas Reed (1887-1920) was known both for the fine quality of his journalism and for his radical political views. Born near Portland in 1911, the son of Charles Jerome Reed, a U.S. Marshal, and Margaret (Green) Reed, John Reed graduated from Harvard College in 1910 and the following year joined the staff of the *American Magazine*. The very first issue of *Poetry* magazine, published in 1912, contained his poem "Songs." Prose books, resulting from his work as correspondent for *Metropolitan Mazazine*, included *Insurgent Mexico* (1914), based on his experiences with the Mexican revolutionary leader Pancho Villa, and *Ten Days That Shook the World* (1919), widely regarded as one of the finest eyewitness accounts of the Russian Revolution. Returning to the United States, Reed formed the Communist Labor Party (as distinct from the Communist Party), appeared before a senate investigation committee, and was later arrested for an "incendiary speech" in Philadelphia. Released without trial, he fled to Moscow in 1920, with a forged passport.

He died of typhus the same year, was given a state funeral, and was buried beside the Kremlin wall. Although Reed never condoned the dictatorial aspects of communism, he became a friend of Soviet leader Lenin. The story of Reed's life and the life of his wife Louise Bryant, whom he married in 1917, was made into the 1981 motion picture "Reds." His *Collected Poems*, from which this excerpt from the six-page, Whitmanesque poem "America 1918" is taken, was published in 1985.

from America 1918

I

    By my free boyhood in the wide West,
The powerful sweet river, fish-wheels, log-rafts,
Ships from behind the sunset, Lascar-manned,
Chinatown, throbbing with mysterious gongs,
The blue thunderous Pacific, blaring sunsets,
Black smoking forests on surf-beaten headlands,
Lost beaches, camp-fires, wail of hunting cougars . . .
By the rolling range, and the flat sun-smitten desert,
Night with coyotes yapping, domed with burst of stars,
The grey herd moving eastward, towering dust,
Ropes whistling in slow coils, hats flapping, yells . . .
By miles of yellow wheat rippling in the Chinook,
Orchards forever endless, deep in blooming,

Green-golden orangegroves and snow-peaks looming over.
By raw audacious cities sprung from nothing,
Brawling and bragging in their careless youth . . .
I know thee, America!

Fishermen putting out from Astoria in the foggy dawn their double-
      bowed boats,
Lean cow-punchers jogging south from Burns, with faces burned
      leathery and silent,
Stringy old prospectors trudging behind reluctant packhorses, across
      the Nevada alkali,
Hunters coming out of the brush at night-fall on the brink of the Lewis
      and Clark canyon,
Grunting as they slide off their fifty-pound packs and look around for a
      place to make camp,
Forest rangers standing on a bald peak and sweeping the wilderness for
      smoke,
Big-gloved brakemen walking the top of a swaying freight, spanner in
      hand, biting off a hunk of plug,
Lumbermen with spiked boots and timber-hook, riding the broken jam
      in white water,
Indians on the street-corner in Pocatello, pulling out chin-whiskers
      with a pair of tweezers and a pocket-mirror,
Or down on the Siuslaw, squatting behind their summer lodges
      listening to Caruso on a two-hundred-dollar phonograph,
Loud-roaring Alaska miners, smashing looking-glasses, throwing the
      waiter a five-dollar gold-piece for a shot of whiskey and telling
      him to keep the change,
Keepers of dance-halls in construction camps, bar-keeps, prostitutes,
Bums riding the rods, Wobblies singing their defiant songs, unafraid of
      death,
Card-sharps and real-estate agents, timber-kings, wheat-kings, cattle-
      kings . . .
I know ye, Americans!

Yoko Usada

Yoko Usada (1887-) was born in Toyama, Ken, Japan. She and her husband came to the U.S. in 1921 and started a men's clothing store and cleaners. During World War II, their family was moved to Minidoka Camp in Hunt, Idaho. After the war, she and her husband moved to Detroit, Michigan. When her husband died, she returned to Hillsboro to live with one of her daughters. Both before World War II and after her return to Oregon in the 1950s, she was a member of the Hood Ginsha—a group of Japanese women who met irregularly to share and enjoy poems that they wrote. The group is no longer active. This poem was translated by Keiko Tomizawa.

Poem　初蝶を見しより老の歩のはずみ

Seeing the first butterfly of spring makes even an
Old man step lightly.

Mary Carolyn Davies

Mary Carolyn Davies (1888-1940) was born in Sprague, Washington, attended schools near Portland, and in 1910 graduated "Class Poet" from Portland's Washington High School, where she was editor of both the annual and the literary magazine, *The Lens*. She taught school on the Crooked River in Crook County and on the coast at Rockaway before attending the University of California for a year. The first freshman to win a much-coveted prize for poetry, she left for Greenwich Village in New York, arriving with exactly $4.85 prize money remaining. Over the next few years she earned her living writing short stories, two serials, children's books, and much popular magazine verse, occasionally finding time to write "what *she* regarded as poetry," which was published in leading literary journals. Married for two years to poet Leland Davis, Mary Carolyn Davies returned to Portland in 1922, having published four books of poems and a one-act play, first produced by the celebrated Provincetown Players, and then by many high schools, including her own Washington High. Part of a generation that elsewhere around the world was known as "the Lost Generation," Davies—though she stayed in America—often used her poems to challenge such social institutions as marriage and war. According to Alfred Powers, Davies was adopted by the Blackfeet Indian Tribe and given the name Pawtuxie (Pinewoman); became president of the Women's Press Club of Oregon; and was the first president, in 1924, of the Northwest Poetry Society, whose members included Howard McKinley Corning, Verne Bright, Charles Oluf Olsen, and Ethel Romig Fuller. "The Circuit Rider" received first prize out of hundreds of entries in a 1924 contest sponsored by R.A. Booth of Eugene, on the occasion of the unveiling of the Circuit Rider statue he presented to the state in honor of his minister father.

Mary Carolyn Davies as a baby

Traps

A trap's a very useful thing:
Nature in our path sets Spring.
It is a trap to catch us two,
It is planned for me and you.
Do not think my cheeks are warm,
Do not wonder if my arm
Would make a pillow sweet for rest.
Not to speak or glance is best—
To smother the thing that calls so clear
Deep in our thoughts at the spring of the year.
If we stop, if we look, if we speak, if we care,
Spring will catch us unaware,
Will put us in a house with four
Chairs, a table, and a door
To enslave us evermore.
She means to tie you firm and tight
To a desk from dawn till night,
To make you strain and make you sweat
Till you forget, till you forget
All that is good and fine and high.
She will give you fear to keep till you die.
She means to tear my flesh to make
A child to steal my hours awake,
To break my hours asleep, to be
Slayer of the youth in me,
Slayer of the youth in you,
Slayer of that which makes us sing.
—Let us never look at Spring;
It is a trap to catch us two.

War

We'd not have had the grit to be in love
Had not war given a shove
To our slow cautiousness, and made us know
That there is no tomorrow anywhere—
That those who care
Should not take chances so.
And so we married and you went away
To fight. And I am glad we didn't wait.
How queer it is to think it should be hate
And bitterness, that gave the shove
That pushed us into love.

❧

The Circuit Rider

God tramps on through the scourging rains,
    God vaults into the saddle;
Rides alone past the dusty plains;
    God's back bends to the paddle.
Cedar branches and sunlight through,
And on, still on, speeds the lone canoe!

God rides out on his ancient quest,
    Healing, saving, commanding.
Here in the savage unknown West,
    Settlement, cabin, landing—
Well they know the steady beat,
In the stillness, of God's horse's feet.

God leads to grace the pioneers
    Who walk each hour with danger;
Knows these grim men for his peers;
    Gives his bread to the stranger—
Doing all that a neighbor can,
God rides still—a weary man.

God rides out—and founds three states;
    Their scourger, their defender;
Guides their loves and tones their hates,
    Leads them into splendor!
God—in the Circuit Rider's breast—
Once more God built a world—Our West.

❧

Appreciations

To Hazel Hall

At your window, stitching into the thin
Cloth, in, in, in,
In, in—
Sitting alone,
You sewed our future to your own.

❦

Joe Hunt

In addition to writing down Kalapuya texts, anthropologist Melville Jacobs also worked with Klickitat. Mainly a Sahaptin language on the Washington side of the Columbia, its speakers also ventured into Oregon's Willamette Valley. Joe Hunt (birth and death dates unknown), or Joe Hollingsworth, as he also was called, was a very elderly Klickitat medicine man who lived for a time on the Grand Ronde Reservation in northwestern Oregon. He dictated several hundred pages of knowledge, learning, and teaching to Jacobs, as well as several hundred pages of myths called *wat'i't'ac*: stories of beings and persons of a former world, before the "Great Change," when all living things—animals, insects, birds, and fish—were once human beings. The following words were dictated by Hunt in March 1928, immediately after reciting for Jacobs a myth about the origin of fire. Originally translated by Klickitat Sahaptin J.J. Spencer and printed by Jacobs in narrative form, Hunt's words have been retranslated by scholars Dell and Virginia Hymes, who say this of their work:

> We now know enough of Sahaptin poetics to recognize Mr. Hunt's lines, the sets they form, and varied, rather intricate repetitions among them, within an overall sequence having three themes: the myths were made, not by me but by the persons of a previous world; Indian people lived by the myths; the myths, and my voice, are preserved by this act. Using space on the page to bring out something of the original patterns, we try to fulfill Mr. Hunt's prophecy: "Later you will hear me well."

I Leave the Myths

i

Where I made the myth from
    (is) not myself.

When country came to be,
    when persons came to be,
then (power) transformed the people,
    the country,

then those,
     those who had been persons,
         those became birds,
             they became fish,
             became deer,
             became fruit,
             they became roots.

All those,
     from them the myths had their being.

ii

Not only in this country,
     as far as land extends,
         there are all kinds of people,
             and so with language,
             and so with food.

As many as were the people here,
     there was no whiteman's law.
[Yet] by law the people came to be,
     have had their being, we [Indian] people, to this day.

Then they have continued since then,
     those who since then would be living on.
Then they were hearing the myths,
     and they think to this day
the country has grown up that way,
     and the myths, since then to this day.

iii

Now those myths are almost all disappearing—
Now I am an old man,
     and I am making myths to you for the last time,
         leaving you the myths.
Later you will hear me well.

Now I give you almost all the myths in this country,
     Klickitat country.
And you now are hearing me.

PART IV

Pioneers on Aesthetics:
Poems by Early Oregon Modernists

Laurence Pratt

Laurence Pratt (1889-1985), author, teacher, poet, and instructor of dozens of Northwest writers and journalists, was born in Kansas, the ninth of twelve children. Although he quit school at age 11 to work as a printer's devil for his brother in Portland, Oregon, he reentered Lincoln High School at age 23 and finished in 2 ½ years. Having worked as paper boy, elevator boy, trucker, laundryman, groceryman, gas meter reader, and musician, Pratt received his BA from Reed College and his MA from the University of Washington. High school principal, English teacher, and professor of English at Pacific University (Forest Grove), Pratt also spent four years as a clerk in the Crown Willamette Paper Company at Camas—an experience which formed the basis for his first book of poems, *A Saga of a Paper Mill*. Married in 1910 to Susie Smith, and the father of two children, Pratt served as president of the Northwest Poetry Society, president of the Oregon Poetry Association, critic for Verseweavers, and was the recipient of poetry prizes from the Portland *Spectator* and *Lyric Magazine*. He was the author of more than a dozen books of poems and prose. Pratt's sometimes jaunty, sometimes penetrating, poems often combined traditional forms, such as the following sonnets, with the everyday, idiomatic speech of the working life he knew so well.

Head Logger

They called me "Slaughter" in the old ring days
when I was mixin' it with heavyweights
and mashin' mugs. I drew some handsome gates
and put the crimps in "Dempsey" Jones's plays.
    But fellows, I was brought up on the bays
    and in the woods near Tillamook—and fate's
    recalled me, drawn me to my rightful mates,
    the hemlock rafts, the woods and waterways.
The wind is fresh out where the logs are tied;
the river's like a springy, swishy mat.
My punch that used to knock the heavies out
    now takes the forest champions for a ride.
    I swing a wicked peavey, spit for spat,
    and challenge hemlock giants to a bout.

Chinese Laborers

Out of the golden Orient they came
far from the dragon haunts, the sphere of pearl,
across jade seas and the white, impetuous whirl
of foam-fast waters, on their lips the name
    of sage Confucius, in their eyes the dream

of soon returning where the nascent sun
laughs through red poppy fields, and rivers run
in languor like some fabled lotus stream.
With slender yellow hands they wielded tools:
they dug a sullen ditch from the muddy lake,
and gouged a scowling tunnel by rough toil.
A falling roof of earth can bury fools
or sages. Dreams are lost. Suns cannot wake
white bones forever smothered in black soil.

Paul Tracy

A plumber by trade most of his life, Paul Tracy (1889-1976) grew up in Silver City, Idaho, attended the College of Idaho and the University of Oregon, worked as an electrician-linesman on the Arrowrock Dam, was a magneto repairman during World War I, and, with his wife Dorothy, had two children. Though he is frequently associated with Idaho poetry (having spent the later years of his life in Caldwell), much of Tracy's work comes from the Baker area and the Owyhee country in southeast Oregon. Of his poetry, often published in *Frontier and Midland*, editor H.G. Merriam once said: "His sense of values is independent and discriminating. Literature means to him life and not escape from life." Tracy's only book of poems, *Owyhee Horizons*, was published in 1968. A year previously, having collected, stapled, and hand sewn many of the same poems in a limited edition, the author introduced them with these words:

> Here at last is my own pack-rat's nest of verses. Gathered over many years it is a tangle of local greasewood thorns, sage bark, and salt-grass. . . . Unlike an Idaho pack-rat who accumulates rather than dispenses, this gatherer offers you a copy—hoping you may read with pleasure—and perhaps quiet laughter.

"Horsemeat" (which appeared in Tracy's book of poems as "Wild Horses") is here reprinted in its original 1930 version, first published in *The Frontier*.

Herder

A David undisturbed, the lonely Basque
Broods by his flock upon a humdrum hill.
Listless he turns a tanned and stolid mask
To crags of basalt deathly still.
Lacking the lute how can the shepherd calm
His heart, or mind, in this forgotten place?
So with the passing sun and stars, no psalm
Is born, nor song to meter words of grace.

Mute like the mid-day owl, this solitary one
Wears out the time with thought of food and grass,
Care for his dogs, his coyote-killing gun.
Filled with the droning bleat the dull hours pass
Till with the dusk he beds the simple sheep
And in a canvas wedge lies down to sleep.

Horsemeat

Wild horses are always feeding in Eastern Oregon.
They nibble at noon. They browse in the twilight.
Even in darkness they rattle the balsam-root leaves.
They eat the dry grass until thirst sets them trotting
In dusty strings miles and miles to water. They trot . . .
Tireless as watch springs. All summer these horses,
With hoofs polished by sand and lava, are grinding dry grasses.
In winter they paw for it in the snow;
They do not stand and whinny for sugar.

You, reader by the electric light, think of the horses,
Momentarily untroubled by gnats, dozing in Eastern Oregon.
Some sleep on their feet. Others are listening . . . watching.
Some lift scraggy manes and watch a shadowy coyote.
They are an unlovely lot who greet the sun in gray wastes.
They are survivors of Conquistadore herds;
Poor relations to the Clydesdale-Percheron aristocracy—
An untamed, unroached, tick-ridden herd.
At night they nod under the nearby stars subject
To similar cosmic draughts and silences.
        And who cares ?

But there is one man who cares. And this man sends riders
To gather the wild horses in Eastern Oregon. He invites them
To the city and pays their fare; he feeds them well.
He is the friend of all wild horses.
He even sends the provincial, unlettered cayuse abroad
In fifty pound tierces so Germany and Holland may judge
How good are the horses running wild in the West.

And while you are reading this, some perplexed European,
Saddened by local woes, is eating horsemeat. And in Eastern Oregon
Some wild little horse, equally sad, is nibbling bunchgrass.
He lifts his scraggy mane, now and then, and looks around.

The Plumber

Down in a corner crouching in a cellar,
Striking in the darkness a fragrant snake,
Jabbing down the oakum, mumbling bits of hokum,
Jabbing all the oakum that the joint will take;
Squatting in the cob-webs, scaring sullen spiders,
Humbling himself before the proud outsiders,
Fumbling and mumbling, rising up and stumbling,
One of the smudge-faced, unsung providers
Of pure water, channelling off the waste.

Back in a cavern underneath a stairway
Flattened in the darkness a tom cat glows,
Glowering at the plumber, swearing at the plumber,
Eyeing the new-comer with the cob-webbed nose!

Down on his knees by the torch that roars,
Roaring at the lead in the cast-iron pot—
Soaring tongues of red, tongues white hot
Bellow at the lead in a burning spot.
Here kneels the plumber at his shrine, winter, summer,
Humbling, mumbling, fumbling in the shadows;
Bowing at his altar, mindful of the nation,
Worshipping obscurely the goddess Sanitation.

The tom-cat glowers and the spiders sulk
Awaiting the departure of the solitary hulk.
Still he keeps a-pounding, pounding down the lead,
Bowing down his head,
Mindful of the living, thoughtful of the dead.

❧

Pioneer on Aesthetics

Your poets keep singing of smoothness
And the beautiful cadence of living:
"The even unhesitant sweep of the swallow."
"The uniform heaves of the tide."
"The steady, unruffled cruise of the moon
through cloud banks . . ."
        And all that.

Life to me is a series of yanks and jerks.

Night jerks a black cap over the sky
And all trees stop breathing.

The sun pops over mountains
With a bright bang!

        Smoothness is not life.
Unevenness is living. Jerks, yanks,
Tuggings are pulsations of being.

        Young chap,
I have been jerked through greasewood
By a bull. Broncos have burned my hands
With a racing lariat. I have been blasted
Into a canal, pitched off saddles, burnt
By high-tension "juice"—and kept awake.

Life is wildcat teeth.

        Some day a hand
Will flick out and jam me into eternity,
Or something.
        Singers, young man, should
Fit measures to this free-for-all.

Haralambos Kambouris

One of untold numbers of Oregon poets whose work is almost unknown because they never sought its publication, Haralambos K. Kambouris (1890-1964) wrote poems as part of the diary he kept as a young Greek immigrant, trying to make sense of his homesickness, dreams, and despair. Born in the village of Piri in the province of Thebes, Kambouris traveled for several years throughout the railroad and mining towns of Oregon, Washington, Utah, and Wyoming trying to find permanent work. He lived for a time (approximately 1912-15) in Roseburg and Glendale, lifted rails on track gangs, and spent some time in Albany and Natron (no longer a town) near Eugene. Kambouris's poems and diary, written in Demotic Greek, the people's language of Greece, reflect the need of all people—literary or not, published or not—to give order and perspective to life's most trying and most significant experiences. They also offer a rare, first-hand account of the European immigrant experience in Oregon—an often overlooked part of the state's history. Other parts of Kambouris's intriguing diary, translated by Helen Papanikolas and C.V. Vasilacopulos, are published in *Talking on Paper*, the volume of Oregon letters and diaries edited by Shannon Applegate and Terence O'Donnell in the *Oregon Literature Series*.

Peripetias

Couldn't the hour be dark
    the day snowy
To freeze the ocean
    Cursed Fate!

To this strange place where you brought me
    Like a crazy man I wander
From town to town I walk
    Where I go I do not know

Upon a hill I sit
    And cry my troubles
My bitterness and groans
    and my despair

With weeping eyes
    Bitter songs I sing
I write them down on paper
    And tears sprinkle them

Written seated on a high hill at Roseburg Oregon the 28th of December 1914, the day Tuesday the hour 2 o'clock in the afternoon

Clara Hoff

Clara S. Hoff (1891-1956) was born in Sweden and lived her last forty or more years in Portland. A registered nurse and an active member of the Montavilla Conservative Baptist Church, she was married and the mother of four children, one of whom became a missionary in Brazil. She was also a member of Verseweavers, a Portland-based organization, founded in 1936. "Devoted to the study, appreciation and development of poetry in the Oregon region," Verseweavers published two anthologies of Oregon poets, in 1945 and 1955. "Plow-Woman in Time of War," one of several poems by Clara Hoff appearing in the second anthology, stands out from most poetry on the subject of war in that it speaks for the often-unspoken realities common to many women in Oregon, and elsewhere throughout history.

Plow-Woman in Time of War

With unaccustomed strides she follows on
Behind the pointed steel. She turns the fields
Of rooted sod: like broken hearts that learn
To bury withered joys, rekindle hope.
Slow soil-stained beads of sweat ooze down her cheek
Through morning hours, while bird-song soothes her heart,
Till shadows slant along the fence-post lines.
This woman wears the mark of labor now—
But toil is sweet to hearts that daily mourn.
Each furrow turned becomes a silent prayer
Which reaches out for strength to do her part.
The woman plows, this is her duty now
While men lean out upon the edge of death,
And brace their souls against the hate and fear
As new to them as toil to women's hands
That now must grip and guide the heavy plow.

James Stevens

Known primarily as a writer of prose, James Stevens (1892-1971) was born in Iowa, was expelled from school in Idaho at age 15 for chewing tobacco, and supported himself from then on in various jobs: as logger and millworker in the summers; in winters, as a truck teamster. After two years with the U.S. infantry in France, Stevens moved to Oregon and continued to work in the woods. His first publication was in the *American Mercury* in 1924, when he was 32. Shortly thereafter he co-authored, with H.L. Davis, the notorious "Status Rerum," an essay blasting the general state of literature in the Northwest. Married in 1929 to Theresa Fitzgerald, Stevens authored several books about Paul Bunyan, numerous short stories, and two novels. The following poems, though written by Stevens, are in the voice of the central character of *Big Jim Turner*, a novel that captures many of life's realities in the Oregon timber industry of the time. The poem "Sunup Hangover" is an example, also, of the belief among growing numbers of twentieth-century poets that poetry did not always have to express "nice" feelings about things, or to use "proper" language, but should also be able to honestly render all of human experience, even if that experience might be somewhat unpleasant.

Sunup Hangover

I am in temper to strike at anyone or anything.
Self-hate and self-loathing are alive in me, too,
Crawling and whining.
Right now nothing could exult me more than a blow on my cheek,
A bruising, bloodying, rocking, dazing blow.
By Jesus, I would exult to it,
Turning the other cheek;
Heart pounding, blood engorging my eyes, hands lusting to tear my brother.

Words obscene and profane gall into my mouth,
Now I can curse what I cherish,
Now I can kill the thing I love.
Swamp dawn.
Gray, sullen, humid, smothering dawn.
Blood lightning in the east,
And thunder.
Not lusty, stirring giant thunder ringing:
Devil's thunder, Old Nick a-growling.
Let hell yammer.
I give a damn, I give a damn for nothing,
Not even for dying.
My testimony is for red hell this morning,
This sunup.

Forest Sunrise

I have seen a thousand suns rise
On forests and forest rivers;
Sunups on the white pine of the Clearwater, on the Missoula tamarack, on the fir,
    cedar, hemlock and spruce of the Tillamook, the Hoh and the Skagit, on the
    Klamath's sugar pine, on the Humboldt's redwood tree, and on the yellow
    pine of the Okanogan and the Deschutes.
All saying the beauty of morning is the best beauty.
Let me not sleep past any rising of yours on forest rivers,
O sun!
Even through the thundercloud I see you there,
With faith for my eyesight.

Verne Bright

Best known today for his book-length narrative poem *Mountain Man*, Verne Bright (1893-1977) also wrote nearly 1,600 poems, which appeared in such magazines as *North American Review, Saturday Evening Post, Life,* and *Poetry*, as well as over fifty anthologies. Born in Missouri, orphaned as a child, he came to Oregon at age 18. *Oregon Teachers' Monthly* published his first poem while he was still in Brownsville High School. Bright served two years with the U.S. Army in Siberia during World War I, attended Pacific University, worked on newspapers, taught English at Pacific University, and served as editor of the Oregon Writers' Project. His contribution to Oregon letters lies in his clear-sighted attention to the complexities—the failures, as well as the successes—in the lives of ordinary people, particularly those living close to and working the land.

Stone Breaker

He had a feud with stone. Stone was a foe
To test his manhood's strength; day after day
He waged a lusty warfare, wresting gray
And meagre tilth from acres where the flow
Of ice had sown a grain of boulders; slow
His tillage grew to fields, his fields to gay
And bannered harvests. But stone had a way
Of growing walls to thwart his sturdiest blow.

Caught in a ruthless battle, stone by stone,
He broke the years to brittle planet dust
With grim Antaean might; with dauntless thrust
He scourged the land, till thinning flesh and bone
Sank to a slow defeat. . . . Now low, apart
He lies, with stone, triumphant, on his heart.

Strange Fruit

Fult said he didn't want to be a farmer;
But old Jake Daniels swore: "By God, you will!"
So Fult, though stormy-hearted, plowed the hill,
Spurning the stony soil. His eyes burned warmer
Than August sunlight with desire for the gleam
Of golden streets, with girls like poppy flowers;
Hungry at heart for youth's impassioned hours
He fed with bitterness his frustrate dream.

He sowed the barren fields with sullen grain
And tilled the acres with unstinting toil:
Dark growths of hate and impotent despair . . .
On an orchard limb one night of autumn rain
He severed his allegiance to the soil—
Next morning Jake found strange fruit hanging there.

H.L. Davis

Perhaps the most famous Oregon writer of his generation, H.L. (Harold Lenoir) Davis (1894-1960) won the nationally prestigious Levinson Prize from *Poetry* magazine in 1919, and the Pulitzer Prize for fiction for his 1935 novel, *Honey in the Horn*—a story of an orphaned teenager who takes a wandering journey through the Oregon back country around 1900. Born in Yoncalla, Davis spent his teen years in eastern Oregon at jobs that included sheepherding, cattle punching, typesetting, and deputy sheriff. He began writing poetry while serving in World War I. Although he is best known for his prose, which he began writing at the encouragement of H.L. Mencken in 1928, and which captures the Oregon frontier both in subject and narrative voice, Davis continued to write poetry all of his life. Together with writer James Stevens, whom he met at a reading by Carl Sandburg in Corvallis in 1927, Davis co-authored (in a Eugene hotel room) the pamphlet "Status Rerum," an attack on the Northwest's literary establishment. The following poems, two of Davis's shortest but also most widely acclaimed, show him as an innovator in several respects: his use of conversational, sometimes vernacular speech; his unpredictable metaphors, their images reflecting a real, rather than idealized landscape; and his use of long lines, which, as he wrote to his friend Howard McKinley Corning, "are supposed to give a feeling for the contour of the landscape."

H.L. Davis age 3

Proud Riders

We rode hard, and brought the cattle from brushy springs,
From heavy dying thickets, leaves wet as snow;
From high places, white-grassed and dry in the wind;
Draws where the quaken-asps were yellow and white,
And the leaves spun and spun like money spinning.
We poured them on to the trail, and rode for town.

Men in the fields leaned forward in the wind,
Stood in the stubble and watched the cattle passing.
The wind bowed all, the stubble shook like a shirt.
We threw the reins by the yellow and black fields, and rode,
And came, riding together, into the town
Which is by the gray bridge, where the alders are,
The white-barked alder trees dropping big leaves
Yellow and black, into the cold black water.
Children, little cold boys, watched after us—
The freezing wind flapped their clothes like windmill paddles.
Down the flat frosty road we crowded the herd:
High stepped the horses for us, proud riders in autumn.

The Rain-Crow

While women were still talking near this dead friend,
I came out into a field where evergreen berry vines
Grew over an old fence, with rain on their leaves;
And would not have thought of her death, except for a few
Low sheltered berry leaves: I believed the rain
Could not reach them; but it rained on them every one.
So when we thought this friend safest and most kind,
Resetting young plants against winter, it was she
Must come to be a dead body. And to think
That she knew so much, and not that she would die!
Not that most simple thing—for her hands, or her eyes.

Dead. There were prints in the soft spaded ground
Which her knees made when she dug her tender plants.
Above the berry leaves the black garden and all the land
Steamed with rain like a winded horse, appeared strong.
And the rain-crow's voice, which we took for a sign of rain,
Began like a little bell striking in the leaves.
So I sat in the rain listening to this bird's voice,
And thought that our friend's mouth now, its "Dead, I am dead,"
Was like the rain-crow sounding during the rain:
As if rain were a thing none of us had ever seen.

Phyllis Morden

Despite its constant presence throughout Oregon's literary history, the natural world was only one of many subjects in the work of a growing number of Oregon poets who found inspiration also in the workings (and dysfunctions) of society. Phyllis Morden (1896-1951), born in Corvallis, Oregon, published poems with such titles as "Hard Winter," "Sunset Plowing," and "Abandoned Farm." But she also, like others of her generation, sometimes used poetry as a vehicle for social criticism, exposing the differences between appearance and reality in the pretensions of the upper classes— whose behavior seems not so much tied to any geographical place as to the universal habits of privilege. Little is known of Morden's personal life, except that she was married and had one daughter, and that her poems received wide recognition in such publications as the *Saturday Review of Literature, American Scholar, New York Times, New York Herald-Tribune,* and the *Washington Post,* as well as regional literary magazines of the Northwest. Perhaps her work as a journalist gave her access to the (Portland? Salem? New York?) society she describes in "City Vignettes."

from City Vignettes

Winter City

A slattern in an ermine cloak,
Drifting scarf of sooty smoke,
And crystal slippers, with a sprig
Of Neon in a frowsy wig.

Dinner Hour

Beyond plate glass, protruding paunches
Refuse domestic cheeses and new wines;
An old man in the alley, on lean haunches
Squats beside the garbage cans, and dines.

Social Leader

Always the perfect hostess . . . and the host . . .
She knows more answers than the famous Mrs. Post.
Her maids she chooses for their ugliness,
Girls without admirers work for less.

Benefit Concert

The violin's whine is shrill, and thin
As the ghost of coffee, swirling in
The eddies of polite applause.
"So lovely!" "Such a noble cause!"

Howard McKinley Corning

Poetry editor of the *Oregonian* from 1965 to 1976, author of three books of poems, and president of the Oregon State Poetry Association, Howard McKinley Corning (1896-1976) was a high school dropout who came to Oregon at age 22. Born in Nebraska, raised on an Ohio farm (where, he later said, he loved to wander the fields "generating my poetic nature"), Corning worked first at a Portland candy company making peanut brittle and fudge, and then in his brother's nursery business. Self educated through the Multnomah County Library, Corning began publishing poems in 1923, and his first book appeared three years later. Active in the literary community in Oregon, Corning worked for the WPA on the Oregon Writers' Project—a job that resulted in his history, *Willamette Landings*. During World War II he worked for the Maritime Administration in the Vancouver shipyards. Married to Virginia Runyon in 1940, with whom he had one son, Corning became a book salesman after the war, published short stories and many articles on Oregon history, edited *A Dictionary of Oregon History*, and wrote a series of reminiscences of Oregon writers prominent in the '30s. In an interview shortly before his death, Corning observed that "Pruning Vines" had been the most consistently popular of all of his poems and was the favorite of (then) Poet Laureate William Stafford.

Pruning Vines

In February, when the sap's below
The inattentive earth, I take my shears
And prune away the too-audacious years.
It's grapes I want and not mere leafy show.
I trim the trailing year's growth to a span,
With only laterals intact for crop;
A snip or two and I know where to stop
To bring a harvest where my hooks began.

It takes some fortitude to cut a vine
Half into dead ends for the cloying mold,
Where growth takes profit as the shears take hold,
Cutting the heart a little . . . as I cut mine.
But since its grapes I want I understand
How to rebuke the heart to fill the hand.

❦

Courtland Matthews

Reading the poems of Courtland Matthews (1897-1974), along with such 1930s contemporaries as Tracy, Stevens, Bright, Davis, and Corning, we now see—instead of the glorified travel reports of the earliest Oregon poets—the Oregon country as full of places where humans live and work, dream and grieve. Courtland Matthews became a poet after an arm injury ended his early ambitions to be a big league baseball pitcher and, later, a violinist. Moving with his mother to Eugene, Oregon, after his father's death, he attended high school from 1913 to 1916, lived again in Illinois for several years, and returned to Oregon in 1922, working for the Siuslaw National Forest in the summers and clerking in the Gardiner Mill Company store in winter months. His later career (in Portland) included work as a salesman, social worker, and publisher and editor of *Western Timber News, Chain Saw Age,* and *Northwest Literary Review,* a short-lived magazine he began in 1935. Although his books include *Aleutian Interval,* a narrative poem based on his service with the Navy during World War II, and a book titled *To the Little Wabash* (an Illinois river), the poems for which he is best known are those which reflect his experiences in the Oregon woods. His wife, Eleanor Matthews, also a poet, is represented elsewhere in this volume.

From a Forest Lookout

The fires flagged at sunset, and the west wind slowly
Pushed the long fog-billows in from the sea—
In across the blue hills, blanketing each wholly,
Hiding lakes and valleys from the crescent moon and me.

Remote from men I waited: I watched the vapors wreathing
Familiar peaks and firs below with delicate blurring twist.
The eerie surf came creeping on, as noiseless as my breathing . . .
Dusk found me on an island in a sleeping sea of mist.

Somewhere beneath the silver miles the ranch-house lamps were lighted
And far-down canyons echoed to the horns of homing cars.
Somewhere flame-ravaged woods in dripping dimness were benighted,
While I, above the spectral sea, kept vigil with the stars.

Shizue Iwatsuki

Born the same year as Courtland Matthews, the poet Shizue Iwatsuki (1897-1984) experienced life quite differently. At age 19 she left her home in Okayama Prefecture, Japan, to settle with her husband, Kamegoro, in the Hood River Valley. After many hard years of strawberry picking, house cleaning, and farming, the couple had a family and an orchard of their own. She is said to be one of the first Japanese women in the valley to learn to drive. At first a self-taught poet, Iwatsuki eventually studied by correspondence with Japanese master Seiki Ota, whose attention led in 1974 to a special emperor's award. By then she had composed nearly 1,500 poems, most of them in the traditional Japanese tanka form: 5-line poems of 31 syllables, arranged 5-7-5-7-7. The following poems, translated by Stephen W. Kohl, are part of a longer cycle based on the internment of her family during World War II in Pinedale, Tule Lake, and Minidoka relocation camps.

from **At Tule Lake Camp**

5   American born
    For two generations,
    Still they are relocated.
    The night, the iron gates
    Are dark.

6   Writing the history
    Of these events
    For later generations
    My own anxieties
    Seem trivial indeed.

7   Twilight calm
    Of summer evening
    I stand and face the moon
    Rising on the edge of desolate fields.

8   White dawn moonlight,
    On the road a frozen rime of snow.
    Muffled footsteps
    Echo sadness.

from **Returning Home**

21 Going home;
Gripping my daughter's hand,
Feeling cheated,
I tell her we're leaving
Without emotion.

22 Through the car window
A glimpse of pines.
Oregon mountains.
My heart beats faster,
Returning home.

23 Four years have passed,
Returning home
Though I have no flowers to offer,
First I visit my child's grave.

24 Evening twilight,
Mother cow chews her cud.
Beneath her
The calf dozes.

25 Home at last
At the dinner table
My husband calls my name,
But lapses into silence.
His heart, too, is full.

26 He was kind to us before,
But now—the shopkeeper
Nervously refuses to serve us.

27 Hard at work
Rebuilding our life,
To help my husband
Today I go
To buy farm tools.

28 Glancing up
At red-tinged mountains
My heart is softened.
A day in deep autumn.

Helen Emerson

Helen Emerson (1898-) began writing poems at age 18, contributed "one bad poem," as she says, to her college literary magazine, then, like untold numbers of other promising writers, "retreated to the status of desk drawer poet." Shortly after retiring from 15 years of teaching at Linfield College (McMinnville), she began to study Japanese poetry, to attend workshops led by Oregon poets, and to publish in literary magazines. She is also the author of a book-length memoir titled *Paris Without Hemingway and Other Places*, an account of the year (1929) she spent in Paris and Munich. Born in Chicago and raised in the Midwest, Emerson received her MA and PhD from the University of Wisconsin. She taught German (and sometimes French) in Illinois, at the University of Wisconsin, at Stanford University, and at Linfield College. From 1944 to 1946, she worked for the Signal Corps in Washington, D.C. Calling herself "a devoted amateur of poetry," Emerson focuses on the human landscape of feelings and memories, allowing readers insights into their own.

Forgive Me, Grandma

When you were with us in the flesh, grandma
—your angular uncompromising flesh—
your high-pitched down-east twang
rasped with a sound of knives on whetstones
to adolescent ears. Victrola concerts died.
It killed Fritz Kreisler, Alma Gluck, Caruso. Besides,
the madding metronome beat of your rocker
on the one loose board in the floor
creaked over printed pages. It felled the forest primeval
and shattered the wing of a skylark.

You had no truck with our singing world.
That hurt. But the sting was sharper
when you brushed off caresses: a grandchild's hug,
a kiss attempted. We did not understand.
Deep in your blood lay distrust of outward show
and all that might betray
a pure integrity. You reared a fence to guard it.

Sometimes, not often, you opened a small gate
and let us see you young.
Boys and girls went Maying. East wind whipped their faces.
They hunted violets and rare arbutus
under fallen leaves. Then, to warm their blood
they played tag, chased each other. . . all the way home.

You throve on what was hard, crisp, cold:
streams running over rocky beds, checkerberries, Jonathan apples.

Where slow rivers flow brown with silt,
we gather soft fruits: paw-paws and persimmons.
Our father, your son, set you here
in soil your roots rejected.

Well, we saw you young like us. You must have felt (you, too)
the pulse of untapped tenderness within your veins.
Where did your young love go
when you were old and your man dead?
To flowers. There was permitted love. The Lord had made them.
Among them you dared be happy.

Once I had a dream about you.
You stood in the garden, aproned, bareheaded.
In one hand you held a trowel.
Your cheeks and your blue eyes were glowing.
You smiled and called to me, pointing to your flowers,
"An't they pretty?"

Cosmos, pinks, petunias, wild Sweet Williams
(you called them Wandering Charlies).
When I smell their breath on summer wind,
grandma, you are there.

Ernest G. Moll

Born in Australia, the son of wheat and sheep farmers, Ernest G. (Gerry) Moll (1900-) lived most of his adult life in Oregon but, unlike most Oregon poets before him, whose work sprang out of the soil of their new surroundings, he never stopped writing about home. Moll was a versatile poet, comfortable with the sonnet as well as free verse, whose subjects ranged not only through the Australian landscape but also through Oregon, classical Greece, and the Old Testament. He was a professor of English at the University of Oregon from 1928 to 1966. He came to America in 1920, received a BA from Lawrence College (Wisconsin) and an MA from Harvard, and worked his way to Europe on a cattle ship. Before coming to Oregon, he taught for a year in Colorado and spent two years collecting and importing 3,000 live Australian birds. The author of twelve books of poems, a textbook, and an autobiography, Moll has received many honors, among them the distinction from the Commonwealth Literary Committee of Australia for the best book of 1940. After his retirement, Moll lived in Brookings on the Oregon coast, where he cultivated a small reserve of Australian bushland, including wattle and gum trees. He now lives in Oroville, California. His most recent book is titled *The View from a Ninetieth Birthday.*

Sheep-Killer

I should have known, when I undid his chain
That darkness had been busy at his brain
As at an anvil, sharpening a fang.
I should have known it by the glint that sprang
Into his eyes when the chain fell and he
Stood stiffly there, as though to let me see
That he had all the time in the world to spare,
If I so felt, to match me stare for stare,
His heart being innocent.

     I watched him go
Out through the gate with just the slightest show
Of hurry in his trot, as though he kept
His body back from where his thoughts leapt
Ahead to the red kill; that holding back
A dog will never show unless the track
He follows is a secret he would keep
From men whose fingers smell of lambs and sheep.

I should have known, had I but had the eye,
That strain in hip and curving flank and thigh
For what must happen in a hawk's neck when
He spots the quail way down there, but with men
Too near in yard or paddock to make safe
The whistling lunge; the tension of that chafe
That is when lust has the red tongue on fire
But cunning is the muzzle on desire.

So he went slowly till I lost him quite
In the thick fog that made another night
Over the paddocks where beneath the trees
The lambs would be hard at it on their knees
Draining the heavy udders. In that fog
A lamb would learn the coming of a dog
Too late even to get upon its feet,
Or in one wild and lost and desperate bleat
To say that death was hard and life was sweet.

He got his fifty in a mile that day,
Crunched through the shoulders in the killer's way,
Ribs broken in to crush the leaping heart.
Though great my loss, I recognized the art
With which the thing was done. What speed, what power,
He must have known for that one breathless hour,

When long restraint was straw before the urge
Of instinct, the red longing, the hot surge
That leapt and thundered and would not be still
Till fifty lambs lay dead about the hill!

He always liked to work the sheep close in,
Sniffing the blood, no doubt, beneath the skin
He dared not tear because of watching eyes.
Why did I trust that shifty compromise!
Why must sheep stand, by fear together drifted,
Helpless as flowers when the scythe is lifted!
Who was at fault, the dog, or I, or the sheep?

But since a farmer needs must have his sleep,
That night I put a bullet in his head,
Gave the world back to God, and went to bed.

Phyllis McGinley

The only Oregon-born writer (so far) to win the Pulitzer Prize for poetry, Phyllis McGinley (1905-78) was born in Ontario. Nationally known as a poet, essayist, and writer of children's stories, McGinley once said her goal was to try "to narrow the gulf betweeen light and serious verse" in order to help lead her readers "into greater poetry." Indeed, although many of her poems—on the topics of family life, religion, politics, and the role of women—are considered "light verse," they also bear serious elements of social criticism. *Times Three*, the book which won the 1961 Pulitzer Prize, contains a foreword in which W.H. Auden points out this often-overlooked depth in her work. Like Edwin Markham and several other Oregon-born writers, McGinley did not live long in the state. She grew up on a ranch in Colorado, attended high school in Utah, graduated from the University of Utah, taught school in New Rochelle, New York, worked as an advertising copywriter in New York City, married, and had two children. Spanning four decades, her writing career included eighteen books and numerous journal publications, honorary degrees from colleges and universities, and membership in the National Institute of Arts and Letters. McGinley has been praised for her "faultless ear and a natural inventiveness," and one of her most important contributions to modern poetry was her ability to delight the reader with tenderness, wit, and the appropriation of traditional forms and sentimental poetic conventions for daring new ends.

Phyllis McGinley age 6

Carol with Variations, 1936

The world now has 7,600,000 men under arms, excluding
navies, as against 5,900,000 in 1913.
New York Sun, *Christmas, 1936*

Oh! Little town of Bethlehem, how still we see thee lie;
Your flocks are folded in to sleep, and sleep your little ones.
Behold, there is a Star again that climbs the eastern sky.
And seven million living men are picking up their guns.

>   Hark, the happy cannons roar—
>   Glory to the Dictator,
>   Death and fear, and peace defiled,
>   And a world unreconciled!

Once more the bells of Christendom ring out a proclamation
Of joy to all the universe, and mercy, and good will;
While brother shoots his brother down, and nation scowls at nation,
And seven million uniforms are decorate at drill.

>   Hail to Dupont and to Krupp!
>   Steel is strong and going up.
>   Let the tidings glad be sent—
>   Tis the Morn of Armament.

God rest you merry, gentlemen, whose will these armies are.
Go proudly in your colored shirts, let nothing you dismay.
(Oh, little town of Bethlehem, how fades your shining star?)
While seven million fighting men stand up on Christmas Day.

>   Sing hosanna, sing Noel.
>   Sing the gunner and the shell.
>   Sing the candle, sing the lamp,
>   Sing the Concentration Camp.
>   Sing the Season born anew,
>   Sing of exile for the Jew,
>   Wreathe the world with evergreen.
>   Praise the cunning submarine.
>   Sing the barbed and bitter wire,
>   Poison gas and liquid fire,
>   Bullet, bomb, and hand grenade,
>   And the heart of man, afraid.
>   Christ is come, the Light hath risen,
>   All our foes are safe in prison,
>   And the Christmastide begets
>   Seven million bayonets.

>   Hear the carol, once again—
>   Peace on earth, good will to men.

Jeanne McGahey

Speaking in retrospect of her many years as a poet, Jeanne McGahey (1906-) says that much of her work is "an addiction to the here and now; . . . a life-long . . . love affair with place." McGahey was born and raised ouside a small lumber-and-mill town in Coos County, on the Oregon coast, and her first job was teaching five pupils in a school on a lake in the dunes. She began working seriously at poetry in the mid-1930s, when she discovered—through a night-school class—a new way of analyzing and reevaluating language (later called the Activist Movement by poet W.H. Auden). In 1941 she was included in New Directions' *Five Young American Poets*, and the following year she received a Bender Grant-in-Aid for poetry. In 1944 she married Lawrence Hart, also a writer and leader in the Activist Movement. The recipient of a Marin Arts Council award for poetry, McGahey edited for three years *the poetry LETTER*, a highly controversial magazine of discussion. In addition to poems in magazines and anthologies, her publications include two children's books, a 6-year radio narrative series, a TV documentary (*The Mayflower Story*), and two books of poems, the second of which was selected in nationwide competition by the *Quarterly Review of Literature*.

Oregon Winter

      The rain begins. This is no summer rain
Dropping the blotches of wet on the dusty road:
This rain is slow, without thunder or hurry:
There is plenty of time—there will be months of rain.

      Lost in the hills, the old gray farmhouses
Hump their backs against it, and smoke from their chimneys
Struggles through weighted air. The sky is sodden with water,
It sags against the hills, and the wild geese,
Wedge-flying, brush the heaviest cloud with their wings.

      The farmers move unhurried. The wood is in.
The hay has long been in, the barn lofts piled
Up to the high windows, dripping yellow straws.
There will be plenty of time now, time that will smell of fires
And drying leather, and catalogues, and apple cores.

The farmers clean their boots, and whittle, and drowse.

Mary Barnard

One of the first Oregon poets to participate in the national and international community of poets of influence, Mary Barnard (1909-) did not, like many poets around her, feel her work had much in common with the poetry being written in Oregon literary circles of the '30s. Born in Vancouver, Washington, the daughter of a lumberman, she lived and went to school for a time in Buxton, Oregon. Barnard received her bachelor's degree from Reed College in Portland, where she first encountered the work of Ezra Pound and other avant-garde poets of the 1920s. Boldly entering into a correspondence with Pound, who was living at the time in Rapallo, Italy, Barnard received encouragement from the famous poet, as well as introductions to such poets as Marianne Moore, *Poetry* magazine editor Harriet Monroe, and William Carlos Williams, whom she met on her first trip to New York in 1936. Returning to Vancouver after several months at the Yaddo writers' colony, Barnard was employed for a time as a social worker, but returned to New York in 1938, as a research assistant and then a curator of the poetry collection at a Buffalo library. Her first book of poems, *Cool Country*, appeared in 1940, in a volume with poets Randall Jarrell and John Berryman. In it one sees Barnard's commitment to Imagist principles (economy of language; no excess adjectives; concrete images; no abstract words; and the musical phrase of free verse over the beat of the metronome) as well as to subjects that are undeniably Northwestern. After returning (in 1951) to Vancouver, where she lives today, Barnard embarked on new lines of scholarship, resulting in *Sappho: A New Translation*, *The Mythmakers*, and an adventurous book of poems, *Time and the White Tigress*. Her *Collected Poems* appeared in 1979.

Logging Trestle

Neither cloud nor rain casts
A chill into the valley
Like that of a trestle fallen into disuse.

The rails move out from the hillside,
Across the piling lengthening its stroke
Where ground slopes riverward.

Abruptly, the rails terminate.
Sky opens between the cross-ties lifted
Each upon five upright timbers. The gray wood

Leads the eye to nothing further.
The broken column stands against cloud
As though an abandoned wharf extended into wind.

Roots

Rain on the windshield,
roads spongy with sawdust
have meant in the end
a love of place that grows into the body.
Blood should be clear amber under tree bark.

Lacking that, there are the roads
extending like root tendrils
under the angles of mountains,
rain sharpening on the windshield at evening.

Eleanor Matthews

Less visible on the literary scene than her husband, Courtland Matthews, Eleanor H. Matthews (1910-79) was nevertheless also a widely published poet. Born in Oregon, she earned her BA at Pacific University and her MA at the University of Oregon. For many years a teacher and chair of the English department of Monroe High School in Portland, her articles and poems appeared in many newspapers, magazines, and anthologies. Her first book of poems, *Ever the Sunrise*, appeared in 1954, and her second book, *The Unseen Wing*, in 1973. An officer and board member of the Oregon State Poetry Association, she traveled many of the by-roads of Oregon with her husband, photographing vanishing sights: country churches, windmills, ferries, and covered bridges. Her poem "The Foragers," which is interesting to contrast with Hall's poem, "Inheritance," was found in a copy of *Fabric of Song, II*, with the following handwritten inscription: "To Ethel [Romig Fuller], who knows how to harvest huckleberries—and many other things, including the affection of everyone who knows her. Sincerely, Eleanor H. Matthews."

The Foragers

My mother's mother gathered lingonberries
Upon some Swedish marsh. My mother ranged
Along the Mississippi for wild grapes.
By Kinzel Lake upon the slopes of Hood
I harvest huckleberries. I look out
Across the veiled blue distances and think
The age-old thoughts of women foraging
Against the family's need. Now I am one
With women of long generations past
And with my daughter's daughter when she stands
Basket in hand, in quest of what wild fruit?

William Everson

The poetry of William Everson (1912-) has been called "a quest for value and certainty in an uncertain and frequently violent world." The same could perhaps be said of his life, in which he spent 18 years as a Dominican monk, publishing many of his works under the name Brother Antoninus. His residence in Oregon was brief, but significant, for it was during the World War II years of 1943-46 which he spent as a conscientous objector in Camp Angel (Waldport) and Cascade Locks that he wrote the poems that would first bring him national attention. Born in Sacramento, California, Everson attended Fresno State College (now California State University) and worked in the '30s as a farmer, in canneries, and as a laborer for the Civilian Conservation Corps. His early books focused on his love of the California landscape (a constant theme throughout his career), although in this and subsequent work we can see a somber awareness of the world's violence, both in the natural world and in the collective nature of humanity. His highly acclaimed book *The Residual Years* (which contains *The Waldport Poems*) includes the long poem "Chronicle of Division"—a record of personal frustrations in the camps and of the disintegration of his first marriage. Converted in 1949 to Roman Catholicism, Everson left his second marriage for a monastic life; in 1969, he left the church for a third marriage; and, through all the years, wrote well over three dozen books of poems and edited eight books on the poetry of Robinson Jeffers, his literary mentor and inspiration. Named by poet Kenneth Rexroth as one of the San Francisco Renaissance poets (later known as "the Beats"), Everson has been both a controversial and a nationally esteemed poet all his life. In 1988, he received a Special Recognition Award from the Oregon Institute of Literary Arts.

The Raid

Then Jesus saith to him:
Put up again thy sword into its place:
for all that take the sword shall perish by the sword.
Matthew XXVI-52

They came out of the sun undetected,
Who had lain in the thin ships
All night long on the cold ocean,
Watched Vega down, the Wain hover,
Drank in the weakening dawn their brew,
And sent the lumbering death-laden birds
Level along the decks.

They came out of the sun with their guns geared,
Saw the soft and easy shape of that island
Laid on the sea,
An unwakening woman,
Its deep hollows and its flowing folds
Veiled in the garlands of its morning mists.
Each of them held in his aching eyes the erotic image,

And then tipped down,
In the target's trance,
In the ageless instant of the long descent,
And saw sweet chaos blossom below,
And felt in that flower the years release.

The perfect achievement.
They went back toward the sun crazy with joy,
Like wild birds weaving,
Drunkenly stunting;
Passed out over edge of that injured island,
Sought the rendezvous on the open sea
Where the ships would be waiting.

None were there.
Neither smoke nor smudge;
Neither spar nor splice nor rolling raft.
Only the wide waiting waste,
That each of them saw with intenser sight
Than he ever had spared it,
Who circled that spot,
The spent gauge caught in its final flutter
And straggled down on their wavering wings
From the vast sky,
From the endless spaces,
Down at last for the low hover,
and the short quick quench of the sea.

William Stafford

The first Oregon poet to win the National Book Award for poetry, William Edgar Stafford (1914-1993) was born in Hutchinson, Kansas, and came to Oregon in 1948. In his early years he worked a variety of jobs—in sugar beet fields, in construction, at an oil refinery—and received his bachelor's and master's degrees from the University of Kansas. A conscientious objector and pacifist, he spent the years 1942-46 in Arkansas and California work camps, fighting forest fires, building and maintaining trails and roads, and halting soil erosion. After the war he taught high school, worked for Church World Service, and joined the English faculty of Lewis and Clark College in Portland, where (with time out for earning a PhD from the University of Iowa) he taught until his retirement. Married to Dorothy Hope Frantz in 1944, the father of four children, Stafford authored 35 books of poems, the first of which, *West of Your City*, was published when he was 46. In addition to the 1963 National Book Award for *Traveling Through the Dark*, Stafford's many honors included Poetry Consultant for the Library of Congress (1965-1967) and the Shelley Award from the Poetry Society of America. He was appointed Oregon Poet Laureate by Governor Bob Straub in 1975.

An enormously loved and admired poet, a generous mentor to aspiring poets everywhere, Stafford traveled thousands of miles in his later years, giving hundreds of poetry readings in colleges and universities, community centers and libraries, throughout the United States and in Egypt, India, Bangladesh, Pakistan, Iran, Germany, Austria, Poland, and other countries. Characterized by a quiet, everyday vocabulary, common speech rhythms, an understated manner, and close observation, Stafford's poems are, in the words of Glen Love, a "repeated encounter with the otherness of the world," in which the individual comes to new realizations about the earth and also the self.

William Stafford age 8

Traveling Through the Dark

Traveling through the dark I found a deer
dead on the edge of the Wilson River road.
It is usually best to roll them into the canyon:
that road is narrow; to swerve might make more dead.

By glow of the tail-light I stumbled back of the car
and stood by the heap, a doe, a recent killing;
she had stiffened already, almost cold.
I dragged her off; she was large in the belly.

My fingers touching her side brought me the reason—
her side was warm; her fawn lay there waiting,
alive, still, never to be born.
Beside that mountain road I hesitated.

The car aimed ahead its lowered parking lights;
under the hood purred the steady engine.
I stood in the glare of the warm exhaust turning red;
around our group I could hear the wilderness listen.

I thought hard for us all—my only swerving—,
then pushed her over the edge into the river.

❦

Deer Stolen

Deer have stood around our house
at night so still nobody knew,
and waited with ears baling air.
I hunt the still deer everywhere.

For what they heard and took away,
stepping through the chaparral,
was the sound of Then; now it's Now,
and those small deer far in the wild

Are whispers of our former life.
The last print of some small deer's foot
might hold the way, might be a start
that means in ways beyond our ken

Important things. I follow them
through all the hush of long ago
to listen for what small deer know.

❦

Fifteen

South of the bridge on Seventeenth
I found back of the willows one summer
day a motorcycle with engine running
as it lay on its side, ticking over
slowly in the high grass. I was fifteen.

I admired all that pulsing gleam, the
shiny flanks, the demure headlights
fringed where it lay; I led it gently
to the road and stood with that
companion, ready and friendly. I was fifteen.

We could find the end of a road, meet
the sky on out Seventeenth. I thought about
hills, and patting the handle got back a
confident opinion. On the bridge we indulged
a forward feeling, a tremble. I was fifteen.

Thinking, back farther in the grass I found
the owner, just coming to, where he had flipped
over the rail. He had blood on his hand, was pale—
I helped him walk to his machine. He ran his hand
over it, called me good man, roared away.

I stood there, fifteen.

Assurance

You will never be alone, you hear so deep
a sound when autumn comes. Yellow
pulls across the hills and thrums,
or in the silence after lightning before it says
its names—and then the clouds' wide-mouthed
apologies. You were aimed from birth:
you will never be alone. Rain
will come, a gutter filled, an Amazon,
long aisles—you never heard so deep a sound,
moss on rock, and years. You turn your head—
that's what the silence meant: *you're not alone.*
The whole wide world pours down.

Self portrait by George Hitchcock

George Hitchcock

Playwright, fiction writer, founder and longtime editor of *Kayak* magazine, as well as a painter and poet, George Hitchcock (1914-) has recently moved back to Oregon, the state of his birth, after many years in California. Great-great-grandson of a Mississippi senator, Hitchcock was born in Hood River where his grandfather—an apple grower and founder of the Agricultural Service at the University of Idaho—had decided to farm. Although Hitchcock lived in the Hood River area only 6 years, he returned to it annually throughout his boyhood, and much of the imagery of his poetry is rooted there. After several years in Eugene, where the family lived on the banks of the Willamette River (Hitchcock graduated from University High School and the University of Oregon), he moved to California, where he held a variety of jobs: 15 years in landscape design, several years at sea as a journeyman shipfitter, several years as a professional actor, and acting coach and stage director for the opera program of the San Francisco Conservatory of Music. He spent the last 20 years before retirement at the University of California in Santa Cruz, where he was director of the writing program. An emeritus professor, Hitchcock is the author of more than a dozen books of poetry, many plays, and four books of fiction. He lives half of each year in Eugene, the other half in La Paz, Mexico.

May All Earth Be Clothed in Light

Morning spreads over
the beaches like lava;
the waves lie still, they
glitter with pieces of light.

I stand at the window
& watch a heron on one leg, its
plumage white in the green banks
of mint. Behind me
smoke rises from its nest
of bricks, the brass clock
on the kitchen shelf
judges & spares.

Slowly the bird opens
its dazzling wings.
I am filled with joy.
The fields are awake!
the fields with their hidden lizards
& fire of new iris.

Glen Coffield

One of several poets to be assigned in 1943 to the Civilian Public Service Camp (Camp Angel) in Waldport, Glen Coffield (1917-1981), a conscientous objector, was activities coordinator at a fine art school there and, together with William Everson and others, started the Untide Press, which published their work. A maverick in the literary world, remaining independent of the academic literary circles that were becoming increasingly influential in Oregon, as elsewhere, Coffield taught English, speech, and drama in high schools in Missouri and Oregon, worked for the Office of Scientific Research and Development, acted in little theater groups in San Francisco (where he managed an opera house for a year), and directed the Grundtvig Folk School (a neighborhood outdoor school) at Eagle Creek, Oregon, for seven years. Graduating from Central Missouri State College in Warrensburg, Coffield did graduate work in English at the University of Missouri, the University of Oregon, and Portland State College. During his lifetime he published more than 65 books, pamphlets, and brochures—both poetry and prose. The editor of twelve different magazines from 1937 onward, Coffield won a special award in 1971 from the American Poets Fellowship for his work in promoting poetry.

Crossing Hawthorne Bridge

One morning while crossing Hawthorne bridge,
The seagulls were soaring in magnificent arcs,
And a slight trace of fog was banked against
The houses on the opposite cliffs. Despite

A chill, the sun was breaking through here
And there, and it was a fine morning.
I am sure the motorists thought so, who caused
The iron girders to tremble, by a trifling weight.

Even the gray battleship, that was moored along
The West dike, for the moment, seemed to belong;
And all things, good and bad, were mingled
In the idea of beauty, accentuated by:

The oneness of time, the weight of being,
And a necessary balance, as in the seagull
That swooped to pick up a lemon rind
From an eddy in the current of the Willamette.

Willis Eberman

Willis Eberman (1917-1979), who lived many years on the Oregon coast, at Seaside and at Cove Beach, was the grandson of a hunter, scout, and guide of an 1843 wagon train from Missouri to Clatsop County, Oregon. Eberman's father Richard, to whom his poem "The Others" is addressed, was also a colorful figure; one of a family of sixteen children, he carried the mail on horseback along the beaches and over the mountains once a week from Astoria to Tillamook. Born and raised in Portland, poet Willis Eberman studied at Reed College and the University of Oregon Extension Department. Like many other poets of his generation, Eberman began writing in traditional forms but later wrote almost exclusively in free verse—a style which, as the century wore on, was becoming more and more acceptable. His subjects were many, ranging from love poems to nature poems to memories of his own boyhood; but the titles of some of his numerous books of poems—*Lines to Be Left in the Earth; This, My Bequest; The Pioneers; Torrent of Time; I, Too, Am a Traveler*—demonstrate also the poet's abiding allegiance to the memory of his ancestors and his sense of connection to them. As John Armstrong, Sunday editor of the *Oregonian*, once wrote, Eberman's voice sings "of how good today's life can, and should be, if only we will look behind the facade of the atomic age—a facade of uncertainties which we have created and which, if we so desire, we can do away with."

The Journey

When it was silent: when the river was
the sound only; that day my twelve year old
grandmother and her father set forth
from the further shore: crude-hewn, perhaps,
and strong, resilient, broad, the canoe;
no sound, but soft cat-lapping Columbia
waves; no Vancouver, much, but the fort. No
roar of continual cars: no interstate bridge.

She made good camp, they say, in the red
sundowns, as far as the hundred-some-miles
to the mouth. I see her moving about with
frugal supplies in the silence; against
sunset, the camp-fire a coin in a furnace . . .

Continual is the journey: and beyond that
time, past barriers: over the over one hundred
years, and beyond the clangor of progress,
we resume the journey past sunset, toward morning.

Elk

Hoofprints of cows: we saw a herd of them
near Silver Point last night. Frightened by lights
of the car, they swerved and crossed the highway,
gaining the bank. We see them often,
before their season of death sends them to hiding
in the Coast Mountains, ungainly rumps and bodies
lumbering forward. Their yearly season of slaughter
leaves them depleted, but now large herds are seen
on the slopes of the mountains.

      Unbeautiful beasts, you do well
to disdain us, for we are murderous foe
even to ourselves: and the earth is ours to destroy
or love once again. We must decide very soon
which it will be.
      Today, bright sunlight shines
on all the clay hoofprints. In hiding, you watch us; and soon
we will ambush you again, killing more than our share.
Hide, frightened beasts. We, too, may have our season,
unless we find love, like a fawn, under the starlight.

The Others

Yes, you have accomplished the west and forded
the final river, father remembered:
I could turn on the tape again, if I wished,
and hear you tell of that journey: the wild darkness,
the crossing, the mail-bags held
high from the saddle; the horse rearing,
struck by the log.
      You saved the mail, and
walked six miles to safety under the clangor of storm . . .
O father I love: heart, hand that I held, I, too, am alone in the dark.

Seventy years ago, some seventy miles from here
to the west, you blazed the coast range, clung
to rock, slashed brush; swam the horse
around Arch Cape at high tide, carrying close humanity's dreams.

Father, forgive me for being afraid of the dark;
let me learn my self does not matter, but only
the mission accomplished, the message delivered,
the others, that wait at the end of the arduous journey.

Vi Gale

Vi (Hokenson) Gale (1917-) was born in Dalarna, Sweden. A naturalized U.S. citizen, she came as a child with her parents via Ellis Island to Oregon, where her father worked in the timber industry near Clatskanie. Married for more than fifty years to James Gale, a fire protection engineer, Vi Gale has published poetry, short stories, essays, and photography, and has translated from Swedish into English. For over forty years she has taught, lectured, and conducted workshops in poetry and creative writing in many colleges and for various organizations throughout the Northwest. The author of six collections of poetry, she is founder, editor and publisher of Prescott Street Press, a Portland-based publishing house which, since 1974, has published books by Northwest poets, an innovative series of postcard poems, anthologies, and books of poems in translation. She has received numerous honors, including the C.E.S. Wood retrospective award for lifetime achievement from the Oregon Institute of Literary Arts. Like well-crafted photographs taken with a macro lens, Gale's poems are a striking contrast to the landscape poems of the previous century. Poems also of discovery, their language is jaunty, conversational, yet economical. Readers will enjoy pairing Kenneth Hanson's poem "First of All," also published in this volume, with Gale's "At That, the Day Ended Well," which speaks with kindly self-irony of being awkward in the presence of someone born in the Northwest, to whom the landscape is nothing new.

Cape Foulweather

The sky. The sky hangs clear, a jay's wing.
The name is unjust. The cape is maligned.

The surf. The surf runs flat as a comb.
Was it a sailor who grumbled at sea?

The wind. The wind springs soft, a cattail plume.
The mapmaker's wife, was it she?

No fuss at all. The place is misnamed.
Nothing blows here to be weathered by us.

❧

At That, the Day Ended Well

All you have to do
counsels a friend
is to find a country.

Likely he's watched
he misses nothing
as I skitter through buckbrush

comic even to myself
as I slog through desert
greasewood and bounce

from tuffet to tuffet
of greenrazor swampgrass.
He has no doubt smiled

with me I'm sure
inwardly for he is kind
as I frown at a strange leaf

new twig or indigenous rock
blocked by a scholarship
sentimentally drawn from hardheads

who distrusted schoolmasters
and chose to believe in trolls.
I thank him for counsel and more

as I ponder the countries
of birth and adoption and those
other landscapes one finds

as I watch him measuring
blue seacliffs and watercourses
and the people who own them

with a clean reasonableness
an admirable sparsity
that leaves me breathless.

James B. Hall

Founder both of the literary journal *Northwest Review* and the creative writing program at the University of Oregon, James B. Hall (1918-) grew up on an Ohio farm, briefly attended Miami University (Ohio), and after service overseas in World War II received his BA, MA, and PhD from the University of Iowa. Much of Hall's writing—five novels, four collections of short stories, and two books of poems—comes from his wide variety of experience in the world: on the farm, as a merchant sailor, as a cannery worker, as husband (he married Elizabeth Cushman in 1946), as father of five children, and in various academic posts. In addition to his pioneering work at the University of Oregon, Hall has edited six anthologies of stories and essays on fiction, culture, and the arts; was founding director of the writers' workshop at the University of California, Irvine; founding board member and president of Associated Writing Programs; and founding provost of College V (now Porter College) at University of California, Santa Cruz. Retired from academia, Hall now lives and writes again in Eugene. The poem below, from *Bereavements*, comes from his experience in World War II. Drafted into the infantry, Hall became a chief warrant officer with service from North Africa to Innsbruck, and, at war's end (assigned to military government detachments), he presided as labor officer over the first waterfront union meeting in Germany.

Memorial Day: 1959

I.

When the long iron boat spat us kicking
On the beach near Mers El Kebir
The sea birds twittered past our let-down
Ramp and we ran laughing at a continent,
Not one truly thinking he could die.
But now I think of Elwood Matson
Surprised that night in his own bivouac
Hole, tent poles and his own Garrand
Gouged through his blanket and his blond head,
For a tank track foraged through the lost
Field of his sleep.

II.

And A. C. Roten: often he danced
On our tent ropes and would sometimes sing
Those low, cold Tunisian stars to sleep.
Married, a picture of small girls hiding
In his wallet, and lucky at reconnaissance,
I did not think that he could ever be
Only some rags at Senid Station, thighs severed,
His throat screaming for its mother . . .
And later Graysted, Kibby, Ethred, and Sidney Hines
Died also by S-mines in the Riviera's green
Unforgiving afternoon.

III.

Much later winter came on us near Hagenau
And the season's old revenge of snow shook
The black intricate trees like thunder.
Beaton, and his patrol, in parkas white as breath
Vanished into those mumbling, low-hung boughs.
Later we found them in a shallow bowl
Of that forest, swaying, trussed in the wind,
Flanks maimed, their heads drowned in the terrible snow.
After that we took no prisoners, fought much
Among ourselves with knives, became beasts,
But still alive.

IV.

Now is this longest day of May again
And while the shrapnel rain rattles this window pane,
I thought to write some formal thing
To say how those alive—being so—see on ahead,
And thought that way to justify their deaths.
But oh when I saw them all once more, again,
I thought: write no lies to those who really died.
Instead let stand this hasty parapet of verse:
For A. C. Roten, Ethred, Matson, Kibby, Graysted,
Paul Sommers, Sidney Hines, John Halstead, and one patrol,
For they are dead.

Madeline DeFrees

Madeline DeFrees (1919-) was born in Ontario, Oregon, and at the age of four moved to Hillsboro where she attended St. Matthew's Parochial School. After graduation from St. Mary's Academy, Portland, she entered the Sisters of the Holy Names of Jesus and Mary, where she was known for many years as Sister Mary Gilbert. Under that name, she published two prose books about convent life and (in 1964) her first of five books of poems, *From the Darkroom*. DeFrees has taught in private Oregon elementary and secondary schools, at Holy Names College (later Fort Wright College, Spokane), at Seattle University, the University of Montana, the University of Massachusetts, and elsewhere. Currently retired and living in Seattle, and dispensed from her religious vows in 1973, she continues to do workshops and readings and to write both prose and poetry. "Scenes Out of Sequence: What the Coastwise Know" was written during a year's residence on a Guggenheim Fellowship in Cannon Beach, and is part of a longer sequence of poems appearing under the title *The Light Station on Tillamook Rock*. "Horatio Alger (1834-1899)" is from another sequence in which DeFrees, whose mother was raised in an orphanage, playfully imagines herself the possible descendant of any number of famous people in history, with whom she discovers she has something in common.

Scenes Out of Sequence: What the Coastwise Know

The old Coast Guardsman walks along the Seaside
Promenade, mourning the light he tended
two decades of its 77 years. A visitor might
think, How picturesque! That stubborn chunk
of rock, a mile off Tillamook Head:
white-painted stone, black tower
pitched above calm seas.

            A closer look would
show such treachery, it swells a book
with tales better left untold. Yet the fateful
stand—romantic, doomed—looking out
to sea. I take my stand with them, follow
my history wherever it leads. Ask the locals
who saw their fishermen put a dory in
south of Haystack Rock

               to take the seasick
private owner to his latest piece of real estate.
Ask the outboard motor crew:

the owner and two others
rescued as they swam, treated for shock. Ask
the fourth who didn't come back
alive. Water takes longer than fire to ready
the body for viewing.

                   Don't invent a necklace
of anemones, starfish worn like a badge
or barrette. Widows and cosmeticians have been
known to faint, regarding three days'
changes. Water-logged, we say, speaking of
boats and floating timber, not unlike
the swollen bulbs of kelp: shape of an amber
beet tossed up by the tide.

                 ❦

Horatio Alger (1834-1899)

Books were the air I breathed, curled in the Morris
chair with the Wizard of Oz or thousands of leagues
undersea—a place I could never go without
Jules Verne. So little time. So much to learn.
Too many distractions. *Set the table.*
Dust the woodwork. Get some fresh air. Go to
the store. Time for bed. Mother hid books
on top of the kitchen cupboard.

                   A Carnegie
uncovered in our family tree would keep me in books
indefinitely. More books than Mother could
whisk out of sight. When my brother brought home
from his paper route a ton of Horatio Alger, I read
them aloud, night after night. *Ragged Dick.*
Adrift in New York. Tom the Bootblack. Fame
and Fortune. One story

                 repeated 119 times. Andrew
Carnegie's autobiography repeats it again.
No wonder I recognize
those long-dead volumes brought from the library
mausoleum. Once upon a time I could breathe
life into their creaky lungs. Candidates for
the oxygen tent, they spoke in
borrowed tongues

like the lines of my early poems.
Fashioned of Mother's platitudes
mixed with rhyme, meter, and Horatio Alger, once
removed, hints of the pure sublime
sneaked into newspaper columns: a long dream of
fame—never a dream of fortune. *Your poem*
in the Oregon Journal helped me in my trouble. This
in a shaky hand from a man

                who sent me a dollar
bill. The poem was "Sympathy." I was
thirteen. Six lines in rhymed couplets. I can
recite them still. Ragged Dick
had nothing on me. This had to be The Little League
American Dream. Like Author Unknown,
like Anonymous, I had arrived,
was secretly famous.

Kenneth O. Hanson

Kenneth Ostlin Hanson (1922-), for many years a professor of English at Reed College, Portland, is an award-winning translator as well as poet. He was born in Shelley, Idaho, graduated from the University of Idaho, was staff seargant in the U.S. Army 1942-46, and studied comparative literature and Chinese at the University of Washington. He came to Reed in 1954. His first book of poems, *The Distance Anywhere*, won the Lamont Award from the Academy of American Poets in 1966. The author of three other books of poems, Hanson has published a collection of translations of the poems of Han Yu, *Growing Old Alive*. Recipient of numerous awards, Hanson has over the years maintained a second residence in Greece, where he lived for two years and several summers before the appearance of his second book of poems, *The Uncorrected World* (1973). Hanson's enthusiasm for his adopted country, where he is living as this anthology goes to press, is apparent throughout his recent work; but nowhere is it as evident as in "First of All," a poem in which the characteristically American quest for the perfect place has not stopped in Oregon, but has gone back the other direction—across the Atlantic, back to the simplicity of an ancient way of life. Readers will enjoy pairing this poem with Vi Gale's "At That, the Day Ended Well." Both poems were the result of a mutual challenge the two poets, along with other friends, gave each other (over dinner in Portland) to go home and write poems about countries; and Hanson has publicly credited Gale with giving him his first line.

Eels at The Dalles

Thin-lipped as adders
they swim upstream
through The Dalles fishladders.
Unlike salmon and sturgeon

distinguished daily
by electric eyes, they
are not counted as themselves
but are listed as "other."

Wavering like water
and fiercely determined
they set their own pace
though it may take forever.

Clinging in bunches
to the smooth cement sides
they are whipped by the current—
waiting to make their move

like lovers who
marry the same mistake
again and again
heading for home.

First of All

First of all it is necessary
to find yourself a country
—which is not easy.
It takes much looking
after which you must be lucky.
There must be rocks and water
and a sky that is willing
to take itself for granted
without being overbearing.
There should be fresh fish
in the harbor, fresh bread
in the local stores.
The people should know
how to suffer without
being unhappy, and how to be happy
without feeling guilty. The men

should be named Dimitrios
Costa, John or Evangelos
and all the women should be
named Elena or Anthoúla.
The newspapers should always
lie, which gives you something
to think about. There should be
great gods in the background
and on all the mountain tops.
There should be lesser gods
in the fields, and nymphs
about all the cool fountains.
The past should be always
somewhere in the distance,
not taken too seriously
but there always giving perspective.
The present should consist of the seven
days of the week forever.
The music should be broken-hearted
without being self-indulgent.
It should be difficult to sing.
Even the birds in the trees should
work for a dangerous living.
When it rains there should be
no doubt about it. The people
should be hard to govern
and not know how to queue up.
They should come from the villages
and go out to sea, and go back
to the villages. There should be
no word in their language
for self-pity. They should be
farmers and sailors, with only
a few poets. The olive trees
and the orange trees and the cypress
will change your life, the rocks
and the lies and the gods
and the strict music. If you go there
you should be prepared to leave
at a moment's notice, knowing
after all you have been somewhere.

Anthony Ostroff

Anthony Ostroff (1923-1978) spent the last nine years of his life in Oregon and died of a heart attack while hang gliding at Cape Kiwanda near Pacific City. Born in Gary, Indiana, he received his BS from Northwestern University, his MA from the University of Michigan, and did postgraduate study at the Sorbonne, the University of Paris, and the University of Grenoble. For twenty years a professor of rhetoric at the University of California, Berkeley, Ostroff became professor of humanities at Lewis and Clark College, Portland, in 1969. The author of four books, he also contributed poems, fiction, and articles to such magazines as *Atlantic Monthly, Harper's, Paris Review,* and *Saturday Review.* Guest editor of several journals; editor of *The Contemporary Poet as Artist and Critic*; visiting professor at the University of Buffalo and Vassar College; narrator of films for the University of California Film Production Service; panelist, lecturer, director, and performer for KPFA radio; Ostroff was also the recipient of numerous awards for his writing, including a Borestone Mountain Poetry Award, a Robert Frost fellowship in poetry, and a Guggenheim fellowship. Intensely musical, with their free-verse forms, wide-ranging in subjects, from Mexico to the Northwest, Ostroff's poems, such as the one reprinted here, are often both a celebration of and an elegy for the strong and yet fragile things of the natural world.

Winter Salmon

In the spawning pool
freshwater clear
and freshwater clean
from the long cold rain,
the winterwash clicks
in the steady rush
of the spawning stream.
Tattered and brown,
Old Silversides,
ten thousand miles
of salt blue
and salt green
behind him, thrusts.
His lifework won
he almost rests
in the roil of the pool,
clenched as one
with the current's muscle
days on end.

Then drawn from his own
drawn line, scales
peeled and gone,
patched red raw
by the gravel wash,
as in a dream
of losing strength
he slowly drifts
backward down
the current's swell,
head still held
headwater high
drifts back, back
until at last,
struck and turned
by strengthlessness,
gills force-filled,
brain-pulse stilled
to water pulse,
he quickens, speeds
to the cells of the stream,
swift as the lunge
past root and rock,
past hurt, past need,
wide-eyed and blind,
downstream.

Beverly Partridge

Beverly Partridge was born in Chicago, Illinois, in 1923. She has lived in Berkeley, California; Hood Canal, Washington; Ashford, England; Aurora, Oregon—a sixteen-year stint working on a sheep farm—and taught at Catlin Gabel School in Portland, Oregon, for another sixteen years. Partridge has conducted poetry and creative writing workshops for teachers and meets monthly with Kwinnen, a Eugene, Oregon, women writers' group. Her poems have appeared in *Fireweed* and *Chadakoin Review*. She has spent the last thirty-two years backpacking, skiing, and farming in Oregon; her work speaks from that base.

January Lambing

That week he came down with the flu
The hard kind, flat in bed for three days
Three days of twins, triplets and singles
The lambs dropped where they chose

Without any shepherd to follow
That week I milked twenty ewes
Gavaged their determined-to-die lambs
And built sudden pens with straw

I called Orion to sing with
I called the County Extension

Flu man, get out of your bed
Take over my bungled job
Let me return to my pots, my pans,
A table full of flowers

*

Still bodies of new lambs
lie limp in a garbage can,
on a truck, on the burn pile,
in the field, where buzzards
care for them

The smoothness of their death
brings calm tears flowing
inside my guts trying
to make their river of blood alive

John Haislip

John Haislip (1926-) was born and raised in Lancaster County, Pennsylvania, but he has been a resident of the Northwest since 1946. Having served during World War II in the North Atlantic with the U.S. Coast Guard, Haislip used the G.I. Bill to attend Johns Hopkins University and then the University of Washington, where he studied with poet Theodore Roethke and received his BA and PhD. He has taught at the University of Idaho, Oregon State University, and the University of Oregon, where he was director of the creative writing program for many years. A group of his poems was included in *Oregon Signatures*, a 1959 anthology of contemporary Oregon poets. His own books of poetry include *Not Every Year* and *Seal Rock*, which received the Oregon Institute of Literary Arts Hazel Hall Award for 1987. A professor emeritus, Haislip taught in Germany in 1983 under a Fulbright award. He was also a recipient of an Oregon Arts Commission Individual Artist Fellowship in 1987. *Seal Rock*, from which two of the following poems have been selected, is a book firmly rooted in place: the village of Seal Rock on the Oregon coast, just south of Newport, where Haislip, a father and stepfather, and his wife, the poet Karen Locke, have established a long, part-time residency.

At Grandmother's

She lay in bed on the second floor,
Dying in quiet that whole season—
While I played catch behind the barn
Each afternoon,
And bounced the ball against the fence,
The wall, the chopping block, the trees.
But never against the empty metal drums,
The wooden well, the sill, the double doors,
Never against the chancy echoing dark.

❦

The Visit

Wandering the base of the high cliff,
Up the long beach, on the gravel bar;
First my father, bent, arthritic.
Next my mother, slow, attentive,
Trailing her idle stick.
They are being watched from the cliff's edge,
Yet neither one would know,
Working the cobbles between the boulders,
They're searching for the perfect agate.

But they've come here to be alone with their son.

All week the weather, calm and luminous.
So every day, on the sheltering deck,
We sat and feasted at every meal.

And stared at the taut horizon.

Talk, they were terribly hungry:
Just look how they fed the gulls;
But oh how they ate memory.

Still my theme is now,
How through this slow dream of gathering
They climb the cliff, and are seen coming
Up the deep path floating,
Floating into my arms.

And their little bag of agates?
It swings from my father's shoulder.
They need to carry what they have found back into the valley.
They want my kiss laid on their old cheeks.
They want the words glittering to wear like pendants,
And my polished heart: firm, translucent, pulsing.

Ralph Salisbury

Ralph Salisbury (1926-) first came to Oregon as an 18-year-old machine-gunner on a training mission to bomb lumber stacks and engage in mock aerial combat with the Navy fliers at Pendleton. Born and raised on a family farm in northeast Iowa, he served 29 months in the Army Air Force during World War II and attended college on the G.I. Bill, receiving his BA and MFA from the University of Iowa. Having taught at Texas A & M and Drake universities, Salisbury returned to Oregon in 1960 to teach in the English department at the University of Oregon, where he was director of creative writing as well as editor of *Northwest Review*. He is married to poet Ingrid Wendt. His poems and short stories are widely published in the *New Yorker, Poetry, Poetry Northwest,* and elsewhere. The father of two sons and a daughter, he has received the Chapelbrook Award, with which he lived a year in England, and a Fulbright professorship to Germany. The son of two storytellers—his mother of Irish, and his father of Cherokee descent (a "hard rock" Tsaragi from the people who fled to the hills to escape the Death March to Oklahoma)—Salisbury has sought to follow the family oral tradition in five books of poems and a book of short stories, which includes chapters of his just completed novel *The Raven Mocker Wars.* Of his work, he says, "Perhaps because of an increased ecology awareness and civil rights awareness, people notice more the writing based on the Indian part of my upbringing, but I hope that my writing keeps faith with all of my people."

Come Near the Western Edge, I Try a Last Myth for the Childhood of My Sons

"The giant is eating the mountain,"
I tell my children while eating
cereal with them.

A gray moustache
is working slowly down the last green
slope before ours. It is a very large mountain
and mostly granite. It is very hard. It is
much harder than limestone, which was
formed from small shellfish under the sea in Iowa.
"Our old home under ocean?"

"Yes, once upon a time
an ocean ate little Iowa."

"Back when there was

Indians?"

"Oh, my sons. It was
not the ocean that ate the Indians. And it was
not their medicine men who made the ocean
leave. Before I was
a baby even. Before Iowa was
a part of the United States. Or even a state
of mind in a settler. Before man; before words became
language. Long before
Hiroshima dissolved like sugar in your cereal."
        "Huh?"
        "Oh, my neighbors," I whisper because I fear
huge ears and the tongue that may crush me
and my two sons. Oh, my neighbors beyond the gray
moustache, through which a dying father speaks.
"Oh, my neighbors, the giant is eating
very slowly just now. The mountain is
hard. It is not
easy eating. It must be
difficult to live
with an appetite huge as a cloud's. Live
well, my neighbors living still
where all will be green
a little longer. Man
was made to eat.
A little conversation is said to help
digestion. Laugh. To end
with a reassuringly familiar phrase, make—
and I am
serious about this—make
a good meal."

My Brother's Poem: Vietnamese War 1969

You tell me   you can not write it
yesterday's pretty village   splinters   and in
your aircraft's cargo compartment   ammunition/rations/med-
icines gone   an American lies   wrapped in his rain-coat
strapped to the floor of that machine generations struggled
to invent   and thousands of hours of lives went to create
the boy's belongings   all he could bear
on his back   packaged beside him
sunset   a shimmer like cathedral-glass
a memory   the instrument-panel glow
as low as devotional candles   showing
in plexiglass   monsoon screams past   your face
above the controls   your own American face

Ellen Shannon

Born in Decatur, Illinois, Ellen Shannon (1927-) has been a resident of Oregon since 1964, when she moved to Cannon Beach and began a 20-year career teaching writing and literature at Clatsop Community College, Astoria. She received her BA from the University of Illnois, her MA from the University of Delaware, and spent several years as a secretary in New York before driving alone across the country, in 1958, in a Ford Anglia. She taught English in Los Angeles for a year, married film and television actor Richard Shannon, had three children, and, in Oregon, embarked upon various scholarly projects, such as writing the history of Astoria's Grace Episcopal Church to celebrate its recent centennial. The author of *The Layman's Guide to Christian Terms, The Expectation Cookbook,* and *A Culinary Dictionary,* Shannon also earned her PhD in 1989 from the National University of Ireland. Having spent more than ten years as a part-time resident in Ireland, researching and publishing three volumes on the work of the noted Irish poet James Clarence Mangan, Shannon is currently supervising editor of the Mangan Publishing Project and is preparing a condensed, trade edition of her research. Her two books of poems, *Memory's Children* and *On the Way to Easter,* speak from the heart of many of life's most significant turning points.

Daughter /

When the night is dark,
midnight or after and very cold,
and the wind flings sleet against the window pane,
there are no words
for my heart's hollowness.
My daughter,
I cannot bear this time
and the thought of you, together.
My first born,
whatever you do is beautiful!
No cruel surgery that this world knows
can cut you from my love.
No night has ever been so black
I could not find you in it.
No hurt has ever been so deep
I could not kiss it whole.

O my child!
Let it be warm where you are,
and your feet not be wet.
Let there be something to wrap you in
warm as the Aran sweater
we brought you one summer long ago.
Let there be arms as loving
as any you left here,
and no harsh words
to hate you with,
and someone kind to say,
Oh, but they love you still.
Of course they love you still!

❦

Ursula K. Le Guin

Although her major writing awards have been in fiction, long-time Portland resident Ursula Le Guin (1929-) has also published four volumes of poetry. Her first publications, in fact, were poems—the first in 1959 in *Prairie Schooner*, a literary journal published in Nebraska. Born and raised in Berkeley, California, the daughter of the respected anthropologist Alfred Louis Kroeber and writer Theodora Kroeber, Le Guin went to college at Radcliffe and to graduate school at Columbia University. In 1953 she married the historian Charles Le Guin and they are the parents of three children. In 1958, Le Guin and her family moved to Portland where she still resides. In addition to publishing more than seventy short stories (many collected in three volumes of stories), two books of essays and reviews, sixteen novels, and her four books of poems, Le Guin has also authored screenplays, young children's books, verbal texts for musicians, and voice-texts for performance or recording. Her many writing honors include Hugo, Nebula, and National Book awards, the latter for *The Farthest Shore*. Le Guin is a highly original writer in all genres, and her work addresses a wide variety of social, political, personal, and environmental problems of our time. The poems included here illustrate the playful as well as the serious side of the poet, as she writes of the complexities of being both mother and daughter, as well as of the devastation wreaked by the eruption of Mt. St. Helens in 1980—a hint, only, of what the dust clouds of a nuclear winter might produce. See *Varieties of Hope* in the *Oregon Literature Series* for her essay on the Mt. St. Helens event.

An April Fools Day Present for My Daughter Elisabeth

Mother of my granddaughter,
Listen to my song:
A mother can't do right,
A daughter can't be wrong.

I have no claim whatever
On amnesty from you;
Nor will she forgive you
For anything you do.

So are we knit together
By force of opposites,
The daughter that unravels
The skein the mother knits.

One must be divided
So that one be whole,
And this is the duplicity
Alleged of woman's soul.

To be that heavy mother
Who weighs in every thing

Is to be the daughter
Whose footstep is the Spring.

Granddaughter of my mother,
Listen to my song:
Nothing you do will ever be right,
Nothing you do is wrong.

🌿

from **Luwit**
Part I: The Grey Quaker

She dances,
she dances,
the lady dances.
Ashes, ashes, all fall down!
Shakti, Shakti,
blew your stack,
your virgin crown
is boiling mud,
forestfire, earthshade,
gas, ash, filth, flood,
your breath death. You are
a darkness on the western wind,
a curtain falling for a thousand miles.
O lady you've blown it,
you're grit between our teeth,
motes in our eyes,
rose-salmon sunsets clear to Reykjavik.
Your face is dirty, seamed, burnt, scarred.
You killed the old man and his cats,
ten billion tiny fish,
and broke the lake your mirror.
Bad luck lady.
The grey Quaker woke
and the cities of the plain
beheld, and shook,
cast ashes on their heads,
crying Lady be good!
Unkind: O plumed
unmaker,
fire-womb,
O dancer!

from **Luwit, Part II**
To Walk in Here

To walk in here is to stop pretending.

What's real? Grey dust,
     a dead forest.
Entropy moves quickly to its end.
O desolation!
     What's real?
     says the fireweed lightly casting
     its words upon the wind.

To walk in here is to stop pretending
that what we do matters
all that much. Less in the long run
than the fireweed: to the others.

To ourselves we matter
terribly.

That there will be summer
ever
is the responsibility of others
more careful than ourselves.

They do not look us in the face.

     The gulfs of air
     are full of blowing rain,
     between us and the crater

     the small, cold rain of autumn.
               (October 1981)

Gary Snyder

For many years a prominent voice and the hero of various counterculture movements on the west coast, Gary Snyder (1930-) is the author of many books of poems, as well as poems in translation. Born in San Francisco, Snyder grew up on his parents' farm north of Seattle, graduated from Reed College (where he was the roommate of noted anthropologist Dell Hymes), and studied Oriental languages for three years at the University of California, Berkeley. Fluent in Japanese, and able to read Chinese, Snyder lived from 1956 to 1964 in Japan and studied Zen Buddhism. Before that, he worked at a variety of jobs in the Northwest, including logger, Forest Service crew member, lookout, and wiper on an American tanker. With Allen Ginsburg, Jack Kerouac, Philip Whalen, and others, he helped to introduce Beat literature to the public. Returning from Japan, he taught at the University of California, Berkeley, and founded a California community of Western Buddism. Like that of many artists of his generation, and the "hippie" generation that followed, Snyder's commitment to reestablishing a meaningful relation between humans and nature led to his open rejection of city life, a return to a more primitive life style, and an embracing of pre-existing mythologies. In addition to numerous translations, among them the poems by Han-Shan (*Cold Mountain Poems*), Snyder has often integrated elements of various Oriental and Native American art forms and rhythms into his own work. The poems below reflect Snyder's identification with people of the working classes, as well as his own experiences in Oregon. Snyder received the Pulitzer Prize in poetry for his 1974 book *Turtle Island*. He currently lives in California.

Hay for the Horses

He had driven half the night
From far down San Joaquin
Through Mariposa, up the
Dangerous mountain roads,
And pulled in at eight a.m.
With his big truckload of hay
    behind the barn.
With winch and ropes and hooks
We stacked the bales up clean
To splintery redwood rafters
High in the dark, flecks of alfalfa
Whirling through shingle-cracks of light,
Itch of haydust in the
    sweaty shirt and shoes.
At lunchtime under Black oak

Out in the hot corral,
—The old mare nosing lunchpails,
Grasshoppers crackling in the weeds—
"I'm sixty-eight" he said,
"I first bucked hay when I was seventeen
I thought, that day I started,
I sure would hate to do this all my life
And dammit, that's just what
I've gone and done."

❧

Bear

Kai was alone by the pond in the dusk. He heard
   a grunt and felt, he said, his hair tingle.
   He jumped on a bike and high-tailed it down
   the trail, to some friends.

Scott stood alone in the dark by the window. Clicked
   on his flashlight and there out the window, six
   inches away, were the eyes of the bear.

Stefanie found her summer kitchen all torn up.

I went down the hill to the beehives next morning—
   the supers were off and destroyed, chewed comb
   all around, the whole thing tipped over, no
   honey, no larvae, no bees,

But somewhere, a bear.

❧

PART V

Contemporary Voices:
Arriving and Leaving Here

Introduction to Part V
Arriving and Leaving

There are those days when looking out my window I dream of being a backup singer for Walt Whitman. I guess it is his verve that gets me. His seer-like certainty that democracy, that rambunctious polyrhythmic choir of his, is a healthy chaos that works because it respects the broadest possibilities we are capable of. Whitman was always after our voice and willing to carouse anywhere to find it. He did not want to hear and celebrate some singular speech, some cultural monotone, some myopic social thought. He wanted our largest appetite, understanding like Ishmael Reed that "the world is here." It has come to us, and we celebrate ourselves best by "celebrating every man and woman and child alive."

This is a good time for people along the margins to ask what does this have to do with contemporary Oregon poetry (1960-1991). It has a lot to do with contemporary Oregon poetry.

As a state we are a particular, *yes*. We are a distinct region with a distinct landscape and climate whose rivers are named after our history, *yes*. Our human beginnings are with the immense journeys of Native peoples, explorers, trappers, and pioneers. While our contemporary poets are respectful of our past and in varying degrees appreciative of our landscape, in the end the scope of their diversity and the nature of modern life doesn't ordain a provincial poetry, a poetry limited to local color.

Contemporary Oregon (like many other states) is no longer so isolated that it brews a profoundly separate story. Farmers and ranchers throughout the country share similar situations, employment possibilities for loggers and mill workers nationwide are declining, roads everywhere in the country are deteriorating, schools (urban as well as rural) are struggling to be more effective at stimulating learning, racial, ethnic, and gender conflicts remain conflicts with all the guilt and innocence they imply, and our wardrobes cross dress with the world. In short, the world is "too much with us."

How could it not be? Modern communication creates larger neighborhoods. Radio, television, movies, telephones, CDs, computers are extremely effective at creating artificial intimacies through electronic figures. In fact *place* in our world is often a sustained electronic experience. Today our covered wagons, our ox carts are our remotes.

We not only have an abundance of poets here. We also have an abundance of poets free to range the significantly more diverse worlds that have formed them.

What else is suggested by this large gathering of poets for consideration in this section of the anthology? Today the body of Oregon poetry is perhaps as large, if not larger, than it has ever been, larger even than the considerable work of the renowned literary pioneers. But it is not an isolated phenomenon. Colleges and universities nationwide have been breeding poets like fruit flies and that is okay—really. After all we don't need more mythical business majors as our messiahs. We are a nation that for the last twenty-three years exposed growing numbers of children to Poets-in-the-Schools programs with residencies designed to sustain young poets and encourage the innovative teaching of poetry writing and appreciation. It is no wonder that there are a lot of skilled poets scattered throughout the country. We have strategically built audiences and husbanded prospective writers to expand our national imagination.

The more than three hundred poets reviewed for Part V, though not comprehensive, nevertheless suggest the idea of a swarm, perhaps something even more exotic like a grist, a volery, a drove, a sledge, a plague, a span, a covey, a muster, a bouquet, a tidings, or an exaltation of poets. Their abundance now, like their abundance in the late nineteenth and early twentieth century, speaks to the general theme of abundance that embraces the American epic. (Notice: the abundance of teachers, the abundance of lawyers, the abundance of middle managers, even the abundance of criminals . . . .) Opportunity to us is as standardized a part as a clutch. And, poetry, whether pedigreed or not, genteel or vulgar, has a right to provoke itself toward some unavoidable market share of attention.

In our democracy we have moved toward the idea, even if reluctantly on some issues, that opportunities are best when they are abundant. We are a country designed to find traces of gold in large pans of sand—*e pluribus unum*.

What else does this section reveal? It reveals that Oregon poets are natives, naturalized citizens, and even resident aliens. Some of the writers were born here; many were not. Some have been here for a long time; some have not. Some came to attend college; some came to teach. Some came following lovers and mates; some stayed because they met them here. Some left because they couldn't find work here; some left because their careers offered other attractive choices. But everyone here has testified to an indelible bond with Oregon that they will not dissolve. Like wolves they have mated for life; like immigrants they make sense of the present by refusing to allow memory to vanish. If one of the definitions of the word *bond* is love and peace, then indeed these poets are in love and in peace with Oregon. Their private allegiance is enough to sanctify them as Oregon writers and attaches them to the precedence of Roger Williams and Anne Hutchinson.

It has been a pleasure to read all the manuscripts submitted for consideration to this section, and it is with deep regret that I could not select at least one poem from each manuscript, because all of the poets I read were skillful. But in the end an anthology is a prescribed space, and the editor like an architect must invent something beautiful that fits.

Let me tell you something about my design. One of the things that occurred to me was that the contemporary literary scene is vaporous like a game in progress or the light you meet before you meet a star. This is not the time for lasting conclusions; this is the time for explorations. I have listed the writers in alphabetical order instead of chronological order to avoid the illusion of permanence. I am not trying to comprehensively define the age.

The next factor that influenced this selection was some preliminary testing of poems in college and high-school classrooms. I wanted a sense of the school room response to many of the selections. The classroom was not a final judge, but a guide for designing doors, windows, and hallways for the exploration of poetry.

Another consideration for the anthology was what I call the *we the people* factor. Who is *we*? What color is *we*? What ethnicity is *we*? What gender is *we*? I would not like to see Oregon misunderstood by its own or others, so I looked for *we*. I am not satisfied with the plurality that I found for this section. I believe the invisibility of works by people of color and a less than representative spectrum of women's voices are a consequence of how unwelcome we can make people feel and how astutely we can engineer reality. But despite those drawbacks, I wanted to be sure that women and people of color were the people who described the features of their own faces and the timbre of their own voices. I cannot pretend that literary expression has no politics. For it is indeed another arena where groups exercise power on behalf of their values, so as an editor, I exercised my value that we include as many *invisibles* as we can.

Finally I chose poems by watching closely how *writers* made choices and discovered their way through their thoughts and feelings. I sought a spectrum of delight, anger, sadness, fear, confusion, faith, mystery, athleticism, acceptance, visions, battles, resurrections, wit, satire, foolishness, geography, uncertainty, confidence, history, duty, obedience, wonder, and love that would effectively celebrate the internal life that enchants the poet.

Primus St. John
February 1993

Paula Gunn Allen

Paula Gunn Allen (Laguna Pueblo/Lakota) attended the University of Oregon. She is at present a professor of English at UCLA. A poet and a scholar, her work has appeared in numerous anthologies, journals, and scholarly publications. She is the recipient of a Native American Prize for Literature, an American Book Award and a Susan Koppleman Award. Her book of poetry is titled *Skins and Bones: Poems 1979-1987* (1988).

What the Moon Said

The moon lives in all the alone places
all alone.
      "There are things
      I work out for myself," she says.
      "You don't have to be depressed about them.
      These are my paces, and walking through them
            is my right.

      You don't need to care
            when I'm down.

      "Or if I'm mad at myself, don't believe
            I'm mad at you.
      If I glare it is not your face I am staring at
            but my own.
      If I weep, it is not your tears that flow.

      "And if I glow
      with the brush of twilight wings,
      if I rise round and warm
      above your bed,
      if I sail
            through the iridescent autumn spaces
      heavy with promise,
            with red and fruity light,
      and leave your breath
            tangled in the tossing tops
      of trees as I arise,
      as I speed away into the far distance,
      disappearing as you gaze,
      turning silver, turning white,
      it is not your glory I reflect.
      It is not your love
            that makes me pink,
                copper,
                gold.

It is mine."
The moon moves along the sky by her own willing.
It is her nature to shed some light, sometimes
to be full and close, heavy with unborn thought
on rising. It is her nature sometimes
to wander in some distant place, hidden, absent, gone.

Dear World

Mother has lupus.
She says it's a disease
of self-attack.
It's like a mugger broke into your home
and you called the police
and when they came they beat up on you
instead of on your attackers,
she says.

I say that makes sense.
It's in the blood,
in the dynamic.
A halfbreed woman
can hardly do anything else
but attack herself,
her blood attacks itself.
There are historical reasons
for this.

I know you can't make peace
being Indian and white.
They cancel each other out.
Leaving no one in the place.
And somebody's gotta be there,
to take care of the house,
to provide the food.
And that's gotta be the mother.
But if she's gone to war.
If she's beaten and robbed.
If she's attacked by everyone.
Conquered, occupied, destroyed
by her own blood's diverse strains,
its conflicting stains?

Well, world. What's to be done?
We just wait and see
what will happen next.

The old ways go,
tormented in the fires of disease.
My mother's eyes burn,
they tear themselves apart.
Her skin darkens in her fire's heat,
her joints swell to the point
of explosion, eruption.
And oh, the ache: her lungs
don't want to take in more air,
refuse further oxygenation:
in such circumstances,
when volatile substances are intertwined,
when irreconcilable opposites meet,
the crucible and its contents vaporize.

Dori Appel

Dori Appel was born and raised in Chicago, attended the University of Michigan, and then spent the next twenty-two years in Boston. She moved to Ashland, Oregon, in 1979. She is a playwright, fiction writer, and clinical psychologist, as well as a poet. Her work has appeared in the *Beliot Poetry Journal*, *Prairie Schooner*, the *New Renaissance*, and *CALYX*. "Being an Oregon poet informs my sense of place and contrasts—living in Ashland as opposed to living in cities like Boston and Chicago."

A Double Life

A girl who loved horses thought
she was a horse. Her brown shoes
that laced were her hooves,
her neck, not long, became long
when she thought about who she was.
She told no one. When they called
her for supper she came at an
obedient trot and tucked her napkin
just above the place where

the martingale had left its mark.
When they took her places she walked
properly and answered courteously,
and thought about the sweet grass
in the field where she greeted
the morning, and the moonlight in
the meadow where she ran at night.
The morning was gold
and the night was silver, and only she
in all the world was awake to its
secret sounds and shadows,
her hooves bright as stars, her
long neck arcing towards the moon.

Diane Averill

Diane Averill was born in Glendale, California, and has lived in Oregon since she was two years old. Many of her poems identify Oregon places and some speak from the point of view of nineteenth-century Oregon women. Her poems have appeared in *CALYX*, *Hubbub*, *Mississippi Mud*, the *Portland Review*, and *Northwest Review*. She is the author of a collection, *Branches Doubled Over with Fruit* (1991).

Racing Snakes

Nail polish was our first cosmetic experiment,
our way of making up with snakes
for stepping on them,
each scale a fingernail.
After we painted their tails crimson and pink
they ribboned off sideways like kitetails.
Sally and I never knew who won.

Later we let them go in woods.
Catching them again was like teasing brats.
Streetfighters of the forest,
we'd feel them tremble in our fingers
and twist like braids in rubber bands.

When prissy Mrs. Cooper scolded us
for cutting across her lawn
I tucked a silky garter
in my training bra and touched

her brass monster knocker.
She opened, I shook my tee shirt
and the snake slithered out
of the stiff cotton cup.

Mrs. Cooper's face was that orange,
Sunday-school-magazine hue
of one who'd witnessed the supernatural.
A blue vein jumped out of my skin,
scribbled on the welcome mat
and cut across her grass.

David Axelrod

David Axelrod was born in 1958 in Alliance, Ohio. For fifteen years, he worked in his family's used auto parts business. He holds an MFA from the University of Montana and is the author of *The Jerusalem of Grass* (1992), a collection of poems, and a chapbook, *The Kingdom at Hand* (1993). Axelrod currently lives and writes in La Grande, Oregon, and teaches creative writing at Eastern Oregon State College.

Skill of the Heart

The morning I lost my job,
I glanced up absently
thousands of feet above me
into the Bitterroot Range,
where winter retreated
and snowmelt erupted from canyons.
Stranded in the anxious lines
of automobiles, idling
side-by-side at traffic lights,
I knew I might never change,
like my father, who stammered
until words twisted his face.
A freak to men who jeered,
he was always filled by
a rage that corrupted every
hope he ever held long enough
to value or recklessly love.

I was laid off from my job
the morning my son spilled
free from his mother's body
and drew the inevitable
knife-edged air in his lungs.
Through his first hour, he slept
in an exhausted repose
unlike any other he or
I would ever know again.

All the length of the valley
to where the Bitterroots
vanished on the earth's curve,
wide fault-lines of light streaked
through low clouds and rushed over
foothills blotched green with sage,
a landscape as intent
and overflowing with the skill
of its own inexhaustible heart
as vistas painted by Sung
masters, who washed raw silk
with India ink and fled
this world a thousand years ago.

Alison Baker

Alison Baker was a resident of Portland in the mid-seventies, graduated from Reed College in 1975, and later relocated and earned a degree in Library Science at Indiana University in 1977. A recent move from Salt Lake City brings her back to Oregon, where she and her husband own a home in Rogue River. Some of her poetry has been anthologized in *The Oregon Anthology of College Poetry* (1977) and *From A to Z: 200 Contemporary American Poets* (1981). Poems also appear in magazine publications such as *Bitterroot, Mississippi Valley Review, New Letters,* and *Kennebec.* Shifting from poetry to fiction writing, her recent focus, she has published short stories in the *Atlantic, Threepenny Review, Ascent,* and the *Ontario Review.*

Flying

The old dog grins. It's been a perfect day,
sky brushed with cloud, grass
fresh-mown this morning, making hay
of the field. He drifts past,

tongue nearly to his feet,
to stand in the diminishing stream
cooling down. I watch the heat
rise in layers, a mirage or dream

of summer. Earlier we drove a deer
from a thicket, heard a sound it made
like "THET!" as the dog came near,
taking off across the meadow toward the shade

of those still woods. I'd never seen
a deer at noon, and he
had never seen a deer at all. His keen
nose drew in great draughts, free

of smog here thirty miles west of town:
wondering at the strange scents
of deer, and grass, and sounds
of birds, and what they meant.

He flushed a pheasant, too,
from undergrowth. I heard a cry
and beating wings, and turned to view
a body hurtling toward the sky,

a mighty motion; and the old boy
leaping after, eyes bright,
tail up, his aging body purest joy
chasing the better flier toward the light.

Jim Barnes

Jim Barnes (Choctaw-Welsh) is a professor of Comparative Literature at Northeast Missouri State University and editor of *Chariton Review*. He also lumberjacked for ten years in Oregon's Willamette Valley. Some of his poems have appeared in the *Nation, Northwest Review, New Letters* and *Chicago Review*. In 1980, he was awarded a translation prize from the Translation Center of Columbia University for *Summons and Sign: Poems by Dagmar Nick* (1980). He is also the author of three collections of poems: *The American Book of the Dead* (1982), *A Season of Loss* (1985) and *La Plata Cantata* (1988). Barnes has also won a Rockefeller Bellagio Fellowship.

A Choctaw Chief Helps Plan a Festival in Memory of Pushmataha's Birthday

We know he liked chockbeer and watermelon
and raced sleek ponies in the dead of night.
We'll give him that. We'll have to open up
the valley to whites and those Chickasaws,
or it's sure no go. But we'll keep it pure.

Now for the other games, let's see, we'll want
the local P T A to have free rein to
search Muskogee archives for stickball rules
and rituals of the eagle dance and how
to mourn his bones, old style, for channel eight.

A lot depends on image. Use your masks.
Don't wear boots. Speak the language if you can, or invent.
And let's have them see us pray.
About the chock: keep it out of their sight.
And strip all the kids under nine or ten.

One more thing: we can get those federal funds.
So look dumb, play poor, form car pools or walk.

Tim Barnes

Tim Barnes is a native of the San Francisco Bay area and graduated from San Jose State in 1970 with a BA in English literature and from Portland State in 1976 with an MA in American literature. Between 1977 and 1988, he worked in the Poet-in-the-Schools program in Oregon and Washington. He currently teaches in the English Department at Portland Community College. His poems, essays, articles, reviews, interviews, and translations have appeared in various magazines, including *Cutbank, Mississippi Mud, Oregon English Journal,* and *Portland Review.* His book, *Mother and the Mangos,* was published in 1991. Although Barnes states, "The landscapes of my poems of recollection are from the Bay Area," he still captures Oregon's "clouds, blossom-soaked Aprils, long rain, fat rivers, and green on green," in much of his poetry.

Winter Fog along the Willamette
1

The hills across the river
turn slowly to mist
this afternoon, all
the way to the coast,
trees fade from
their forests, farms
leave their chickens
and goats, housewives
look out windows
into a vanished
yard. Toddlers drift
from their trikes.

The crow and his cry
are lost where rivers
wave to their beds.
A sigh that is almost
a shudder
breaks from the bull
in the field as he chews
the thoughtful grass
down to simply nothing.

2

It is similar to snow,
to TV static, an
interference of air.
Your best friends
evaporate in the distance,
the way roads blow
away into winter.
No knobs or wheels
can recall them.

There is nothing to fix,
now, nothing to focus.
Your hands, your eyes,
no longer hold
what you wish,
which, at this moment,
is only your body—
that it might remain with you
in any weather
on earth.

Judith Barrington

Judith Barrington is a poet born and raised in Brighton, England. In the early 1960s, she spent most of her time in Spain, working for a wine company based in a castle near the French/Spanish border, and eventually moved to Oregon in 1976. She is the author of two poetry collections: *Trying to Be an Honest Woman* (1985) and *History and Geography* (1989). Much of Barrington's work has been published in journals and magazines, including the *Women's Review of Books, Northwest Magazine,* the *Kenyon Review, Ms. Magazine,* and others. She is a recipient of grants from the Metropolitan Arts Commission and from the Money for Women Fund. Her second book, *History and Geography,* was selected as a finalist for an Oregon Book Award from the Oregon Institute of Literary Arts. She is also the founder of The Flight of the Mind, an annual summer writing workshop for women writers held in the foothills of the Oregon Cascade Mountains. She has frequently been called a "poet of place," and the landscape and people of Oregon have had a crucial effect upon her work.

Beating the Dog

She lowered her belly into heather
and froze. Her nose explored
the breeze, sorted smells of weather
from what mattered. I saw how her eyes stared.

She was so young then, downwind
from two sheep on a hillside purple under blue;
there were farmers with guns in my mind
as I yelled NO. I was young too.

It was no use, my yelling.
The sheep lifted their heads too high
and bolted, swerving, almost falling
over tussocks, while the sky

tilted and spun as I ran,
the dog ran, we barked and yelled
and the four of us, alone up there,
ploughed through bracken and hare-bells.

She heard me at last, left
the sheep heaving and bleating
by a gorse bush. Her eyes softened,
she crouched, and then I was beating

the dog with the leash,
farmers and guns in my mind
as rage washed over the hill
like a storm's hot wind.

I remember how she screamed twice
before I sank down in the heather.
It doesn't matter that she licked my face—
the sorry tears; it doesn't matter

that she barked and skipped through the stream
or that she never stared that way
at a sheep again. Ends and means.
How could things be simple after that day?

Gloria Bird

Gloria Bird (Spokane) was raised on both the Spokane and Colville Indian Reservations and has been a resident of Portland, Oregon. She earned her BA at Lewis and Clark College, an MA at the University of Arizona in Tucson, and plans to continue toward a PhD in Native American literature. Her poetry has been published in *High Plains Literary Review, Mr. Cogito, American Indian Issue, CALYX, The Pointed Circle*, and *TAMAQUA*. With Elizabeth Woody, she co-authored the introduction to *Dancing on the Rim of the World*. A recipient of a 1988 Writer's Grant from the Oregon Institute of Literary Arts, Bird is one of the founding members of the Northwest Native American Writers Association. She currently lives in Santa Fe, New Mexico, and teaches at the Institute of American Indian Arts. Her recently published book of poems is *Full Moon on the Reservation* (1993). "The Women Fell Like Beautiful Horses" is an excerpt from a series in progress on Chief Joseph and the Nez Perce Wars.

The Women Fell Like Beautiful Horses
1. Kowtoliks, a boy

I threw back the teepee flap,
running. Patsikonmi
was gathering morning wood.
The roar of guns and horses flew up around us
as we fell to our hands and knees.
She drew in her breath; I heard the bullet strike.
Soldiers were shooting everywhere,
children and men fell before bullets
pelting like rain, the hurt
my throat could not scream through.

She was telling me, motioning
to move away from the bad place.
I watched her death blossom
from the wound in her breast.
She died and I ran away
from the beautiful woman who fed me
into the bushes, the voice of guns from the *tewelka*,
the enemy, the shrill bone whistle and wailing
surrounded me.

My Digging Stick
Atsipeeten & Her Grandmother Intetah

She talks to me while she works,
Spruce peeled, then hardened in the fire,
like this, bowed for digging, pointed
as a new antler turning in.

I am watching her hands,
notice the rivers of her veins, and the smoothness
of her fingers rubbing
the long wood she has chosen bending and calling to form.
I have drilled the hole in, Atsipeeten,
and am wrapping this bone handle
tight, like this. She is piercing me
with her bird looks.

I nod my head yes
I have been watching,
I am watching. Someday
I will make a digging stick, too.
I watch Intetah, my grandmother, talking

to the digging stick she has made,
These things I do
so that you will work for me
as my own hand. You and I
the roots, keh kheet, camas, kouse
will know well.

       ❦

Olga Broumas

Olga Broumas, born in Syros, Greece, moved to the United States to study architecture at the University of Pennsylvania in 1967. Subsequently, she received an MFA in creative writing from the University of Oregon, where she taught in both the creative writing program and women's studies. She has also been the director of "Freehand," a fine arts program for women cofounded by Broumas in Maine. Her published books include *Beginning with O* (1977), *Perpetua* (1989), and *Black Holes, Black Stockings* (1985). She has won the Yale Younger Poets Award, as well as National Endowment for the Arts and Guggenheim fellowships. She currently teaches at Brandeis University and makes her home in Provincetown, where she is a licenced bodywork therapist.

Cinderella

> *. . . the joy that isn't shared*
> *I heard, dies young.*
> Anne Sexton, 1928-1974

Apart from my sisters, estranged
from my mother, I am a woman alone
in a house of men
who secretly call
themselves princes, alone
with me usually, under cover of dark. I am the one allowed in

to the royal chambers, whose small foot conveniently
fills the slipper of glass. The woman writer, the lady
umpire, the madam chairman, anyone's wife.
I know what I know.
And I once was glad

of the chance to use it, even alone
in a strange castle, doing overtime on my own, cracking
the royal code. The princes spoke
in their fathers' language, were eager to praise me
my nimble tongue. I am a woman in a state of siege, alone

as one piece of laundry, strung on a windy clothesline a
mile long. A woman co-opted by promises: the lure
of a job, the ruse of a choice, a woman forced
to bear witness, falsely
against my kind, as each
other sister was judged inadequate, bitchy, incompetent,

jealous, too thin, too fat.   I know what I know.
What sweet bread I make

for myself in this prosperous house
is dirty, what good soup I boil turns
in my mouth to mud. Give
me my ashes. A cold stove, a cinder-block pillow, wet
canvas shoes in my sisters', my sisters' hut. Or I swear

I'll die young
like those favored before me, hand-picked each one
for her joyful heart.

Sweeping the Garden

for Deborah Haynes

Slowly learning again to love
ourselves working. Paul Eluard

said the body
is that part of the soul
perceptible by the five senses. To love
the body to love its work
to love the hand that praises both to praise
the body and to love the soul
that dreams and wakes us back alive
against the slothful odds: fatigue
depression loneliness
the perishable still recognition
what needs

be done. *Sweep the garden, any size*
said the roshi. Sweeping sweeping

alone as the garden grows
large or small. Any song
sung working the garden brings
up from sand gravel soil through
straw bamboo wood and less
tangible elements Power
song for the hands Healing
song for the senses what can
and cannot be perceived
of the soul.

Lois Bunse

Lois Bunse was born in Portland, Oregon. She graduated from Willamette University in 1962 and later earned an elementary teaching certificate from Oregon College of Education in Monmouth. After a stint of substitute teaching around the Salem area, she worked in Oregon Poets-in-the-Schools: "my favorite job, second to teaching dance!" Currently living in Lincoln City, an Oregon coastal town, she writes poetry, feeling "strongly regional," yet wanting that to include countries she has never visited—"like Finland." Her poetry has appeared in *CALYX, Hubbub, California Quarterly,* and *Calapooya Collage.* "The Kalavala" is the Finnish epic.

Right in the Kalavala It Says

a woman created the world.
She probably looked up from the dishes,
bubbles of creation studding her fingers

stepped to the back door,
looked over the yard,
saw nothing but whitecaps, and said,

"Let's have a little land here."
Low lands emerge, hardly hills.
Then she says, for fun, "Stars!" They arrive,

soften when they see how young she is.
She steps back, snapping her dish towel.
Soapy constellations slide down her ringed glass.

Out the window she sees men
pointing their arms, already naming things.
Humming, she knows her landscape will stay.

John Bush

John Bush was born in 1952 in Burns, Oregon. He has attended Eastern Oregon State College and received a BA in English from the University of Oregon (1976). In his senior year, he won an undergraduate creative writing prize. Over the years, John Bush has worked as a fisherman, ranch hand, builder, and teacher's aide. He now owns an antique shop in Lincoln City. Some of his poems have appeared in *Intro 7, Beacon,* and *Underpass.* "Puller" is one of the crew on a fishing boat. His job is to pull in the lines.

Puller on the *Ann*

I pull for father.
I pull for *Ann*.
I pull for myself.

Ann carries me.
At night, inside her, asleep,
I forget I was born.
These waves gurgle up against her
like flowing blood.
Waking, I see this pregnant woman
has oak flowing through her veins.
I pull for *Ann*.

As the sun rises,
I lower my lines.
I am young.
There are schools of silvers and chinook.
When I feel good
I give the fish I catch
a quick solid rap,
head to deck.
On my own forehead, sweat and sea, salt of everything.
I pull for myself.

Grasping that vast wheel,
my father wants me.
He makes short tacks,
keeping with these salmon.
We land a splitter;
clasping hands,
I am more his brother than son.
I pull for father.

I pull when I'm tired.
I pull selfishly,
the sun over the edge of the world.
Between this dome of stars,
phosphorescent wake,
father guides *Ann*
over the surface of nothing.
We are thieves in the dark,
running home,
with a hold full of fish.

Henry Carlile

Henry Carlile was born in San Francisco and grew up in the Pacific Northwest. He attended the University of Washington and since 1967 has taught at Portland State University. During 1978-80 he was a visiting lecturer in the Iowa Writers' Workshop. His publications include *The Rough-Hewn Table* (1971), which won the Devins Award, *Running Lights* (1981), and *Rain* (1993). Carlile is the recipient of two Pushcart prizes, *Crazyhorse* magazine's 1988 Poetry Award, and grants from the National Endowment for the Arts and the Ingram Merrill Foundation. He lives in Portland, Oregon.

Train Whistles in the Wind and Rain

In some Havana of the heart I still
imagine my father, his broken English
explaining why that morning he left
he never looked back but went on
into his life. And was it a good life?
The last time I saw him was before
the war, on Christmas Day. I was two,
watching the toy train he'd brought
slow down until, minutes after he left,
my mother wound it too tight and broke it.

I gave his name up for a stepfather's, but
whenever I thought of it, and I tried not to,
I hated him for leaving, for not writing.
I hadn't a photo, even, to tell what he had
looked like, only his shadow, and images
of trains. Later, in Klamath Falls,
my mother told me tales to scare me
from the tracks: horrible stories of hoboes
who tortured children, and of a kid with
both legs cut off at a crossing.
But nothing kept me away. On my tricycle
I watched the trains roar past, huge
Mallets, four-eight-eight-fours, with pusher
engines to scale the Siskiyous, until
my mother, missing me, switched me home,
pedaling and howling for my life.

In Seattle, Uncle Andrew took me to the yards
to watch the engines shuttling boxcars.
And standing by the tracks, clutching his hand
as the switchers passed, bathing us in steam,
I didn't know I wouldn't see him again, that
somewhere in the Ardennes a German mortar
round would fall behind the lines where
he stood drinking coffee beside his tank.
Mother, not his mother, though she had nurtured
him after my grandmother's religion tore the
family apart, hung a gold star in our window.
That Seattle morning's all I remember of him.
I can almost see his face, almost hear him,
mother's youngest brother, explaining
the complicated mechanisms of pistons
and drivers, of boilers and steam valves,
as the engines rumbled and huffed, bellowing
steam and smoke, their bells clanging.

And years later, a young man, just broken up
with my fiancee, I took my grief to a river,
as I always had, and stood knee-deep
in the chill winter current, casting
toward a far bank where the steelhead lay,
their icy blue backs freckled with black,
their noses aimed upstream, fins sculling
them in place. But nothing hit that day.
One by one they broke ranks to let my lure
drift past, then reclaimed their places.

I was almost ready to leave when I heard
the far whistle of a freight, one of the
last steam engines, surviving dinosaur,
its carboniferous breath blooming beyond
a far curve of pinkish, bare alders,
where the tracks followed the river,
then curved to cross a bridge upstream
from where I stood. Like soot, a flock
of crows started from the deep boom of
its drivers, the screech of trucks on rails,
the headlight, though it was almost noon,
swiveling its lizard's eye. And suddenly,
something, not nostalgia for trains,
or the woman who had left me, or my

father, or my uncle, caused my eyes to brim
and scald as they had once in St. Paul
when I leaned off an overpass to stare down
a passing engine's funnel and got an eyeful.

So tell me why, this late at night,
I love to hear that far hoot through the rain.
Why does it comfort me, when it's not steam
but air sounds the whistle, not coal
but diesel quakes the house and rattles windows?
Tell me why so late in life, engine, father,
uncle, lover, your loss gathers to a sweetness
in one voice to sing a past more
perfect than it was.

Raymond Carver

Raymond Carver was born in Clatskanie, Oregon, in 1939, and died of lung cancer in 1988 while living in Port Angeles, Washington. In the 1980s, he was recognized as an important American fiction writer, and his works garnered numerous honors. He was awarded three O'Henry Prizes for fiction. *Cathedral* (1989), a collection of short stories, was nominated for both a Pulitzer and a National Book Critics Award, while *Will You Please Be Quiet Please* (1992) was nominated for a National Book Award for fiction. He was a Guggenheim and National Endowment for the Arts fellow and was elected to the American Academy and Institute of Arts and Letters. Raymond Carver's work has been praised for the richness of its brevity.

Where Water Comes Together with Other Water

I love creeks and the music they make.
And rills, in glades and meadows, before
they have a chance to become creeks.
I may even love them best of all
for their secrecy. I almost forgot
to say something about the source!
Can anything be more wonderful than a spring?
But the big streams have my heart too.
And the places streams flow into rivers.
The open mouths of rivers where they join the sea.
The places where water comes together
with other water. Those places stand out
in my mind like holy places.

But these coastal rivers!
I love them the way some men love horses
or glamorous women. I have a thing
for this cold swift water.
Just looking at it makes my blood run
and my skin tingle. I could sit
and watch these rivers for hours.
Not one of them like any other.
I'm 45 years old today.
Would anyone believe it if I said
I was once 35?
My heart empty and sere at 35!
Five more years had to pass
before it began to flow again.
I'll take all the time I please this afternoon
before leaving my place alongside this river.
It pleases me, loving rivers.
Loving them all the way back
to their source.
Loving everything that increases me.

Still Looking Out for Number One

Now that you've gone away for five days,
I'll smoke all the cigarettes I want,
where I want. Make biscuits and eat them
with jam and fat bacon. Loaf. Indulge
myself. Walk on the beach if I feel
like it. And I feel like it, alone and
thinking about when I was young. The people
then who loved me beyond reason.
And how I loved them above all others.
Except one. I'm saying I'll do everything
I want here while you're away!
But there's one thing I won't do.
I won't sleep in our bed without you.
No. It doesn't please me to do so.
I'll sleep where I damn well feel like it—
where I sleep best when you're away
and I can't hold you the way I do.
On the broken sofa in my study.

Tina Castañares

Tina Castañares is a physician and writer from Hood River. Born in 1949 in Los Angeles to a Mexican father and a North American mother, she settled in Oregon in 1983. Her poetry and book reviews have been published in *Northwest Magazine,* the *Northwest Review of Books, Medical Self-Care,* the *Hood River News,* and elsewhere. As a medical doctor, she works chiefly with migrant farmworkers and is a frequent lecturer and consultant to Northwest groups about Hispanic issues and health policy reform. She met her husband while camping at Santiam Pass; they share a deep affection for central and eastern Oregon, areas which inspire much of her poetry.

In Eastern Oregon
for Pablo
The sky is still,
your kayak paddle dipping in the sea,
the lapping of the water.
You solo in your quiet boat.
I am a fire glowing
half a mile away.

Warm your weary hands
and sleep beside me,
keep me burning through the evening winds.
Come to shore from time to time.
I am that kind
of friend.

Three Deer
three deer
inspecting one another's feet
heads low
between bites of grass
then moving on
planting every step
with restraint
with that—
catch—
to each swing of limb
before it lightly lands.
a morning fog

surrounds them.
morning chill
a blanket,
dim serenity beneath it.
all the green shades of the woods
becoming bluish
in this mist.
only popping twigs
to break the silence
and for insect ears
the soft
exquisite
stepping
of the deer.

Marilyn Chin

Marilyn Chin was born in Hong Kong and raised in Portland, Oregon. She is both a poet and translator, and her first book, *Dwarf Bamboo* (1987), was nominated for the Bay Area Book Reviewers Association Award. Recently, Chin has published poems in *Ploughshares, Parnassus,* the *Iowa Review, Kenyon Review,* and *The Norton Introduction to Poetry.* A recipient of numerous awards, including a fellowship from the National Endowment for the Arts, the Wallace Stegner Fellowship from Stanford University, and the Mary Roberts Rinehart Award, she teaches creative writing at San Diego State University.

The Floral Apron

The woman wore a floral apron around her neck,
that woman from my mother's village
with a sharp cleaver in her hand.
She said, "What shall we cook tonight?
Perhaps these six tiny squid
lined up so perfectly on the block?"

She wiped her hand on her apron,
pierced the blade into the first.
There was no resistance,
no blood, only cartilage

soft as a child's nose. A last
iota of ink made us wince.

Suddenly, the aroma of ginger and scallion fogged our senses,
and we absolved her for that moment's barbarism.
Then, she, an elder of the tribe,
without formal head-dress, without elegance,
deigned to teach the younger
about the Asian plight.

And although we have traveled far
we would never forget that primal lesson—
on patience, courage, forbearance,
on how to love squid despite squid,
how to honor the village, the tribe,
that floral apron.

Gruel

Your name is Diana Toy.
And all you may have for breakfast is rice gruel.
You can't spit it back into the cauldron for it would be unfilial.
You can't ask for yam gruel for there is none.
You can't hide it in the corner for it would surely be found,
and then you would be served cold, stale rice gruel.

This is the philosophy of your *tong*:
you, the child, must learn to understand the universe
through the port-of-entry, your mouth,
to discern bitter from sweet, pungent from bland.
You were told that the infant Buddha once devoured earth,
and hence, spewed forth the wisdom of the ages.

Meat or gruel, wine or ghee,
even if it's gruel, even if it's nothing,
that gruel, that nothingness will shine
into the oil of your mother's scrap-iron wok,
into the glare of your father's cleaver,
and dance in your porcelain bowl.

Remember, what they deny you won't hurt you.
What they spare you, you must make shine,
so shine, shine. . .

Linda Christensen

Linda Christensen is a native Oregonian who was born in the coastal town of Bandon and raised just south of the border in Eureka. An English teacher at Portland's Jefferson High School for the past fifteen years, she has published poems as well as articles about teaching writing. Some have appeared in *Oregon English Journal,* *Language Arts,* and *Northwest Magazine.* Selected by US West Foundation as one of three outstanding educators in the western states, she has recently written a book on critical teaching. Influenced by the Oregon coast, her poetry reflects "the ocean, the sand, the rain, the fishermen, and the people who worked there."

He Looks for Worms

in my garden—
pink worms sashed
in purple
pushing
like thin tongues
through mulch
manure compost
to touch air.
He collects
smooth ropes of their bodies
in jars brown
with earth.
Their loops slide
the ridge between glass
and dirt,
eyeless tips
flicking like fish at dusk
across knife slices
of blue
like the arms of so many women
trapped in canning jars
on the wide green shelves
of our basement.
At night,
when he sleeps,
I unscrew the lid
and spill them
back to earth.

How to Act Male at My Mother's House over the Holidays

Stretch the entire length of the couch
and give orders
like how about a beer
or
anything to eat around here
Use the subtle approach
like
maybe I'll have that piece of pie now
Say it
while you switch channels with the remote control
Say it
while you flip from the Rose Bowl
to the Cotton Bowl
to the Dust Bowl
Say it
after dinner
while the women
are still taking dishes from the table
Say it
while we scrape the leftovers
and stack the plates
Say it
while we pull meat off the turkey
so it'll fit in the refrigerator
Say it
while we transfer the mashed potatoes, cranberry sauce,
gravy, peas, waldorf salad, radishes, stuffed celery
from their serving platters
into their storage bowls
Say it
while we wash the plates and pots and pans
Say it
while your mother or grandmother or sister or wife or
daughter stacks forks, spoons, knives back into the velvet
slots of the silver box
Say it
when there's someone standing here
who'll listen.

Gerald Costanzo

Gerald Costanzo was born in Portland, Oregon, and is a graduate of Milwaukie High School. He has received degrees from Harvard in 1967 and from Johns Hopkins in 1969 and 1970. He has taught at Carnegie Mellon University in Pittsburgh since 1970. He is the founder of *Three Rivers Poetry Journal* and Carnegie Mellon University Press. Some of his poems have appeared in *American Poetry Review,* the *Georgia Review,* and the *Nation.* Costanzo has won the Devons Award for his first book, *In the Aviary* (1975), and has since published three books, including his latest, *Nobody Lives on Arthur Godfrey Boulevard* (1992). "But the clincher for his Oregonianism, however, lies in the fact that he was the Rose Festival candidate for Prince from Rose City Park Grade School and rode on a float depicting Johnny Appleseed, from which he waved and lofted roses to the multitudes . . . wearing white shoes, a white suit, and a rose boutonniere."

Dinosaurs of the Hollywood Delta

> *Joe DiMaggio, who was married for three years to Marilyn Monroe, has ended a 20-year standing order for thrice-weekly delivery of roses to her crypt. The florist said Mr. DiMaggio gave no explanation.*
> —*The New York Times*, September 30, 1982

In times of plenty
they arrived from everywhere
to forage among the pallmettos
of Beverly and Vine, to roam
the soda fountains and dime stores
of paradise. For every Miss Tupelo

who got a break, whose blonde
tresses made it to the silver screen,
whose studio sent her on a whirlwind
tour to Chicago, and to the Roxy
in Manhattan where she'd chat
with an audience, do a little tap

dance, and answer questions
about the morality of the jitterbug,
thousands became extinct.
Their beauty, it was said,
drove men to wallow in dark
booths in the Florentine

Lounge dreaming of voluptuous
vanilla, though the rumor persists
that they were dumb.
They were called *Jean, Rita, Jayne,*
Mae, and *Betty.* The easy names.
No one remembers now

how the waning of their kind
began. Theories have pointed
to our own growing sophistication—
as if that were a part of natural
selection. At first we missed
them little, and only in that detached

manner one laments the passing
of any passing thing. Then posters
began to appear. Whole boutiques
adoring their fashion: heavy rouge,
thick lipstick. The sensuous puckering of lips.
Surreptitious giggling.

We began to congregate on street corners
at night, Santa Monica and La Brea,
to erect searchlights
and marquees announcing premieres
for which there were no films.
We looked upward

as if what had been taken from us
were somehow etched in starlight above
their sacred city. We began
to chant, demanding their return—
to learn, for once, the meaning
of their desperate, flagrant love.

Tom Crawford

Tom Crawford was born in Michigan but has lived on the Oregon coast for the past twelve years. A poet who has held a variety of jobs—cook, shoe salesman, cannery worker—he describes his most interesting job as a patrolman for a land company: "I was supposed to keep the poachers out so that the stockholders could get first crack at the deer . . . they didn't." Crawford has published three books of poetry: *I Want to Say Listen, If It Weren't for Trees,* and *Lands.*

Otis Cafe

You can believe in the eight plastic hands—feminine,
that never tire of serving
while blue saucers and chocolate donuts
spill forever down the yellow wall in front of you
a greeting to COME IN
A restaurant where you might think
what's best is nothing new,
old photos curling away from the walls
of dead loggers and fishermen, stumpage and gill nets
the camera couldn't lie about
and their wives, resigned, who never entered the picture
though they stood there, though you know they cooked

You have to go back in time to order your food here,
the building, clapboard
and grandfathered in to an ancient grill and two mud roads
that diverged in a wilderness,
the loudest sound then, wind through tall trees

Be sentimental
The booths give you the privacy of history,
honey-grained wood and light through the window
are a way in,
and if you get loud, so is the kitchen loud

It's emotional to cook here or to eat
the German potatoes and black mushrooms
and not feel something: civility, the affection of soup?
A country built on a hustle and a sneer?
Doesn't longing keep us all a little hungry,
the waitress taller, (the height she wanted to be),
the nose not so squat
When it rains here the windows fog over
and if it weren't for the black coffee
in front of you, steaming, you'd want to leave,
you'd think that you had dreamed this all up

Kathleen Culligan

Kathleen Culligan, the oldest of eleven children in an Irish Catholic family, was raised near Chicago in Naperville, at that time a sleepy farm town. She received her BA from St. Mary's College, Notre Dame, in1968, and her MA in English literature from the University of Illinois in1970. After she and her husband moved to Oregon in 1975, they lived in Silverton, where she taught English and art history at Mount Angel Seminary. Culligan relocated to Portland in 1988, and currently teaches writing at the University of Portland and serves as the director of Oregon Writers' Workshop. She has published essays in various journals, and her poetry has recently been published in *Fireweed*. Culligan's observation of Oregon's landscape has often acted as a starting point for her work. "The beauty of Oregon—whether large-scale or small, domesticated or wild—is arresting. All of it, urban and otherwise, offers glimpses of life's cosmic dance in all its infinite variety."

Something Learned about Fish
Carrying the fish on a willow branch
run through their gills, he drops them
on the lawn, next to the garden hose.
In his other hand he carries a knife.
He slips the first fish off the branch,
holds it belly up and cuts the length of it,
gutting it with his thumb and throwing
the glistening, dark pink offal in a pail.
Then he takes his knife and makes the scales dance.
They fall like fire works, iridescence
glueing itself to hair and hands and feet.

By the time I discovered Hemingway
I already knew about fishing for walleye,
and about ducklings losing a leg
as they swam placidly around the lake.
A stuffed walleye hung on the back wall
of my grandfather's bar, the corners
of its mouth curving upward as if
it were trying to hide its deadly rows of teeth.

I like fish, but I didn't try walleye until recently.
The flesh is good but full of tiny bones
I didn't know were there until I felt them
at the back of my throat, the old fish
still trying to make life tough for us.

Hemingway and my grandfather shared
a male toughness you don't see much
any more. Born the same year, they died
decades apart, Hemingway by his own hand,
my grandfather gradually becoming gentler,
lighter, as if everything about him were trying
to put aside matter and become pure spirit
even as he lived, an old man without weight,
taking no space, wisping away.

Walt Curtis

Walt Curtis has spent all of his 49 years in the Pacific Northwest, living in Oregon since 1953. He was born in Olympia, Washington, and graduated from high school in Oregon City. His most recent collection of poems is *Rhymes for Alice Blue Light* (1984). He has also published in such magazines as *Atlantic Monthly*. Some of his nature poems, such as "Salmon Song," "Snag on the Molalla," and "Ode to a Douglas Fir," underscore the poet's remark that he has "always identified with the Oregon landscape." Curtis is recognized as a colorful figure and famous street poet laureate of Portland.

Cabbages in the Garden

They are nine in number.
Their outer leaves are of odd animals,
rhinos', an armadillo's ears smashed flat.
Rooted solid,
their heads are little green suns
or ugly crystal balls.
Poor cabbage has no close neighbors,
except rhubarb, with her red limbs
and elephant's ears.
The cabbages in my garden are so sad:
they are like moons fallen out of sky.
I want to cry
viewing them so forlorn and serious.
Worrying about coleslaw and sauerkraut,
I promise never to eat them.
Instead, I will send them to an orphanage
in a big basket tied with Easter ribbons.

John Daniel

John Daniel was born in Spartanburg, South Carolina, and grew up in the suburbs of Washington D.C. In the late sixties, he moved to Portland where he attended Reed College. After this he worked as a chokersetter for Weyerhaeuser where he first experienced hiking and climbing in the Cascades. From 1978 to 1982, he lived on a ranch in Eastern Oregon and worked as a Poet-in-the-Schools—Lakeview, Paisley, Elgin, and La Grande. During the eighties, Daniel returned to California, where he won a Wallace Stegner Fellowship at Stanford and a subsequent lecturer's job. He came back to Oregon and published his first book of poems, *Common Ground* (1988), then left to become a writer-in-residence at Austin Peay State University in Tennessee. He has published a book of essays, *The Trail Home* (1992).

Dependence Day

It would be a quieter holiday, no fireworks
or loud parades, no speeches, no salutes to any flag,
a day of staying home instead of crowding away,
a day we celebrate nothing gained in war
but what we're given—how the sun's warmth
is democratic, touching everyone,
and the rain is democratic too,
how the strongest branches in the wind
give themselves as they resist, resist
and give themselves, how birds could have no freedom
without the planet's weight to wing against,
how Earth itself could come to be
only when a whirling cloud of dust
pledged allegiance as a world
circling dependently around a star,
and the star blossomed into fire from the ash of other stars,
and once, at the dark zero of our time,
a blaze of revolutionary light
exploded out of nowhere, out of nothing,
because nothing needed the light,
as the brilliance of the light itself needs nothing.

❦

Efrain Diaz-Horna

Efrain Diaz-Horna was born in 1945 in Talara, Peru. He attended high school in Lima and in 1965 came to Oregon to attend Mt. Angel College, where he received a BA in sociology. For two years he worked in Peru's land reform program, and later returned to the US to attend the University of Wisconsin, Madison. He holds MA degrees in social work and public administration, and currently works for the State of Oregon. Diaz-Horna has been writing, drawing, and painting since he was a child. Some of his poems have appeared in *Express* (Peru) and the *Hispanic* (Portland). He is the author of a collection of poems, *The Many Faces of Love* (1983). Efrain Diaz-Horna has been a member of the Oregon Council for the Humanities and chaired the Oregon Hispanic Commission.

For John Sinclair
April 24, 1993

I.

The pertinacious swallows
Proclaim the enigma of life:
The day is perennially short,
The night is long,
Very long (too long!).

II.

My dear friends
Listen to the grave news:
John submerged himself in the night
In his human eagerness
To kiss the avid earth.

He departed suddenly
(Hard nudge of life)
And he left us alone
Struggling with the solitude
With the voracious abysses,
With the cold wind of the ages,
And missing the warmth of his kindness.

Blessed human ritual!
O sad and solitary gesture!
O bittersweet genius of the hours!

Harken,
The heavy-hearted rustle
Of the birds of memory
Tell us:
John has departed, period.
John, aye! will live on, comma.

III.

The guitars moan,
The millenary drums roar.

The bagpipes cry,
The Scottish melodies are reborn.

The Andean flutes sing,
The infinite pains are stanched.

Our saddened hearts shed their tears,
The sagacious crepuscles are announced.

IV.

John:
The liturgy of our friendship
Sustains us in this sad day,
In which the guitars, the lemons,
The cherry trees, the remembrances,
And the bagpipes
Salute you,
And the love of your family,
And the torrent of the rivers
Dampen the fertile earth
That sweetly covers your torso.

The birds of hope sing,
The vital trees sigh,
The jungle bells ring,
And the faith of your memory
Nourishes our daily dawns.

❦

Sharon Doubiago

Sharon Doubiago was born in Long Beach, California. She holds an MA in English from California State University, Los Angeles, and for many years has traveled the American West as an itinerant writer and artist-in-residence at numerous schools and colleges. She has been a sometimes resident of Ashland. Her poetry has appeared in *CALYX, ACM, Bumbershoot Literary Magazine,* and *Quarry West.* Some of her books are *Psyche Drives the Coast: Poems 1975-1987* (1990), *Oedipus Drowned* (1988), and *Hard Country* (1982).

Love Song for a Man Whose Mother Killed Herself

Your open mouth like the ocean
where you allow me, swimming.
Beneath all things, the Bible says
are the waters
but men don't usually open this way.
They are always ships headed for some horizon, the rescuers

dragging the lake for days for her body, you said.

You have opened yourself so wide
you are the water your mother drowned in.
She lies at the bottom of you,
the dark deep water that covers you.

I see her face sleeping with open eyes
looking towards the sun.
I am wanting

the secret of this watery garden
the secret the leaves hide
and the wind
call it the world
the secret she would not live without.

It is deep going between here and the new country.
In the night we are seen waving back to the shore.
Voices call for us. I emerge
over your body to see the earth in light.

You have opened to me.
You are the first man who has ever opened to me.
Somehow you have made yourself
the man she would not live without.

❦

Albert Drake

Albert Drake was born and raised in Portland, Oregon, and educated at the University of Oregon. From 1966 to 1991, he was a professor of English at Michigan State University. He has published poetry, fiction, and nonfiction and is the recipient of two National Endowment for the Arts grants. His two novels, *Beyond the Pavement* (1981) and *One Summer* (1979), reflect the author's statement that "place is important to me." This sense of place, sharpened by years spent away from Oregon, also became the primary motivation for writing his poetry books, *Riding Bike* (1973), *Returning to Oregon* (1975), and *Homesick* (1988). He has now retired and lives in Portland.

Garage

You walk from sunlight into the smell
of mushrooms, damp and exotic. Blackness
is an anvil. Creosote, canvas, hot rubber
recall friendly old toys. Oh oil! Metal!
Spores float through the dark air like ideas,
saying *you can make things here.*
As your eyes adjust you see stains
across the floor like butterfly wings,
and the massive workbench set for a picnic
with tools, wrenches whose cool metal
is bright with promise.
Walls are a calendar of old license plates;
rafters support each other like drunken friends.
This oily cave is cozy, like a darkroom
where things can develop.
Dust breathes, "Come in, come in."
Tools say they will fit smooth handles
to your hands. You become maker.
Be assured: what wants to be done,
can be!

❧

Barbara Drake

Barbara Drake was born in Kansas and moved to Oregon in 1941, when she was two years old. Following graduate school at the University of Oregon, where she received her MFA, she went to work at Michigan State University. Returning to Oregon in 1979, she accepted several visiting-writer jobs, including two years at Lewis & Clark College and one semester at Whitman College in Walla Walla as their "Johnston Chair" in 1982. In 1983, her college textbook, *Writing Poetry*, was published and is currently in use all over the country. In addition, Drake has published two books of poetry, *What We Say to Strangers* (1986) and *Love at the Egyptian Theatre* (1978), as well as several chapbooks and poems in numerous magazines and anthologies, ranging from *Northwest Review* and *North American Review* to *Sulfur* and *American Sports Poems*. In 1986, she was awarded a National Endowment for the Arts fellowship to work on her poetry. At present, she teaches at Linfield College in McMinnville as an associate professor and is the English Department chair. She is currently working on a third book which contains a large section of poems dealing with country living in Oregon.

Stink Ant

I am watching television,
a nature show. I don't know
which one it is—about the jungles
of South America.
I'm feeling comfortable,
a wool blanket tucked around my knees,
slippers on, cocoa,
the usual securities.

A stink ant appears on the screen,
a solitary stink ant the commentator calls it,
whose neighborhood is the jungle floor.
There it goes—ta da ta da, happy stink ant.
Till high above a mushroom shoots its spore
which lands on the ant's poor head
and gives its brain a little spin.
Then all it wishes to do is climb
a lofty blade of grass.

Now, high above the jungle floor,
the stink ant rants and raves and roars
and clamps itself immovable
upon that stem and dies.

The stink ant conveniently dead,
a little bouquet of mushrooms
grows out of the vase of its head.

Thank God for my blanket,
my cocoa and my couch,
my healthy lack of ambition
in my television watching condition.
At times like these it's easy to imagine
the desire to get up in the world
is nothing more than a fungus infection.

❧

Shy Child

for Bellen

They said "shy" when you started school
as if they meant leaping convulsively
like an unsteady horse,
or somehow inadequate.
And they said,
"fails to interact,"
and sent the school social worker
out to look at "the home."
How garrulous she was,
this mouth flapper,
drinking coffee in our kitchen,
stealing suspicious glances
out of the corners of her rhinestone glasses.
There were the giant paper people
we had taped from the ceiling,
and the murals you'd drawn
of acrobatic children
smiling and turning flip-flops
like multi-colored eels.

I was polite.
It was for your good, I thought,
to be polite.
And you leaned into my lap
and gave her the cool look
of your wide green eyes.
I let politeness flow
like a cold stream around a rock,

and soon the social worker left
hungry for something
terrible and broken and malnourished.
You, after all, were just shy.
Well—when I was little, so was I.

But maybe shy is short for "shining,"
or maybe it means:
"seeing without being seen,
like a green bird in a green tree,"
for you sat down then
to draw another picture,
a scene in which people spoke
in comic strip balloons.
The people you drew said, "Please."
They said, "Thank you. May I have some?"
They said, "Fine thanks," and "How are you?"
And you drew a small person down in the corner of the picture,
a small person grinning and sticking her tongue out.
We taped it to the refrigerator.

Jeremy Driscoll

Jeremy Driscoll was born in Moscow, Idaho, in 1951. He came to Oregon for his high school and college education; following graduation, he became a Benedictine monk at Mount Angel Abbey. After five years of study in Rome, where he earned a doctorate in ancient Christian theology, he returned to teach theology in the graduate school at Mount Angel Seminary. Driscoll has published two books of poetry: *Some Morning* (1980) and *The Night of St. John* (1989). Some of his poems have been set to music and have been performed in live concerts in Portland, Rome, and Barcelona. He sees his poetry "as flowing directly out of his experience of being a monk at Mount Angel Abbey." His fellow monks sometimes say that "some of what the earth and the heavens say at Mount Angel is what Driscoll means to say in his poems."

Praying

Everything that's along the water has a reflection.

I like when I can go down along the lake about four
and maybe find you there,
maybe not.
I like going with the hope,
and waiting.
Everything is more by one again.
The water is going to reflect the sky
and it goes right over the trees.

Every tree pokes the water.
And maybe you are there among the trees somewhere.
Maybe you might poke the water and I would see.

I want to stop and feel the damp shade.
I want to stop and hold a feeling just
as still as the water holds the trees.
I want to stop and wait for you
and try, if I see,
to hold you in my looking just as
still as the feeling
and the water holding the trees.

Libby A. Durbin

Libby Durbin was born in Toledo, Ohio, and raised in West Virginia, "the land of my imagination." Oregon has been her home for the past forty years. Her work has appeared in such publications as *CALYX, Calapooya Collage, Northwest Magazine,* and *Portland Review.* After raising her children, she has worked as press bureau assistant at the Library of Congress, researcher for the Oregon Department of Human Resources, and as a psychotherapist. While earning a MA in psychology, she established a sleep lab at Portland State University. Most recently she has worked as executive director for the Oregon Writer's Workshop.

Between Jobs

All day he reads the tablecloth,
                head bent on his hands, body curling
    into itself. Under the sleeves
of his workshirt, his biceps are white
                as Indian pipe that breaks
in the woods at a toe's scuff.

We know not to bother him. Not when
                "Happy" Morgan, broke for months, tore
    his telephone off the wall in a rage.
We play a game on the neighbor's stone steps—
                start at the bottom, climb with each
right guess, until we reach "Heaven."

Up there we can wave at cars, talk about
    the fancy California one we saw once.
                Strange men hike by, toward Ohio,
a rumor of work; some eat rhubarb pie
    at our side door. Last year my father
brought surprises home in his pail:

three orphaned crows, ravenous; rank-tasting
                May apples; flying squirrels from trees
    he felled. I worry about trees,
their roots above ground, creeks
                out of their banks, veins big
as my finger on top of his arm.

At bedtime, his shirt's still ready
                for work, rolled above the elbows.
    Now he lets us climb on his lap.
Ear on pocket, I listen for his heart,
                cradle his arm across my lap, track
its soft blue tributaries until they're tucked away.

❦

Alice Ann Eberman

Alice Ann Eberman was born in Myrtle Point, Oregon, and grew up in small western Oregon logging towns. Reflecting upon her poetry, she comments: "As a poet, I write about where I've lived, what I know, and what I'm coming to know." Recent works include a series of poems about the people of the Coquille River Valley—the native Coos and Coquille, the white settlers, and the descendants of both. Currently a teacher of literature and creative writing at Crescent Valley High School in Corvallis, Oregon, Eberman was one of the winners of the Oregon Council of Teachers of English's Teachers-as-Writers Competition in 1987 for her poem entitled "Last of the Coos Full-bloods." In 1989, she was nominated by *CALYX* for the CCLM-GE Younger Writer's Award for Poetry. Some of her poems have appeared in *CALYX*, *Fireweed*, *Northwest Magazine*, and *Oregon English Journal*.

Finding

To land, hers by blood,
she brought her white husband.
To the land, made his by fences,
he brought, from his old country,
thick, big-uddered deer.
In clean, white-washed barns,
she helped him milk the slow beasts.
And lost her Coquille name.
Her husband could not go deep enough in his chest
to find the sound.
The name he gave her
sank in her like rocks.

She looked for omens,
birds flying against walls,
wild animals creeping in the door.
She looked
until, hearing him call her to the barn one day,
she knew she could no longer wait for signs.
To Siletz she flew, to her people.

And she stayed.
Her fingers, crooked from milking,
grew straight,
and the soft plump of salal in her basket
buried the stiff squirt of milk in an empty bucket.

And her name came at last to find her.

❦

Ed Edmo

Ed Edmo (Shoshoni-Bannock) works with the Poets-in-the-Schools programs throughout Oregon. A poet and traditional storyteller, his works explore Northwest tribal culture and political issues. He is the author of *These Few Words of Mine* (1985) and lives in Portland.

Indian Education Blues

I sit in your
crowded classrooms
& learn how to read about dick
jane & spot
but

    I remember
    how to get a deer

    I remember
    how to do beadwork

    I remember
    how to fish

I remember
the stories told by the old
but

    spot keeps
    showing up
    &

        my report card
        is bad

Juan Epple

Juan Armando Epple was born in southern Chile in 1946 and grew up in Valdivia, where he also went to college. He came to the United States as an exile in 1974 and has earned his master's and doctor's degrees from Harvard. He has been a member of the modern languages faculty at the University of Oregon since 1980. Epple writes both short fiction and poetry. His stories and poems have been published in several languages. Some of his poems have appeared in *Literatura Chileña Review* (Center for Inter-American Relations) and the *Eugene Anthology.*

The Oregon Trail
a Jack Kerouac

Alguien pasó antes por aquí
alguien se aventuró por estas mismas huellas
destituídas
se detuvo a oler el esplendor del bosque
aún no talado
bebió en las aguas, todavia gratuitas, de un estero,
y en el reflejo, apenas aquietado, quizás reconoció
su primer rostro:
un asombrado habitante de sí mismo.
Alguien usó la mágica entonces suficiente
de su lengua nativa
para deletrear la arquitectura simple de una casa
negada en otras tierras.
Alguien viajó llevando un hijo a cuestas
un hijo cuyo país se hacía en el camino.
Alguien tuvo estos ojos que hoy vuelven a buscar
la tierra prometida
que debió estar aquí
en este espacio anónimo
desdibujado hoy por frias carreteras
donde hay que circular a altas velocidades

The Oregon Trail

to Jack Kerouac

Someone came this way before.
Someone ventured down these same,
nonexistent roads
and stopped to smell the forests
that no one had cut down.
Someone sipped the water from streams
that didn't cost a cent.
In his quivering reflection he recognized
a frightened visitor of himself.
Perhaps he even dreamed about building a makeshift house
on the shore of some river.
Someone used the precarious magic of his native tongue
to establish and defend a space
that was denied him in other lands.
Someone traveled with a son on his back,
a son whose country was being made on the road.
Someone had these eyes that today try to capture
a remote landscape that should have been here
if it had not been erased by these highways.

Translated by Stephen F. White

William Ferrell

MT. HOOD

William Ferrell has lived for 37 years in Oregon in such places as Portland, Eugene, Umatilla, and Redland. During the Vietnam War, he was discharged from the Air Force as a conscientious objector and subsequently worked for five years as a psychiatric nursing assistant. He has attended the University of Oregon and Portland State University and has published poems in *ODE*, *Portland Review*, and *Mr. Cogito*. "Because I'm an avid outdoor type, my subject matter is often of the natural world."

The Ground War 2/17/91

for Jill

A mourning dove mourns.
I have a wealth of sadness.
A mockingbird mocks.
In my inner ear
I am off balance.
Falling over I
hear all the birds,
the whistles, the songs,
the coos, the cries.
They nest in my heart
and sing in my head.
But the febrile blood
is not my blood,
the keen eye is not my eye.
I am slow to flight,
mammalian, descended
from the trees never to return.
My thighs are like tree trunks,
my feet like roots.
Instinctively, I flap my arms
tweeting at the sky,
flailing at the great
invisible air.

Phil George

Phil George (Wallowa/Nez Perce-Alaskan Tsimshian) was born in 1946 in Seattle, Washington. He is a champion traditional Plateau dancer, a Vietnam veteran and a former U.S. House of Representatives intern. His first chapbook, *Kautsas* (1978), is sold exclusively at the Nez Perce National Historical Park in Spaulding, Idaho.

The sweat lodge was almost universal for all tribes north of Mexico. It was usually a small round house made of sod, sticks, or hide; an individual entered and hot rocks and water were placed inside to cause steam. After remaining for a time, the participant would then plunge into snow or cold water. The sweat lodge was used for religious purposes, to purify oneself, as well as to cure disease. Special rituals were also conducted there.

Old Man, the Sweat Lodge

"This small lodge is now
The womb of our mother, Earth,
This blackness in which we sit,
The ignorance of our impure minds.
These burning stones are
The coming of new life."
I keep his words near my heart.

Confessing, I recall my evil deeds.
For each sin, I sprinkle water on fire-hot stones,
The hissed steam is sign that
The place from which Earth's seeds grow
Is still alive,
He sweats,
I sweat.

I remember, Old Man heals the sick,
Brings good fortune to one deserving.
Sacred steam rises;
I feel my pores give out their dross.
After I chant prayers to the Great Spirit,
I raise the door to the East.
Through this door dawns wisdom.

Cleansed, I dive into icy waters.
Pure, I wash away all of yesterday.
"My son, Walk in this new life.
It is given to you!
Think right, feel right,
Be happy."
I thank you, Old Man, the Sweat Lodge.

John M. Gogol

John M. Gogol was born in Westfield, Massachusetts, and has been a "confirmed Pacific Northwesterner" since coming west in 1964 to do graduate work and teach at the University of Washington in Seattle. He came to Oregon in 1970 to teach at Pacific University in Forest Grove; however, in 1974 he gave up teaching to concentrate on full-time research, study, and writing about Native American art and literature. From 1979 through 1985, he was editor and publisher of *American Indian Basket and Other Native Arts* magazine, as well as co-editor and publisher of *Mr. Cogito* literary magazine and Mr. Cogito Press. His poetry has appeared in such publications as *Columbiana, Haight Ashbury Literary Review, Kansas Quarterly, Mississippi Mud,* and *Portland Review*. In addition, he has authored numerous articles and published translations of hundreds of poems of Polish, Russian, and German poets. Gogol reflects on his own works: "The themes of most of my poems relate to my interests and writings on Native American themes, particularly dealing with Oregon and the Columbia River plateau region."

Boy in a Cherry Tree
for Danny

He was born in a cherry tree,
       he often said,
dad migrating with motherless son
       from field to orchard,
from Missouri to Marysville,
from the Sacramento to the Columbia.

He became a rider of ladders,
galloping among the fruit trees
of Hood River and Wenatchee,
rose with the sun
and raced those wooden steps
through green-soaked trees,
ever higher toward that blazing flower,
fingers flying through crimson clumps,
heaping boxes and pails
till palms bled red
as if nailed
      to that wooden elevator to heaven.

Life drains
      from the weary bodies of workers
who forever ride those heavy ladders

into the setting sun.
Now the squeezings of fruit
drown his dreams
     in whirlpools of rose petals
that soak the cement,
and he will never again see
the white whirlwind of blossoms
that shatter each spring's soft soil.

The next time
you hold a handful of plump cherries,
remember my rider of ladders
mounting his wooden steed,
riding the orchards of the West.
Even without him
there will be youthful laughter
from among the cherries,
and tomorrow will be lovely
in the orchards of Oregon.

Cecelia Hagen

Cecelia Hagen was born in San Diego and grew up in Norfolk, Virginia. Her father was a career marine who later became a TV announcer. Hagen holds an MFA in creative writing from the University of Oregon and has been a fiction editor for *Northwest Review*. Some of her poems have appeared in *Willow Springs, Puerto Del Sol, Exquisite Corpse, 5 A.M.*, and *Northwest Review*, and she is currently the managing editor for the programming magazine *Windows Tech Journal* in Eugene.

My Children Are the Bright Flowers

My children are the bright flowers.

I admire them: I'm dirt.
They know nothing of what it's like
to be laced with minerals
but they need all the salts I've got.

They look up
to sun and rain.
I look up to them,
and also rain.

I keep them colorful, bless them
with my million mouths each night.

I love to hold them this way—
nobody else
can recall their time as seeds,
their brown waiting.
They ask over and over
for stories about themselves,
every grasping root
within my grasp, for now.

They have their lovely sway,
I have this transubstantiation.

I never imagined this
unfurling of desire,
never realized the zeal
with which I'd spread myself so thin,
so wide, so deep.

Michael S. Harper

Michael S. Harper was born in 1938 in Brooklyn, New York, and moved to West Los Angeles when he was thirteen. He received an MFA from the University of Iowa and has taught at Lewis & Clark College, Reed College, Haywood State University, and currently Brown University. He is the author of nine books of poetry, most recently *Healing Song for the Inner Ear* (1985).

We Assume:
On the Death of Our Son, Reuben Masai Harper

We assume
that in 28 hours,
lived in a collapsible isolette,
you learned to accept pure oxygen
as the natural sky;
the scant shallow breaths
that filled those hours
cannot, did not make you fly—
but dreams were there
like crooked palmprints on
the twin-thick windows of the nursery—
in the glands of your mother.

We assume
the sterile hands
drank chemicals in and out
from lungs opaque with mucus,
pumped your stomach,
eeked the bicarbonate in
crooked, green-winged veins,
out in a plastic mask;

A woman who'd lost her first son
consoled us with an angel gone ahead
to pray for our family—
gone into that sky
seeking oxygen,
gone into autopsy,
a fine brown powdered sugar,
a disposable cremation:

We assume
you did not know we loved you.

Jim Heynen

Jim Heynen attended school in Oregon, taught part-time at Lewis & Clark College, and also has written and published poetry. He currently resides in Minnesota with his wife and family. He has described himself as an Oregonian "mostly because I eat mussels, and I compost or recycle leftovers from my household." His works have appeared in such publications as *Redbook*, *South Dakota Review*, and *Poetry Northwest*. He is the author of five books of poetry: *A Suitable Church* (1981), *How the Sow Became a Goddess* (1977), *Maedra Poems* (1974), *Notes from Custer* (1975), and *The Funeral Parlor* (1976). He was awarded a fellowship by the National Endowment for the Arts, and has worked as a Poet-in-the-Schools in Oregon, Washington, Idaho, and Alaska.

During the First Three Minutes of Life

The piglet
sucks

naps
wakes up

sniffs the
nipple next door

bites
its brother's ear

naps again
snores

wakes up
shivers

jumps straight up
twists an ankle

squeals
looks around for the sound

leaves home
gets lost

pees
on the run

stops on a window
frame of light

looks up
into the sun.

Garrett Hongo

Garrett Hongo was born in Volcano, Hawaii, and was raised on the North Shore of Oahu and in Los Angeles, California. He attended Pomona College, the University of Michigan, and the University of California, Irvine. Hongo began to write poetry as "a way to express my love for lost lands—Hawaii, Japan, and rural California—and for people for whom there were no poems—Japanese Americans, Blacks, Chicanos—working people of all kinds." His first book of poetry was *Yellow Light* (1982). Hongo won the Lamont Prize and was nominated for the Pulitzer for his second book, *River of Heaven* (1988). His poems have appeared in such publications as *Antaeus, Crazy Horse, Field,* and the *New Yorker*. At present, he is directing the creative writing program at the University of Oregon.

The Cadence of Silk

When I lived in Seattle, I loved watching
the Sonics play basketball; something
about that array of trained and energetic
bodies set in motion to attack a more
sluggish, less physically intelligent opponent
appealed to me, taught me about cadence
and play, the offguard breaking free
before the rebound, "releasing," as is said
in the parlance of the game, getting to
the center's downcourt pass and streaking
to the basket for a scoopshot layup
off the glass, all in rhythm, all in
perfect declensions of action, smooth
and strenuous as Gorgiasian rhetoric.
I was hooked on the undulant ballet
of the pattern offense, on the set play
back-door under the basket, and, at times,
even on the auctioneer's pace and elocution
of the play-by-play man. Now I watch
the Lakers, having returned to Los Angeles
some years ago, love them even more than
the Seattle team, long since broken up and aging.
The Lakers are incomparable, numerous
options for any situation, their players
the league's quickest, most intelligent,
and, it is my opinion, frankly, the most *cool*.
Few bruisers, they are sleek as arctic seals,
especially the small forward
as he dodges through the key, away from
the ball, rubbing off his man on the screen,

setting for his shot. Then, slick as spit,
comes the ball from the point guard,
and my man goes up, cradling the ball
in his right hand like a waiter balancing
a tray piled with champagne in stemmed glasses,
cocking his arm and bringing the ball
back behind his ear, pumping, letting fly then
as he jumps, popcorn-like, in the corner,
while the ball, launched, slung dextrously
with a slight backspin, slashes through
the basket's silk net with a small,
sonorous splash of completion.

Christopher Howell

Christopher Howell was born in Portland, Oregon, between the villages of Russellville and Montavilla, in 1945. He is a graduate of John Marshall High and has attended Pacific Lutheran, Oregon State, and Portland State universities and holds an MFA in creative writing from the University of Massachusetts. His work has appeared in many journals, including *Iowa Review, Ironwood, Hudson Review* and *Poetry Northwest,* and he has published five collections of poetry, most recently *Sweet Afton* (1991). He now teaches in the English Department at Emporia State University, Kansas.

Bird Love

My wife is on the floor in front
    of the TV set
exercising, her long gorgeous legs

scissoring the grateful air. It is like
butterflies
filling the room each time her body

unfolds. From the quince outside a cardinal
looks on, piping time,
utterly in love. And why not love

such plumage as the skin can be? On a morning
such as this,
after a long night of rain and lightning,

what is more beautiful than a bird
or a naked woman
bathing in the newborn air and in whatever
music she can find? And this love
the bird in me says
is the exact unsentimental recitation of the breath

and we can't help it. I know. I look at her
now, foolishly, from my perch
and I can't help singing, simply
(lift flex kick flex) singing
and I don't care what I sing.

Carol Imani

Carol Imani, who was born in Berkeley, California, is an ex-New Yorker who moved to Oregon about ten years ago. She is also a graduate student in English, a mother, and a freelance writer. As a poet, she recognizes some of her work as a response to the landscape in which she finds herself; and one poem in particular, "like a wandering jew," was written "about the experience of moving from one part of the country to another." Her work has been published in *The Anthology of Eugene Writers #1*.

like a wandering jew

Transplanting my wandering jew into a larger pot,
it was wedged in tight, like my Uncle Paul who worked for the Brooklyn Navy Yard
and came home late from the bars, reeking and snorting
about the "bloody" this and the "bloody" that,
was tight;
its stems cascading to the floor, heavy with foilage
like the mane of a Renaissance wench,
or Sophia Loren's
as she sauntered down a noisy celluloid alley
swinging her hips and flashing her eyes,
its new leaves standing stiffly curled in the centers of old ones
like heartbreaking eighteen year old boy soldiers
who *believe* in their country.

I was surprised
the roots didn't shatter the pot wide open, and

pulling it out I stood bowlegged, wedging it between my thighs, prying all around
        with the flat of a knife
                the way you loosen a cake,
        then out it came, like
                a baby or a pail of wet sand
                the roots tamed to the pot's shape
                        and a great heap of casualties,
                stalks that broke loose,
spread out on soggy newspaper, waiting to be picked over like Miss America contes-
tants,
                the prettiest little shoots, the finalists
        recycled into a container of water
    there to grow strange emphatic fingers (slimy translucent roots)
                the losers piled into the garbage.

        And so,
        the worst over,
                I untangle the stems
        like a hairdresser busy with the final, tender fluff-out
    stand back
    and it looks
shorn, diminished,
        oriental-airy, and
                I remember reading
            that wandering jews like crowded pots
    (like a tenement family of real jews?) turn of the century,
all in one steamy Manhattan apartment, fighting and tripping over one another)
                and
            oh, my wandering jew
                did
            I
            do you wrong?
                    ❦

Lawson Fusao Inada

Lawson Fusao Inada is the author of *Before the War* (1971), *Legends from Camp* (1992), and co-editor of two major Asian-American anthologies: *AIIIEEEEE!* (1976) and *THE BIG AIIIIIIII!* (1991). His poetry has appeared in collections of major American publishing companies and is part of the *Encyclopedia Britannica* filmstrip series on American literature. In 1980 he was one of twenty-one American writers invited to read at the White House for "A Salute to Poetry and American Poets." Inada is the recipient of two National Endowment for the Arts creative writing fellowships, and is the former chair of the Coordinating Council of Literary Magazines. In addition, he has served as educational consultant for numerous school systems around the United States. Currently, he is professor of English at Southern Oregon State College in Ashland, as well as co-owner of Kids Matter, a new media and publishing company for children.

The Shovel People

It happened by accident: I was in the middle
of my yard in the middle of the morning
in the middle of a hole I was digging
to plant a tree, when, all of a sudden,
I heard some cats screaming in the neighborhood—

so, before I knew it, I was dashing down the street
to break up a fight or rescue something
with a shovel in my hand, and,

after everything got peaceful, for some reason
or another, there I was, still with my shovel.

Have you ever just stood around with a shovel?
Well, I never had—not when I wasn't digging—
so I decided to take advantage of the situation
and see what would happen, so I started walking.

At first, I carried the shovel in my right hand,
then switched to my left; either way,
the shovel was swinging along as I walked,
in rhythm with me, and, once or twice,
I let the handle drag in back,
just for the feel of it, just for the sound.

You might say I was "digging" it, as they say,
because while I looked like a serious man
going to or coming from work, some shoveling job,

I was actually having fun, feeling like a kid
who does things just for the fun of it.

And walking around with a shovel is fun!
For instance, just to feel "official,"
I switched the shovel to my shoulder
and marched along like I was on some kind of patrol!
Here he comes, there he goes—Mr. Shovelman to the rescue!

Maybe I was a farmer, maybe I was a street worker,
maybe I was a construction worker—all of which I'm not.
But I could be, I thought, if I want. Why not?

Also, since this is a free country,
I walked with my shovel to the corner grocery
to get a candybar I imagined a shovelman would eat—
something solid but also chewy, with lots of nuts.
And, of course, as a polite person,
I left the shovel outside first, leaning up against
a phone booth for a soft brown dog to watch.

Then I went home—shovel on my shoulder,
munching. I know what you're thinking: "Well, so what?"

Well, I'll tell you: I'm a poet and a teacher
and a son, father, husband. I'm not a weird person.
So I'm not saying that we should all walk around
with shovels on our shoulders and in our hands.
That might look silly, or like we're carrying weapons;
plus, we're not all farmers or workers or soldiers.

But I'll tell you: With that shovel I not only had fun
but felt like I was ready for anything that needed shoveling.
I looked around and noticed what there really was—
mostly things to leave alone, as is, to not shovel:
trees and flowers and sand with ants and rocks just sitting
where they were, in "empty" lots and people's gardens.

Oh, sure, I could have shoveled all those things,
but I had my own tree to plant, my own hole to fill up,
which I did. But I still kept the shovel in my hand.

It began to feel like a friend, so I thought to myself:
"Well, it's a beautiful summer day, and this tool
has helped me dig a hole, take a walk, go on patrol,
think about what I could do if I want, pet a dog,
eat some candy, and just generally appreciate

everything around me that doesn't need shoveling,
and since I planted a tree which gave me
a feeling of accomplishment for a job well done,
and since the tree will grow to give me beauty, shade—
well, I wonder what my friend the shovel would like to do now?"

So the two of us walked up the hill to the middle
of the pasture with the smooth stream running through it.
I washed my hands, I washed the shovel, and in so doing
dipped its full length in the water, then held the handle
as the blade made waves in the water, like a paddle
on a boat called "Planet Earth," and I was the Captain.

Then the two of us laid back on the grass and let the sun
dry us, shine us, as birds flew, cows chewed, breezes blew,
and I dreamed about how life would be, could be, with The
    Shovel People.

Peter Jensen

Peter Jensen was born in Brooklyn, New York, in 1942. He was
raised in New York, and since 1969 has called Oregon his home. He
currently teaches English at Lane Community College and works
as a researcher and fundraiser for the Oregon Natural Resources
Council. A prolific writer, he has published more than one hundred
poems, much prose, and two books of poetry: *This Book Is Not a
Mask for Tear Gas* (1970) and *When Waves Sprout Birds. . .* (1985).
He is currently working on his third book. Since moving to Eugene,
Oregon, in the 1960s, he has "spent 22 years planting the roots of his poetry all over
this state." Like most first-generation Oregonians, he tells of loving his new home, yet
laments: "It hurts to see the last of the ancient forests and the salmon so threatened."

Barracuda

With my belly on the sand
twenty feet under bluegreen water
off Gray Cay in the Bahamas, I swam beside John
a Black fisherman, greatgrandson of slaves.

We pointed our spears up under a stone
ledge at clawless, spiny lobsters
that waved their sticks back at us.
I let go, and my spear jumped in its sling.

I pulled a large, struggling lobster
from its den, and so did John.
We turned to rise like Black and White angels
to John's boat floating above us like a cloud.

But John put his hand on my shoulder
and pointed at a five-foot pencil that hung
in our way: a barracuda just under the waves
was waiting for us to rise. I saw its gun

barrel eyes and razors in its slowly
opening, closing jaws. With our remaining
breath, we did what John had me rehearse:
we blew out bubbles and whined like outboard

motors, and swam with speared, spiney lobsters
right at that hanging mouth, which backed off
slowly with its side fins, and when we
closed, it turned and shot away

like a torpedo into the bluegreen veil
of sunlit tropical water, the color of dreams.
When we surfaced with a gasp, my father
took a picture of our masks and lobsters
dangling on our spears. My parents were
surprised how quickly we kicked our flippers
and launched our bodies over the side
into John's small boat, as we laughed

and tried to catch the breath we had lost
to that barracuda. That air tasted so good
as we bit it and swallowed hunks
of oxygen like cartoon bubbles.

Later, I was to know that same fear
facing racists, their tear gas, guns, and dogs,
and I recalled our funny gulps
as John and I pulled our face masks off

like two actors at a colorful fair
and joined my parents in the free world of air.

David Johnson

David Johnson is a native Oregonian, born in Eugene, who has spent most of his life rambling hills, strolling beaches, and climbing the mountains of his home state. After high school graduation, he served in the Navy as a photojournalist. Following his stint in the military, he attended the University of Oregon, but interrupted his studies to start Eugene's first underground newspaper, *The Augur,* to edit *Bullfrog Information Service,* a Pacific Northwest alternative magazine, and to design and produce the *Willamette Valley Observer,* an alternative weekly based in Eugene. Currently, he is a contributing editor at *What's Happening,* a weekly Eugene newspaper. Yet Johnson confides that "the few poems that have appeared in literary magazines are closest to my heart." Such publications include *Foreground, Denali, Fireweed, Big Rain,* and *Bandon Undertow.* He has also self-published *Butch Beneath the Stars* (1978), a long poem about the mythic marriage between Butch Cassidy and Amelia Earhart. In addition, he has authored a science fiction novel entitled *Backspace.*

from **Three Poems Burnished by Your Waterfall**
Li's Poem

One supposedly random dawn
I awoke, startled to find
Your name perched like a small, triumphant wren
On my lips
Did I say that?
Do I mean this?
Yes . . . yes . . . yes

Vaudeville in the Garden

Eight Steller's jays
In a tree of white blossoms
Who are we? Who are we?
They mime
Bobbing all juicy and fat.

(Answer: Plums)

Harold L. Johnson

Harold L. Johnson was born in Yakima, Washington, "in the middle of the Great Depression." Following high school graduation, he relocated to Portland to study literature and art, and he has been a resident of that city for nearly forty years. Since college and following a stint in the military, he has taught in the Portland public schools. In addition to publishing a chapbook, *Dry Boats* (1984), his poems have appeared in a few small magazines, including *Northwest Magazine*.

The Names of Summer: A War Memory
for Jerry Conrath & Joann Geddes

Early in the war, when I was eight or nine
they began to show up on Sundays
at the Washington Junior High School diamond—
the first baseball players I'd seen in uniforms,
twenty or so, wearing white uniforms with red
caps and stockings. At first, they all looked
alike, like a handful of toy soldiers
and their uniforms seemed like a big white
lily that tore into particles as they piled out
of the army truck that brought them to the field.
"Japs," someone among the watching neighbors said.
An American soldier, the driver, relaxed in his khakis,
looked at magazines, smoked, and napped behind the wheel
during games. He counted heads when they reloaded for camp.

I hung near the benches to drink in the hitting
and catching and heard their talk, which was just like
mine. I heard the pitchers' fear of Yamaguchi, a great
lefthanded hitter. Often, he slammed balls
over the rightfielder's head clear to Eighth Street
and he could punch it to left when he took a notion.
Fujitani was a block of muscle behind the plate
in his armor that snicked and clunked as he worked.
He could whip off his mask, spring after a bunt
like a grasshopper and fire to first or second
in one motion. Duncan Matsushita threw
heart-breaking curveballs that dropped suddenly
into the strike zone and he seldom walked batters.
I began to cheer for my favorites. They laughed
that I could pronounce their names, no stranger to me

than Deuteronomy, Malachi, Ecclesiastes
which I'd been hearing all morning at church.
After a couple of Sundays, they drafted me as their batboy.
Manager Saito gave me staccato instructions
how to retrieve the bats and how to line them up.
Sometimes foul balls looped over the backstop
and bounced into the weeds across the street
and my job was also to hustle after those.

      For the rest of the summer
on Sundays, I was waiting at the diamond
when the truck arrived and the players hopped out
and started playing catch and playing pepper and
talking. I would ask, "Where's Sadaharu?"
"Oh he signed up for the army," somebody would say.
And that was all they said when somebody signed up.

The war. During the week, I played ball, trying
to imitate Kitagawa's nifty pickups at short, or Hongo's
fluid throwing motion from left. And I heard news
about the war, about how we had to beat the Japs,
those funny-talking, slanteyed sneak-attackers
of Pearl Harbor (which we had to remember).
I read comic books featuring heroic American
marines in combat against the bucktoothed and craven
enemy in the islands of the Pacific. In one story
a group of marines, victorious, found among other
graffiti on an abandoned cave wall, stick figures
of ballplayers and the legend "Babu Rusu stenks!"
      But Pentecostal Sunday
mornings sealed off the rest of the week, and the town,
except for a few gas stations, rested. First came
Sunday school, then came church with all the singing
and praying, testifying and the collection plate. Weekly, I
faced the sermon, sin-ridden, trapped, to begin the forced crawl
across a wordy Sahara in that hot hall while the overdressed
saints fanned themselves and chanted, "Preach, Brother!" Then
after an aftermath of waiting for the grownups to finish
laughing, shaking hands and hugging, we cruised home
in the Chevy. I tore into the house, changed clothes
and sprinted to the Washington diamond. Then the players
would arrive in their fresh white uniforms and red
caps and stockings. Balls popped into gloves and the gloves
smelled heavenly of linseed oil

and leather. A just-used glove felt damp, warm,
pliant and protective to my small hand inside. Games
lasted throughout the afternoon and the sparkling white
uniforms picked up streaks and smudges of green and brown.
After a game, the catchers would be covered with dust, and
orange stains from the mask printed their faces.

One Sunday before the game, Yamashita told me,
"Sadaharu's in Italy." "Fighting in the war?"
"Yeah," he said, "fighting the Germans." I could imagine
Sadaharu doing swift heroic deeds for our country.
After the warmup, Manager Saito would gather the players at home plate—
he managed both teams—and read off the lineups.
The suspense was like waiting to break out of church, to see
who would be on which team. How will Yamaguchi
handle Matsushita's curveball this Sunday? Will Kitagawa
be playing short or second—I know
I'd put Tanaka in center more often.
Then one time Manager Saito said, "Well,
this is the last Sunday, Hallie," and school started
and other seasons washed over that summer.
But now here come the names . . . Genesis,
Exodus, Leviticus,
Inaba, Nakasone, Yamaguchi,
Watanabe, Morita, Kitagawa,
Shimura, Fujitani, Matsushita. . . .

Brigit Pegeen Kelly

Brigit Pegeen Kelly was born in Palo Alto, California, in 1951. She
studied at Indiana University and the University of Oregon, earning
degrees in fine arts, nursing, counseling, and creative writing. She is
the winner of a Yale Younger Poets Award, a National Endowment for
the Arts Fellowship, the *Nation*/Discovery Award, two New Jersey
Fellowship Awards, and the Cecil Hemley Memorial Award from the
Poetry Society of America. Some of her poems have appeared in the
Georgia Review, the *Nation*, *New England Review*, and *Kenyon
Review*. She currently teaches at the University of Illinois and is author
of *To the Place of Trumpets* (1988).

Those Who Wrestle with the Angel for Us

for Dion

i.

My brother flies
A plane,
      windhover, night-lover,
Flies too low
Over the belled
        and furrowed fields,
The coiled creeks,
The slow streams of cars
           spilling
Like lust into the summer
Towns. And he flies
       when he
Should not, when
The hot, heavy air
       breaks
In storms, in high
Winds, when the clouds
         like trees
Unload their stony fruit
And batter his slender
        wings and tail.
But like the magician's
Dove, he appears home safely
         every time,
Carrying in his worn white
Bag all the dark
       elements
That flight knows,
The dark that makes
        his own soul
Dark with sight.

ii.

Even when he was a child, his skin was the white
Of something buffed by winds at high altitudes

Or lit by arctic lights—it gleamed like fish scales
Or oiled tin, and even then he wished to be alone,

Disappearing into the long grasses of the Ipperwash dunes
Where the gulls nested and where one afternoon

He fell asleep and was almost carried off by the sun—
In his dream he was running, leaping well, leaping

High as the hunted deer, and almost leaping free,
But like the tide, my gentle-handed mother hauled him back

With cold compresses and tea, and after that he favored
The dark, the ghostly hours, a small boy whistling in our yard

As he dragged a stick along the fence rails, and listened
To the slatted rattle of railroad cars, and knew by

Instinct how railroad lines look from the air, like ladders
Running northward to the stars, to the great constellations.

And he began then tracking his way through the names
Of all our fears, Cassiopeia, Andromeda, the shining Ram,

Tracking the miles and years he logs now, the lonely stretches
Where he finds the souvenirs that light our narrow kitchens—

Buckles and pins, watches and rings—the booty
That makes our land-locked, land-bound souls feel the compass

In our feet, and see in those who never speak, who
Slouch in with the dust of the northern wind on their backs,

The face of the angel we ourselves must wrestle with.

Ger Killeen

Ger Killeen was born in Limerick City, Ireland, later moving to Dublin to attend University College, Dublin. After graduation and traveling through Europe, he and his wife settled in Oregon. Currently residing near the coastal town of Neskowin, next to a forest, Killeen states that most of his life has been spent in cities and towns much different from rural Oregon and that the transition to living in the country, near the ocean with "a world of wildlife on his doorstep" has affected his poetry writing. "These days I even hear traces of Oregonian speech patterns entering my lines," the Irish poet admits. His work has appeared in both American and European magazines, including *New Irish Writing, The Rake, Limerick, Poetry Broadsheet, Calapooya Collage,* and *Hubbub.* He is the author of one chapbook, *A Trace of Exaggeration,* and a collection of poems entitled *A Wren,* which was the winner of the 1989 Bluestem Award for poetry. A second collection of poetry called *Trysts* is forthcoming.

A Full Bucket

The wind from Alaska
nuzzles the rafters
of the small barn where
I stable my old Arabian mare.

She chomps alfalfa hay
in a corner
while under a dim bulb
I fork dung to a barrow.

Distant bells!
Never the same peal
twice: Her hoofs shifting
on the stone floor.

That Caedmon woke
in such a place
warm with the smells
of animals

and felt the angel
of song come touch and heal
his silence
is not beyond

believing— the very
handle of the pitchfork,
lustered by years of hands,
is a solid shaft of moonlight.

I spread new alder
shavings for the horse's
bed and the air
blooms with their green scent.

I fetch her grain
in an old basin,
and fresh water,
a full bucket.

The Sowing Fiddle

Beyond the invisible hills,
in the great towns' market squares,
in red skirts and frills
bears are turning slow reels

to the songs ground
out of barrel-organs
by the morose, bony hands
of bewildered apes. The sounds

carry on the bituminous air,
the catches and wheezes,
all the way here, here
to my acres' soft floor

where I execute gavottes
in the heady musks
of Jack-In-The-Pulpit
and Rich-Man's-Margaret.

So, I'll hum you these tunes—
"Ruth In The Cornfield,"
"The Lovers And The Loons"—
across my knees I'll play spoons

of stolen gold, and from the hump
on my shoulders I'll fling wheat-seeds
and weed-seeds and jump
through haysheds with my flaming lamp.

And over the hills, in fours
and threes, the hulking bears
will stumble and the sad apes bray
such music as would wring tears

from a rainbow. And all their hobbled works
I'll gather to the keeping of my wild park
and saw my sowing fiddle
dawn to dark.

Lee Crawley Kirk

Lee Crawley Kirk was born in Wenatchee, Washington, but moved to Portland as a child. She has been a mother, a farmer, a bookkeeper, an antique dealer, and a bookstore clerk as well as a writer of articles, stories, and poems. Her poetry has appeared in the *Christian Science Monitor, Blue Unicorn, Fireweed, Calapooya Collage,* and the *Gamut.* In addition, she has published prose in regional and national magazines and newspapers.

With Stars in My Forehead

I do not want to live the lives
of other women, soft and succulent
as ripe peaches, pliable as a rubber hose.
I want to live with lightning under my tongue
and storms between my teeth,
with rain and wind at my elbows;
I want to walk with stars in my forehead
and the moon balanced on one shoulder.
I'll carry the sun on my back.

Let the dirt of prairies and deserts
and mountains sift from my fingernails
in a long bright wake behind me. Let me
feel oceans squirting between my toes.
I want thunder to rattle the windows
where I live; and eagles and frogs
to leap into the air when I speak.

I will pull my life out of worm holes
and plunge it into volcanoes,
hurl it away from me like a molten boomerang
that grows larger, coming back.
I will eat grass, and rocks,
and trees five centuries old.

I am a landscape of fields of wheat,
of mountains and canyons and valleys,
of ice water and superheated sand.
There are feathers under my skin
waiting to bloom like sails.

I will scream when I feel rage,
and when I am placated by my own nature,
I will let my silkier side come out:
as succulent as ripe peaches,
supple as a rubber hose.

❧

Amy Klauke

Amy Klauke grew up in Illinois and moved to Oregon in 1984 to attend the University of Oregon's MFA program in creative writing. There, she received the Graduate Poetry Award in 1985. She has continued to live and work in the Eugene area as a three-year poet-in-residence, a volunteer for the Council for Human Rights in Latin America, a five-year assistant editor of *Northwest Review*, and co-editor of *Skipping Stones*, a multicultural forum for children's art and writing. A finalist in the Lane Regional Arts Council poetry competition in 1987, Klauke's work has been published in various magazines and journals, including *Cottonwood*, *Cimarron Review*, and *Renditions*. She has also taught modern American poetry for a term at the Chinese University of Hong Kong. For this author, Oregon provides the "quiet simple lifestyle and strong presence of the natural environment," making it "an ideal place for her life, poetry, and work."

As You Pass

Take me back to the morning your mother
tucked blankets into your arms
sent you down the road to live
with a wealthy family who ate spicy
sausages and tolerated you in exchange
for help with the house. There's your father
weeping as you pass, *Hijito*,
with your *mochila* full of books, too big
for your soft shoulders, your round head
already turning away. There. Let me
come to you before you become
accustomed to loss, before you fix
your eyes on the road you follow
into solitude, into war, that goes nowhere
but away. Wait. I see you *Soldadito*,
pulling on that armor which is so shiny
but so tight. Stop there.
Let me accompany you. Let me
be the vigilant one, stoking
a tenderness in you so sweet
it keeps you from tossing
that gem, that fire,
your love, into the ditch
where I am on my knees in the mud
and grass, searching for it.

❧

Recognizable Terrors

This is the third night
slugs have appeared in the kitchen
rubbing slick bellies on the tiles
and waving antennae. They are so *quiet*
is what I mind, and their lack
of definable weapon. No teeth,
claws, stinger. Heartless

to squish them the way we do,
or flush them cleanly away.
Out of sight, out of
mind, I say, and pad back
to bed with slippers on
my flashlight swinging its thin way

through the dark. I sense another
out there, mine, remorseless, coming
for me over the polished floor.

Marilyn Krysl

Marilyn Krysl was raised in Eugene, Oregon. She received her BA and MFA at the University of Oregon. Currently, she is professor of creative writing at the University of Colorado, Boulder, and the author of *Saying Things* (1975), *More Palomino, Please, More Fuschia* (1980), *Diana Lucifera* (1983), and *What We Have to Live With* (1989). Her book *Midwife* (1989) is being used in a number of nursing programs around the country.

Feet

They are the last to leave
the womb. The woman feels two little fins
fluttering, this is the last time

you fly. Now they're weights, they keep you
down to earth. Flat as the land
you stand on they go *flop, flop,* a pair of
turbot, each in its separate tureen,
and instead of a pair some of us have two lefts,
we put them in our mouths, and they're not

pretty. You never saw your father
without socks. Now when your lover undresses
the foot is the one appendage you don't want to look at,
to touch. Feet are

indecent, certainly unfit for jewelry, and not exotic—just
odd. Likely candidates for dropped
tins of tomatoes, something to step on while
dancing. Even the Chinese failed to find
any grace in them, wrapped them in bandages
and tried to kill them. And the prima ballerina
tucks one under her wing like a flamingo
and tries to sublimate the other into her leg
and if she's good we believe for split seconds at a time
that they don't exist at all. All around the world
women stand at their mirrors, sighing, "If only
we could end at the ankles." They get

cold, they lack any interesting
orifices, all you can do is make clumsy
passes under the table
and like two great brooches grandmother gave you
you can't give them away. White elephants,
they belong in a museum,
keep them in a glass coffin
and charge admission. When you walk
slap, slap, they remind you you're not going
anywhere. And when you feel shame and look down
they seem to confirm it. *It's a miracle,* they say,
that once or twice you managed to dance, and they

smell. And when you finally lie down alone the last time
there they are at the bottom of the bed,
the only thing left upright. Tombstones.
Feet are the last thing you see

before your eyes close.

Barbara La Morticella

Barbara La Morticella was born in Cincinatti, Ohio, and grew up in New York City and Long Island. Oregon has been her home since 1968. She sees much of her work springing from city scenes in Portland and the flora, fauna, and people of the Tualatin Mountains. Her work has appeared in such newspapers and magazines as the *Oregonian, Calapooya Collage, Womanspirit,* the *Portland Poetry Festival Anthology,* and *Confluence.* Ms. La Morticella co-hosts KBOO's regular poetry show. Her most recent book is *Even the Hills Move in Waves* (1986).

Valentines

My daughter is looking at babies
and cooing: almond eyes
          she says
thick black hair, big nostrils—

"Sounds like a gorilla," I scoff.

My daughter is looking at babies
and my heart cracks.

One part is humming
"Keep your dancing feet free, girl!"

and the other is looking at babies, too—
carried away on the curves of two little feet
over one of the world's oldest seas.

———————————

Once she cried whenever I left the house.
Later, she admiringly studied my every move—
Me, who was only a smudged figure
in my own copy book!

Now she's packed up and gone
without even a look back,
following her own life on its
shimmery path.

But when she gets to where she's going,
she'll find me, for I'm
tucked into the plush lining
        of her bones,
wrapped in red silk—

The valentine my mother gave me,
   and her mother, and her mother
      and her mother before.

Jay La Plante

Jay La Plante was born in 1962 in Browning, Montana, on the Blackfeet Indian Reservation. He moved to Portland, Oregon, in 1985. He received a BA in English from Portland State University in 1989. Since then he has worked with the Northwest Indian Child Welfare Association developing materials on child abuse and neglect prevention. LaPlante writes poetry and short fiction and has received the Branford Millar Award in Poetry from the *Portland Review* in 1988. He writes about his cultural heritage and how history reflects itself in contemporary American Indian society.

Mona

She has long black
hair like a real Indian
woman's,
pulled together tight
into a tail.

She quickly
braids its length
with one hand
and wraps it in
a blue rubber band.

She puts on
the new dress (that
she worked on all
summer) with orange
and yellow ribbons.

She wears the
moccasins with
scuffed soles
and beadwork designed
especially for her.

She grabs the shawl
that she was honored
with when she wore
the Blackfeet Princess
banner a year ago.

She says a prayer
to Grandfather
to help her dance good
and leaves the teepee
for the dance lodge.

She is ready.

She turns heads as
her number is called
and she walks into
the arena, keeping plenty
far from the others.

She digs her foot into
the sawdust and smooths
out a groove where
her feet will stay
until the singers start.

She is slightly nervous.

She closes her eyes
and lowers her head,
quickly asking again
for Grandfather to shine
upon her today.

She wraps her shawl
around her shoulders,
hands rest on her hips,
and looks towards
the announcer's stand.

She hears the announcer
cry "O-ke, Two Medicine
Singers, take-it-away,"
and the drum starts as the lead
singer screams into the P.A.

She steps from the groove
tapping the dust lightly,
and begins her routine,
body moving slowly at first,
then faster.

She feels the earth below her
tapping back, and she
is comforted by the gentle
rhythm that lifts her
to a renewed confidence.

She listens closely
to the song, and in her head

sings along because she
has heard this one
at many celebrations.
She knows the time is
right so she does her
backstep, shawl fringe
and dress fringe
swaying in unison.

She hears the end of the song.

She stops on the mark,
her foot coming to rest on
the ground at the same
time as the final
beat of the drum.

She hears the people
clapping as she returns
to the spot where she began,
this being an old habit
and will bring luck.

She takes down her
shawl and stands patiently,
showing off her number
to the judges, who are all
coming to write it down.

She hears the announcer
say "O-ke, clear the arena.
Clear the arena," so she walks
from her lucky spot and
talks with another woman.

She'll have to wait now.

She knows that this
was only the first round
and that she'll have
to dance even better
if she gets to the finals.

She returns to the teepee,
slips the moccasins off,
and pulls the new dress over
her head, laying it on the
mattress where she'll sleep.

She says a prayer to
Grandfather, thanking Him
for watching over her,
and a tear forms in her eye.
She wipes it away.

She pulls on her jeans
and a sweater, and ties her
tennis shoes fast so she
can go find the man she
met during the two-step.

She can hardly wait.

Nela Ladd-Bruni

Nela Ladd-Bruni was born in 1948 in Anchorage, Alaska, of Sicilian and Welsh/Indian parents. Her childhood years were spent on the outskirts of Anchorage, at Lake Daniels on the Kenai Peninsula, and in British Columbia, Canada. She returned to the U.S. in 1960, traveling extensively in Arkansas, Missouri, Florida, California, and Oregon. Ladd-Bruni graduated from California State University, Los Angeles, and the University of Oregon. She has taught English, writing, and special education classes in Los Angeles, Alhambra and South El Monte. Currently, she teaches for a small private college in Eugene, resides in Cottage Grove, and is at work on a chapbook, *Grow Back Your Flesh.*

Enemy and Friend

I want to call these birds home in the chill
of the morning I am rushing through.
The flock of ten stretches over the tiny field
the sun is warming, and shows me no attention,
sweeping to complete the work their eyes must see
and I cannot. Among the rustle of Lightcaps's sheep,
one nimble Toulouse gander cries out its warning
then marches aside. The young vultures
flag the sweet grass and posts, blackish wings
circling a fence that cannot keep them out.
In pairs they gather to eat, and I hear hissing,
try to see the lamb dead at the water trough.
What they saw high above me belongs to them,
a gentle animal turned to meat, its mother now

close with other sheep, and feeding as they do,
convivial. Shredding the carcass with un-mannered grunts,
the vultures clasp and eat until the flesh is gone.
I feel a joy carry the field, the sheep and vultures
nod, and the gander goes among them as Christ might do,
blessing enemy and friend. They clean their bills
in the dry grass, and I sense contentment.
Wings droop, then scissor out as they eye the flock.
But the hospitality of the sheep is finished.
The vultures move and rise, believers seeking heaven,
the air is thick with feather and talon, and I imagine space,
space will take them.

Wing K. Leong

Wing K. Leong was born in Canton, China, in 1934. He migrated
to Hong Kong in 1953 and remained until 1962. He holds a BA
in fine arts from the Chinese University of Hong Kong. Leong left
Hong Kong in 1962 and moved to Portland. He has studied
calligraphy with Lloyd Reynolds and graphic art at the Portland
Museum School. For the last eight years he has owned and operated
the Chinese Art Studio, which sells imported Chinese art objects
and art supplies, including his own work. Wing Leong teaches
Chinese watercolor painting at Portland Community College and
painting and calligraphy at his own studio.

葡萄秋熟

葡萄粒粒似珠垂，甘美秋嘗正合時。
葉上螳螂將躍動，昂頭伸爪欲何之。

Ripe Autumn Grapes

Clustered, dangling like pearls: grapes,
And Fall the fitting time to taste their sweetness.
Mantis on a leaf about to spring
Head up, arms out, bound for where?

Kerry Paul May

Kerry Paul May was born in Condon, Oregon, in 1956 and lived there until 1969, when his family moved to Madrid, Spain. He returned to Oregon in 1974 to attend the University of Oregon, earning a BA and MFA by 1982. Some of his poems have appeared in *Pacifica Awards Magazine, Rhino, University of Portland Review, Three Rivers Poetry Journal,* and the *Northwest Review.* "I always bear in mind my roots," says May. "Where I grew up few people read poems; I would like them to read mine."

The Gift

What had you hoped to gain, son?
A trophy? The gift of fresh meat?
You knew the elk would gather
Just below, grazing on the last
Green shoots of grass before they
Descend further to the valleys,
Hard prairies and lake beds. There
Was nothing to stop you from
Sighting in on the largest bull,
A six-point, his antlers clean
And smooth, his coat already
Thickened, heavy with winter fat.
From his center of seven cows
He had arced his large headdress
And surveyed the dim afternoon
Light evading the sparse treeline
For a scent of anything that
Moved. There was nothing to keep
You from squeezing off three good
Rounds into his heart or throat,
Just like I taught you on all
Those weekend trips together.
Such blasts you knew for sure would
Drop him quickly and without pain.
There was nothing, nothing, that is,
But him alone when he turned your
Way and held his stare, not chewing,
His ears cocked, his eyes unflinching,
No twitch, no steam-breath drifting
From his fine black snout. Maybe

It was glare from your gun barrel
The fire of your fluorescent vest,
Your round outline frozen against
The flat treeless skyline he saw,
Or your own pulsing breath. But
He dropped his head once again,
Unconcerned. And it was there, in
Your sights, that you saw something
Only a few will have chance to see—
The dark, quiet herd making their
Slow way down from the mountain,
Into the approaching winter, alive.

(1925-1985)

❧

Sandra McPherson

Sandra McPherson is a professor of English at the University of California, Davis. She was born in San Jose, California, in 1943 but spent 18 years of her adult life in the Pacific Northwest. She has published in numerous magazines and anthologies and is the author of five books of poetry: *Radiation* (1973), *The Year of Our Birth* (1978), *Elegies for the Hot Season* (1982), *Patron Happiness* (1984), and *Streamers* (1989). McPherson is the winner of National Endowment for the Arts and John Simon Guggenheim fellowships.

Lament, with Flesh and Blood

for my daughter

I do not know much about innocence
but it seems you are responsible
for this evening lake's young blue that laments
how fishermen joke and loons laugh. Sybil
of leeches, you're young but you're scary,
dangling your thin, taut, clarifying legs
at fish cleanings in the estuary.
Fog stars the knives that slip out pike eggs.
Blue's future is black. The present is rain.
The past is rain the wind blows back.
Still you sit—Audubon, catch that blue vein!—
a tiny funnel bisecting your cheek.
I want you to run to me with your kiss.
Still you brood in the lake like wild rice.

❧

Juan Mestas

Juan Mestas was born in Cuba and raised in Cuba, Spain, Puerto Rico, and Tennessee. He has a PhD in Hispanic languages and literatures from the State University of New York at Stony Brook and has been writing and editing since his student days in Puerto Rico, where he edited *La Escalera* (a sociopolitical journal published at the University of Puerto Rico, 1967-1974) and *Guajana* (a literary magazine, 1967-1969). His latest work is a study of the poet José Martí, *José Martí y la clase obrera* (1993). Mestas is vice provost and dean of students at Portland State University. He wrote the following poem in Spanish and translated it into English.

Ephesus 91

Hoy regreso a tus fantasmas
y los míos
me saludan impacientes.
Sombras ancestrales y domésticas
inevitables compañeras de viajes no emprendidos,
de muertes anticipadas,
aguardan detrás de mis mármoles y tus desvelos,
detrás de mi niñez, de tus espantos íntimos.
Aguardan y acechan,
amigas de confianza y desconfiadas,
enemigas entrañables,
imágenes que persigo y me persiguen
sin encontrarnos nunca
ni dejarnos.

❦

Ephesus 91

Today, I return to your phantoms,
and my own
greet me with impatience.
Shadows ancestral and domestic,
inevitable companions of untraveled journeys,
of anticipated deaths,
await behind my marble and your vigils,
behind my childhood and your intimate fears,
await and watch,
trusted friends who mistrust me,
dearest enemies,
images I pursue, that pursue me,
never to meet,
never to part.

❦

Gary Miranda

Gary Miranda was born in Bremerton, Washington, in 1938 and grew up in Seattle. Oregon became his spiritual growing-up place when at 17 he entered the Jesuit seminary in Sheridan. After one year circumnavigating the globe, three years in Athens, Greece, and seven years supporting himself as a poet in Cambridge, Massachusetts, he returned to Oregon. He is the author of two books of poetry, *Listeners at the Breathing Place* (1979), and *Grace Period* (1983), and a translation of Rainer Maria Rilke's *Duino Elegies.*

Horse Chestnut

I fell from one once. Judy Cole
used to put five of them, whole,
in her mouth. My brothers ran to tell
my mother: It's Gary—he fell
from a tree but he isn't dead
yet. As I write, there is one outside
my window. I have a weakness, still, for
women with large mouths. The doctor
put two fingers into my head,
tingly with novocaine, and said
to my mother: Look, you can see
where the skull is chipped. Sometimes we
made pipes, or necklaces. My mother
groaned and looked away. I could never
figure out what connection they had
with horses.

Later, Judy Cole was named Miss
Seattle. Mostly, what I remember is
blood all around and me lying
there thinking: so this is dying.
Every one of them has two inside,
like testicles. I wasn't afraid
really, just convinced. By the time I began
to think I loved her we had been
children too long for it to matter.
Sixteen stitches. I saw her once later,
when she was married. My mother
said: I don't want to see you near
that tree again—understand? I still tend
to confuse dying and love. And
no one I've ever loved has died,
exactly.

Love Poem

A kind of slant: the way a ball will glance
off the end of a bat when you swing for the fence
and miss—that is, if you could watch that once,
up close and in slow motion; or the chance
meanings, not even remotely intended, that dance
at the edge of words, like sparks. Bats bounce
just so off the edges of the dark at a moment's
notice, as swallows do off sunlight. Slants

like these have something to do with why *angle*
is one of my favorite words, whenever it chances
to be a verb; and with why the music I single
out tonight—eighteenth-century dances—
made me think just now of you untangling
blueberries, carefully, from their dense branches.

❦

Rodger Moody

Rodger Moody was born in Williamsport, Indiana. He holds a BA in English and an MFA in creative writing from the University of Oregon. He has taught poetry workshops for the Fine Arts Work Center in Provincetown, Massachusetts, the Oregon State Penitentiary, and the Oregon Coast Council for the Arts. Some of Rodger Moody's poems have appeared in *Calapooya Collage, Hubbub, Indiana Review, Mississippi Mud,* and *Poet and Critic.* He is editor of *Silverfish Review* in Eugene.

Night Shift

Driving
as if my Yellow Cab
could satisfy
the ache in my headlights to see
beyond the dry mouth
of July heat lightning,
I stop and get out
squat to touch the bluegrass
that edges the curb,
and become again the boy
who climbed trees.

Four years old
I watch Dad's intent hands weave
cord around a basket
to shape a net
for the dirt court
across the street.

Twenty-one
he played guard
with the local boys.
And I sat
beneath the kitchen table
when Dad
home early from work
embraced Mom
with good news:
his promotion to
night foreman. And much

the way the tingle in reaching the top
limb of a bare sweet gum
leaves the skin in a crisp wanting
I didn't know what it meant
until years later
though since that day I
can't recall
when I last saw him
hug her
in the light.

Erik Muller

Erik Muller was born in New York City. He holds degrees in English from Williams College and the University of Oregon. Muller has taught at Southwestern Oregon and Lane Community colleges. Some of his poems have appeared in *Hubbub, Western Humanities Review,* the *Beloit Poetry Journal,* and *Prairie Schooner.* Recently, Erik Muller, Peter Jensen, and David Johnson have collaborated on a collection of poetry entitled *Confluence* (1992).

Mare

She stands taller than any friend of mine
   could ever stand
And beautiful has no way to criticize herself
   but is what she is.
She looks at me. And I must seem to her
   another animal
Without horse sense but the known human smell
   and upright posture.
Or maybe I resemble a strolling cedar post
   but that doesn't spook her
As she waits with her long head curved over.
   Stopped at the fence
I stand looking at her smooth strong neck
   while she grazes,
Then raises her head so her eyes fix over my head.
   I begin hearing
Her nostrils taking deep crackling breaths.

Many times I've seen two horses stand close,
   I guessed all day,
Head over back, not meeting each other's gaze.
   Once in the West
I saw two pickups parked in opposite directions,
   cabs in so close
The ranchers were talking, I bet, over idling engines.
   So I know the better
Part of an afternoon can be spent this way
   deepening my breaths
Of a wind that brings us the smell of rain,
   I and the mare standing,
Looking out our different ways another long moment.

Michael Niflis

Michael Niflis was born and raised in Missouri (Carthage, Springfield, Independence). He played lead guitar on a weekly TV show in Indiana and owned and operated an insurance business. After earning a teaching degree, he moved to Oregon, where he teaches during the winters and skippers his own commercial fishing boat in the summers. Some of his poems have appeared in the *New York Times, Esquire, Harpers,* the *New Republic,* and the *Nation.* "The matter in my poems . . . like some of our migratory birds, seems to reach well beyond the borders of our state."

Old Movie Monsters

for Boris Karloff

> *"I just love things that scare me to death."*
> —a high-school girl

There is something kind of nice
about a healthy monster . . .
pieced together with old body snatchings

or nourished by hot blood.
He drags one foot, has a fetching eye
or drools Hungarian accent

through bloody teeth
or enters only doors that squeak
or gets hairy in moonlight

or has only masters with hunchback assistants
or can be stopped only with silver bullets,
mirrors, hawthorn, and holy things;

or the way he shuns all sustenance
save the blood of young women
or furiously rattles his bars and snorts

or effortlessly snaps his bonds
or raises his coffin lid
O. . . so . . . slowly

letting one white hand crawl out;
or loves old castles with bats, rats,
graveyards, and night electrical storms . . .

or is pitied by high school girls
when tracked down at night
with torches, guns, and yelping dogs.

Thunderstorm

I fully intended to write
a poem today about a woman
with dark eyes

but a bird
suddenly stopped singing
and a distant summer

thunderstorm began to walk
heavily across the prairie
with iron boots

and the orchard to speak
in low voices; my long hoe
leaned against the house.

I decided to sit
on the dry porch boards to wait
looking westward with love

at the thickening darkness.

❦

Verlena Orr

Verlena Orr was born and raised in Cottonwood, Idaho. She has lived in Oregon since 1963 and worked as a secretary, social worker, and teacher. She is currently in the Developmental Education Department at Portland Community College and the Talented and Gifted Program of the Portland Public Schools. Some of her poems have appeared in *Poet & Critic, Cutbank, Hubbub,* the *Portland Review, Cincinnati Poetry Review,* and *Slow Dancer* (England). "Raised in Kamiah, Idaho, on a Nez Perce reservation, my themes tend to be rural and draw on childhood experiences and landscapes." Orr is the author of *I Dance Naked in a Dream* (1989).

Learning the Language from Dad

It begins under the John Deere.
At first it sounds like thunder
over by Cottonwood, twenty miles west.

But it is the incantation
of the slipping crescent wrench,

that sacred oath of B's like bells
S's that steam in a long train
coupled with "ings" that ricochet
in the walls of the abandoned granary
echo the canyon
clear down to Seven Mile Grade.

Pigeons fall from the hay mow
at the top of the barn
then rise like death.
The sow lifts her snout
from her morning slop.
Old Jack runs under the milk house
where cream in the separator goes sour.
Silver, the new palomino, lays
his ears back, ready to throw any rider.

The loose two-by-four falls in the shed
crashes like the end
of a long celebration.

Simon J. Ortiz

Simon Ortiz (Acoma Pueblo) was born in 1941 in Albuquerque, New Mexico. While living in Oregon, he taught at Lewis & Clark College and worked for the Portland Metropolitan Arts Commission. His latest collection, *Woven Stone* (1992), is an omnibus of his three previous works, *Going for the Rain, A Good Journey,* and *Fight Back: For the Sake of the People, For the Sake of the Land.* He is currently living in New Mexico.

Running and Fear

Within my knee, the pain's inner animal heart
waits for me to lurch.
Any curb will do, any hole will be sudden enough.
The small animal will gnaw
once set free from the nerve it hides under.
So I fear.

My tremble is urgent, knowing its partnership
with pain is certain.
The fear is not wasted for we know after all
how humbly we are driven to acceptance.

Arriving and Leaving Here

The wind's cold teeth gnaw at my skin
as I run up the street.
Far from prairie and canyons and mesas,
I mark this place by the pines
on street corners, church steeples,
run-down front porches, gas stations.
The trail around Laurelhurst Park
is asphalt but it runs up and down
little hills so it's close enough
to my wish and imagination.
I know it's not imagination
this place needs; it's for us
to realize it for its own power,
its transformations and the part
it has in our present lives.
The truest imagination is what it offers
to us, bringing us to knowledge
no matter where we are, what place.
The hills and the asphalt trail
of Laurelhurst Park are of themselves
and have their own power, just as prairie,
Southwest canyons and mesas do.
And we have to accept that
when we arrive here and leave this place.

Walter Pavlich

Walter Pavlich was born in Portland in 1955. He attended Woodstock
Grade School, Franklin High School, the University of Oregon (BA), and
the University of Montana (MFA). He has worked as a firefighter and a
Poet-in-the-Schools of Montana and Oregon. Pavlich now lives in Davis,
California, where he writes poems, short fiction, and essays full time. He
has published five collections of poetry, most recently *Running Near the
End of the World* (1992).

Three Hearts of the Octopus

Not one is going anywhere
except to inspect the transparent corners
for a way out. A purple shore crab
rises on sideways tiptoes

using a buddy as a stepladder
to push off into the impossible.
Its cruel reflection at the water top
and ascension of bubbles
keep sending hope to the downfallen.
Children have intimidated
the octopus all morning
dirty hands in a saltwater grotto.
It has painted itself
white from the inside.
No one stops the woman
from dropping pennies
on its billowy head.
Stories say fishermen sometimes
turn one inside out
like a pillowcase.
In schoolroom aquaria
they often pull themselves
into the night leaking away
in the sound of janitors' keys.
They live less than five years
mate once
all hugs
then both die floating
like weak sacks pushed
by the wavery currents.
It wasn't suicide one night
when a Newport octopus
took its eyes
good as any human's
over the top of its circle of water
translating the air with its arm
its skin exit-sign green.
The slow arms' exodus began
wading out of the water
onto the floor. The following morning
they found it glued to the glass door
wound around the handles and limp.
As three hearts' compasses still set
stuck on Yaquina Bay.

Myrna Peña-Reyes

Myrna Peña-Reyes was born and raised in the Philippines. After she received her BA in English, she came to Oregon to get an MFA in creative writing. While in Oregon, she met an American who is now her husband. She has worked as a secretary, clerk in an office supply store, and has taught composition, literature, and creative writing on the collegiate level both in the Philippines and in the United States. Her poems have appeared in U.S. publications such as *Northwest Review, The Forbidden Stitch* (anthology), *Making Waves* (anthology), *Sequoia* (anthology), and the Philippine publications *Solidarity, Graphic, Sands & Coral*, and *Equinox I* (anthology).

No More War, 1945

Riding back by water buffalo
to the bomb-burned city
that was home,
out of the jungle,
down from the dark hills,
our four years' hiding over;
"Is the War really gone,
it won't ever come back, ever?"
we asked Father walking beside the bulls.
"Yes," he said, stepping lightly
on his lame leg.

No soldier, he had been resting one day
when, panicked by the guns of a Jap patrol,
he ran down toward the river
and tumbled over a cliff.
It was weeks before the *hilot* came.
That was soon after Mother's death.
For a year Father nursed her cancer
with no drugs—no doctors—
only the occasional *mananambal*
to try to ease her.
(When she cried out loud,
especially at night,
she frightened the children.)

Years later, wanting to know
what it was like for him,
I learned Father chose not to remember
what I know. . .

hilot—traditional bonesetter; *mananambal*—traditional healer

Run—run—
rumors of a Jap patrol
a "guerrilla" band
(they killed anyone)—run—
where will we hide?
—shaking with malaria
or dysentery—run—
we learned not to complain
crouched under the circling planes—
awakened at night—
no questions—
"take what you can"—
our bundles on our heads
run—run—
My fear stretched farther
than the dark—

But on that day at the end of running,
riding home on those slow bulls,
Father stepping lightly on his lame leg
(when he said "no more war"
we thought we would never die),
there was so much sun—
it flowed on the ground
and flooded the sky.

Paulann Petersen

Paulann Petersen was born in Portland, Oregon, and grew up "under the sign of a neon wolf"—the sign above her grandfather's fur shop. She attended Franklin High School before leaving for college. Since college, she has lived in Klamath Falls and taught English at Mazama High School. In 1986-87, she was a Stegner Fellow in poetry at Stanford. Her poems have appeared in magazines such as *Hubbub, Sequoia, Oregon English Journal, Calapooya Collage,* and *Calyx.* Her first book of poems, *Under the Sign of a Neon Wolf,* appeared in 1989. She currently teaches at West Linn High School.

The Moon Recounts the Birth of the Sun

The first twin out of the womb,
I rose, chilled and pale,
busy making my peace with the air—
until I saw my mother still labored.
A huge knot lurched in that belly
I'd so recently left,
shoving first against her ribs,
then toward the knees she clutched.
I watched my brother lunge inside her,
amazed there'd ever been room for me.

For days she strained with that pain,
crying for me to help her,
but what could I do? No way
to wrench my brother from her womb,
nothing to do but stay by her side
until she wedged between two trees
and pushed him out.

From the first moment he was
gorgeous—golden, pink,
glowing with the pulse of heat.
The other women gathered to oooh and ahhh.
"Twins—how lovely," they said,
looking from him to me,
careful to skirt the problem of such
unequal light and size.

True. I would become my father's
darling girl, showered with stars,
set by his own hand to plump and dwindle,
to reign in the night sky.
But even so, I have good reason
for being withdrawn.

How can others blame me if I'm chaste?
What do they know about someone
still wrapped in the silver caul
of her mother's pain,
someone whose only light is gathered
from another's dazzling face?

Moles

One fumbled into sunlight
and the neighbor pushed his shovel at me
saying   kill it   don't be a fool
just bash its head   you know
how they ruin a lawn
while I stood and stared
at its beautiful hands digging
back into the earth.

But these are a different kind.
Nana said, they're beauty marks
be glad you have so many.
Ollie said, you wait, someday
a man will kiss them one by one.
A surgeon cut out suspicious ones
and then came back to remove
their widening scars,
wiring my skin to make it hold.

At night I pleaded   go home
dig back into my blood,
be beautiful.

Amanda Powell

Amanda Powell is a recent arrival to Oregon; her grandfather was an Oregon cowboy before he moved East. She teaches Spanish and literary translation in the Department of Romance Languages at the University of Oregon. Her poems have appeared in *Ploughshares, Sinister Wisdom, Sojourner, Oregon English Journal* and the *Women's Review of Books.* She has held a Centrum Foundation Fellowship and a Massachusetts Artists Foundation Fellowship in poetry. Some of her translations have appeared in *Sor Juana's Answer.*

Square Dance at the Fairgrounds

for Danny Kaiser

Night everywhere, night in our cherry-red lipstick,
we four women grinning without thought of tickets or payment
passed the ticket-taker and his two grinning, elbowing friends

and in under the klieg lights of the sheep sheds; night
black under the prize sheep's blue-felt hooded jackets that guard against soils

working into the fleece by night;
night spilled in the oxen's stiff-sweated, pitched agitation
when the whip cracks, the beefy driver shrills, the massy granite block's
          just budged,
and those packed inches the stone lurches down the fairgrounds

too are night.   And night is the otter-gleam
of the women's softball-team champion in her swimsuit
shouldering out of the dunking tub to dangle her legs again

from the hinged, puddled platform ($.50/three throws to topple her, all for uni-
forms for the team). Each water drop beams a circling midway,
its neon orbits tangible as the glass buttons and plastic pearls that stud

the men's best blue-satin Western shirts nipped into belted jeans, the smocked and
tucked promises edging the women's designer jean's or ruffled dirndls,
all local people ably partnered and handing themselves or the others around

each figure of the square, as they are woman or man accordingly certain
of each neat step in its turn, while our galaxy
flows some 1.3 million miles per hour down the lavish night.

We came here to dance. We're city people, *artistic* as I imagine
the square dancers to confirm with neutral tone and nod
much like forefinger tapped to forehead, explaining it all—

how we can't square our set or recall who's partnered with whom,
let alone which of the women are men and (as our friends join in) which one
of the men *is* being a man and should go first, do-si-do your partner, your corner,
and allemande

left—night narrowing between the nearing hands and then
as they meet, night clasped there.
The farm—and small-towns-people, kindly forebearing, discern

our need for remedial instruction and the slower tunes
while night circles in the caller's recitative and I'm whirled
by a tender, querulous Marxist who, when the band takes a break, imparts

analyses of square-dancing, historical, social, material, from 18th
to 20th centuries, with and by whom to be swung (now, *swing* that lady!)
is to fly, pure and simple, in a body, a long pink skirt someone gave me

and wide red belt, in the night, at the fair, among stars that,
as they whirl from our lives, are asking, what is night? what is class?
          what are species and genders?
Sheep-fleece, ox-sweat, scuffed sawdust hills, hayfields, hands—all now
          to the grand right-and-left with your answers.

John Quinn

John Quinn was born in Albany, Oregon. His career has followed numerous avenues, ranging from the military to dealing in antiques and fine art. He has spent much of the last twenty years teaching in Japan. He is currently living in Boulder City, Nevada. John Quinn's poems have appeared in magazines from the *Hudson Review* to *Gray's Sporting Journal*. "I suppose one day I'd like to come home, but since I've been away, I've gotten rather used to the finer things of life (food on my plate, a roof over my head) that Oregon has never indicated any willingness to provide me." His books include *The Wolf Last Seen* (1987), and *Easy Pie* (1987).

In Oregon

for Linda

Fast as antelope in pumice dust
headed dead-away across the lava
flats at Jordan Valley,
we were hungry trout
in the first clear pools above a reservoir.
We were the sharp sound,
fourteen tongues at once, of chukars
scolding boatmen from a rocky ledge.
We were soft as deer drinking water.

Down through jack-pines, we
were mountain water moving
stone. A man is strong
as a woman makes him
with her tongue. My name
was on your lips:
the feel of wind
as soft as valley rain.

Close in as love
in apple time, fat and slow
for sleep, we were all the animals
that make a year. You were
November's thick coastal slope,
my last huckleberry hunger.
The dense wealth of your long body
made my winter's rest
when we were all of that
and innocent
in Oregon.

The Trough at Rockwall Spring

In Memory: John Duckworth, Sr.
Sheriff, Wallowa County, Oregon

Somebody brought it up here
all the way from Wallowa,
up the old Washboard Road
before they straightened it,
logged it, mapped it and wrote
its name down in a book.
Somebody in a buckboard, up
through virgin tamarack,
damndest tree in the woods—
green spring and summer,
yellow in the fall, winter bare
as an elm tree on Main Street.
Hardly evergreen at all.

Somebody with cattle grazing
the breaks and draws down McAllister
and Tope and all the nameless
creeks and swales the loggers
later numbered, logged and left,
nameless and growing again.
Somebody brought it to water
their stock. White faces, splay-footed
from climbing around this country
like goats, cougar-shy till fall
when they'd appear, fat, and make
their own way down the Washboard
with calves or with the coming snow.
You'd see their tracks along the road,
and the drovers around a stump fire
down in the horse pasture
waiting to take them home.

Somebody muscled it down the ridge
and set it in the rock, laid
up stone to hold it in place,
and fenced the top to keep
the water clear. They built
the trough at Rockwall Spring
a good long time ago, and now
it waters mostly elk and deer,

but I see where somebody,
likely some old man, more
memory than sense, came up
and cleaned it out again this year.

❦

Jarold Ramsey

Jarold Ramsey was born in Bend, Oregon, and raised on a wheat and cattle ranch north of Madras. Ramsey was educated at the universities of Oregon and Washington. He has published numerous poems in such periodicals as the *Atlantic*, the *Nation*, *Christian Science Monitor*, *Iowa Review*, and *Prairie Schooner*. He has published four books of poetry: *The Space Between Us* (1970), *Love in an Earthquake* (1973), *Dermographia* (1983), and *Hand Shadows* (1989). Ramsey is an Ingram Merrill and National Endowment for the Arts fellow who has produced impressive essays and critical books on Shakespeare, modern poetry, and Native American literature. He is also the co-editor of *The Stories We Tell: An Anthology of Oregon Folk Literature* in this series.

The Kit

In the butt of my father's deer-rifle, a cannon-like 30-40 Krag left over from the Spanish-American and Boer Wars, there was a secret tunnel, concealed by the butt-plate of knurled iron. You loosened two screws and removed the plate—and thereby exposed a smooth-bored hole in the wood of the stock, about the diameter of a man's thumb and maybe five inches long. And thrust up tightly there, wrapped in a piece of rotten red flannel, was a Survival Kit! When I was alone in the house with that gun, I used to reach in there and gingerly withdraw the kit and spread it all out on my lap. The contents were: a hank of old fish-line; a snarl of leader and a No. 10 hook; ten waxed matches; a pearl-handled penknife with the tip of the blade broken off; three galvanized nails; the stub of a pencil and a blank sheet of paper folded up very small; one extra cartridge for the Krag; and a brittle stick of Wrigley's Doublemint Gum.

Oh, how I wanted to become a survivor! I'd close my eyes tight, forget my father, and there I was, stranded by an early blizzard at a lake in the High Cascades, my life in my eager hands. Hacking branches and bark for shelter with the pitiful knife, and hammering it together with the three nails, jigging for trout through the frozen lake, and snaring rabbits; tending my fire like a priest, hoarding those waterproof matches until I could learn to strike fire infallibly from stone; writing it all down day by day with the paper and pencil, how I was making it, like Commander Robert Falcon Scott—

Day 27. Very cold, snow this morning and again at dusk. Ate the rest of the rabbit for dinner, must make a new snare! No planes for over a week now, but so what? The lone cartridge was in the Krag's chamber, ready for a deer, or a blundering search party, or Despair the Bigfoot; as for the chewing gum, I nibbled a crumb every morning to sweeten my smoky tongue, and put the rest by to exercise my willpower. My rescuers could have it. And at night, the wind searching in the treetops overhead, my banked fire glowing before my shelter, I wrapped up in the red flannel rag and crawled into the tunnel in the gunstock. Oh, you haven't really slept tight, you haven't begun to survive, until you've slept inside your father's gun.

Judith Root

Judith Root was born and raised in Portland. She has received BA and MA degrees from the University of Oregon. Ms. Root has been a visiting writer at universities in Washington, Minnesota, Iowa, Missouri, North Carolina, Texas, California, and Idaho. Her poems and stories have appeared in the *New Republic, Poetry, American Poetry Review,* and *William and Mary Review. Weaving the Sheets* (1988) is her first collection of poems. "Although I have lived and traveled throughout the United States . . . most of the poems I have written are set in Oregon."

Free Will and the River

Every street in town
ends at the tanker
where the river used to be.
Without Alaskan oil the ship
rides high, blocks wind,
blocks light angling through clouds
that release rain so slowly
the drops seem to turn around,
rise and fill the clouds again.

Year after year the process
repeats itself until we count on it
like we count on the salmon
whose return to spawn
determines when men fish,
when they drink.

If I were part of this cycle,
I'd pour beer at Charlie's Place,
chalk birthdays (Dutch—Aug. 11,
Spook—Aug. 20) on the board
behind the bar and stuff my tips
into hard finger rolls,
the clink of coins backing up
the jukebox bass shuddering
in my apartment wall.

Someday, I'd tell myself,
the difference between tips
and rent will pay my way
downriver to the city where
windows in tall buildings
throw back sunlight
and someone, safe from nature's
whims, controls weather
with metal discs, pipes and fans.

Once in a glass tank there,
I watched a tiny albino
catfish bob like a hypnotist's
charm, skin translucent
in artificial light that lulled me
back to clouds gathering
at the river's mouth, racing
the tanker out to sea, playing tag
with all my expectations.

William Pitt Root

William Pitt Root was born in a Minnesota blizzard, and he was raised near the Everglades. He has spent most of his life living in the West or trying to get back—ranging from Oracle, Arizona, to Port Townsend, Washington. He has taught at Reed College, the University of Montana, Amherst College, SW Lousiana, and Michigan State University. He has also worked in the Poet-in-the-Schools programs in Oregon, Vermont, Texas, Mississippi, and Arizona. Of his half dozen books, *Faultdancing* (1986) is his most recent. Currently, William Pitt Root is director of creative writing at Hunter College in New York City.

Girl Near a Waterfall
After Suzuki Harunobu (1725?-1770 A.D.)

She is not thinking of being painted

This is why
my hands burn so, her spirit
trembling through this brush
my fingers become

Innocence
has no part in the capture
of innocence—what net
for birds
is made of air and song

She is the woman

I am the man

This is the canvas

The Penultimate Labor

To silence the frogs—
now there's a labor
to put a knock
in the knees of a hero.

For to silence the frogs
one first must truss up
        the frog-loving clouds
        and pack them into buckets
        big enough to keep them from spilling,

must force each frog-green reed
        back into the earth

and pluck each lilypad drifting
     like a green cloud
     out of its skyblue pond,

must rid the lakes and rivers
     of all water
     and all mud
snare each mosquito and dragonfly
suppress the moon

then halt earth in its turning
     lest sunrise or sunset
     inspire the last frog in the world
     in some forgotten bay
     to break cover with his homely
homily of love—his unquenchable croaking!

Lex Runciman

Lex Runciman was born and raised in Portland, Oregon. He is a graduate of Jesuit High School and Santa Clara University, and holds graduate degrees from the University of Montana and the University of Utah. He is currently on the faculty of Linfield College, McMinnville. Runciman is the author of two books of poetry: *Luck* (1981) and *Admirations* (1989). He is the editor of Arrowood Books and the co-editor of a collection of essays by Northwest writers, *Northwest Variety*. In 1989, *Admirations* won the Oregon Book Award for poetry.

Fathers and Infants

On 17 separate screens—
I counted them between rounds—Carl
"The Truth" Williams jabs and jabs, slips
the Holmes' right, shakes his head no,
that knockdown in the third an earlier lifetime,
seconds and minutes adding up as we watch,
bell and commercial simultaneous and loud.
They're pushing beer, and it pours colder there
than it ever is, cold, pure, and by the time the song
is half done, we're most of us looking down
the White Sale aisle or maybe watching the escalator stairs
rise and slide flat under the seamless floor.
My Jason's sound asleep, the Nuk still stuck
in his slack mouth. Rosy around the lips,

he's still breathing, buckled in his layback stroller.
Radios, stereo-chairs, the big projection TV
with its half-size, pale screen—this
is Home Entertainment in the anchor store.
Lingerie is one floor up, with dresses, the beauty parlor.
Next door is Appliances, four spendy rows
of energy efficient, no fingerprint freezers,
refrigerators, dishwashers—your Whirlpools and
Maytags—even trash compactors somebody wants.
Downstairs it's donuts, a snackbar in the economy basement.

This guy belonging to a plaid umbrella stroller,
his daughter in a blue dress and matching bonnet, says
"Look at Holmes. 35. He's fat."
Fat or not, right now his one fight's a measured ring,
Everlast right cocked like a hammer, and his cheek
swollen, like it's overstuffed with cotton.
The anonymous daughter in the plaid stroller
(I'd call her Rebecca on account of the bonnet),
she pats her soft knees, open palms up and down,
up and down, her legs kicking too—all of her
bouncing so insistent the stroller wheels
roll back and forth in the carpet dents.
The bell again, beer, or cars, something
MADE THE AMERICAN WAY. Soccer crowds riot. . .
Reagan. . . Nicaragua. . . News Digest. . .
Rebecca's rubbing her eyes with her fists.
Was it five years ago Boom Boom Mancini
killed that guy—Korean. I saw the round on tape—
nothing like this fight. Four days
I prayed for Benny Kid Paret, for all the good
it did him or my fifth grade parochial soul.
Listen, the kids are all asleep, except Rebecca
and she's just cooing with every punch.
Six of us here, counting the sales guy, each of us

thirsty, each of us sure we need a new truck.
Jason's out like a light. Then his mother's back,
a kiss for us both, packages under one arm.
So we're turning, ready to stroll towards Parking,
and I see Ali standing second row ringside,
grinning, waving a towel over his head.
He knows a sad fight when he sees one.
Ali, Ali, Ali, Ali, you can read his chanting !ips
and the crowd's with him. He's leading his own cheers.

Vern Rutsala

Vern Rutsala was born in Idaho and, aside from time spent in Europe and the Midwest, has lived in Oregon most of his life. He is the author of eight books, most recently *Selected Poems of Vern Rutsala* (1991). Among his awards are a Guggenheim Fellowship, two National Endowment for the Arts fellowships, a Masters Fellowship from the Oregon Arts Commission, the Carolyn Kizer Poetry Prize, and the Northwest Poets Prize. "However intentional your point of view the home truth . . . can't be denied." He teaches at Lewis & Clark College, Portland.

The World

I move back by shortcut
and dream. I fly above
it all, the dark stain
where swamps soak up
the lake's extravagance,
stubble hills, the valley's
green finger. This is the place
of pure invention, secret
as old wood
under a hundred coats
of paint. I invent
my own way back, invent
these wings, this
Piper Cub of tissue paper
I glide in, circling the valley
chasing my shadow across
the lake, twisting each layer
back through air.
The town scatters out
along the highway and I cut low
buzzing the school, signaling
my old teacher's chalky bones.
I bank away approaching town
along the old road
that rises from a low plain
where the land tastes bad,
where dust even slips
under rich men's doors.
I trace it like a route
on a map and it climbs

kept company by a creek
with a mouth full of boulders.
I finger wind for updrafts
slowing above the dump,
then sweep around the lake,
past Indian Village
and summer homes,
steering hard I top
the mill, my steering wheel
an old lard can lid
on the end of a stick,
my seat a log set back
in the woods, the shade cool
and safe in the arc cut
by the rope swing
thirty years ago.

Lela and Others

for Kirsten

Tonight you are away sleeping
in sea breeze, dreaming I think
of horses, and I remember
the other day when we
went through the old album,
remember talking as best I could
about that random evidence,
all circumstantial or less.
I knew most of the faces
but the occasions were lost—
Aunt Jenny shading her eyes
and standing on a rock
in the lake. Her dark ship
finally came in, I know, but why
was she there with black hair
and a trim figure I can't
recall?
            We smiled at the pictures
of my father that my mother
cut in half, scissors trimming
away an old girl friend.
Was it Lela? The mysterious Lela,

the album's Madame X,
who turned up so often
in the early pages and then
dropped from sight for good?
There is always a Lela—
but who is Lela?—looking
as helplessly young as my father
looked at twenty-five.
                    More
evident even than Lela
was that cousin I never liked
who squinted at us from page
after page as if the album
were a chronicle of his
life in the sun. He's gone too—
a bad death in California.
                              We looked
at all the relatives on all
those lost days standing
by their cars as if pretending
to leave or arrive, car doors open,
feet poised on running boards.
In the pictures of the farm
there was an odd formality—
no clowning, no bottles tipped
to mouths, no uncles' hats
on children—the men
looking away from the camera
with their large bare arms folded,
aloof and distant.

There was that one
we both liked: Your great grandfather
in a sepia field beside plow horses
and your grandfather in the middle
distance, the whole somehow
telling us of the brown mystery
of the lost, those powerful docile
Dobbins, those strong men gone
to dust.
            Then a turned page caught
my breath—your grandmother
scarcely older than you are now.

I remembered every feature
and how they grew hazy
those last days.
                    We went through them
all and I became garrulous with
the garrulous uncle, tough and wild
with that crazy cousin, cunning
with one aunt, tight-fisted with another,
and spoke sotto voce of that great aunt
who went bad in Butte, Montana—
the whispered family skeleton, no longer
even a whisper.
                    I felt them all converge
with their broken stories and the past
with Lela's slim hand gripped
my wrist an instant then let go.
And our past mingled in, offering up
my memory of your birth
and how some long tension, some
crimped deep fiber in me
relaxed for good when you arrived.
❦

Maxine Scates

Maxine Scates was born in Los Angeles, California. She has an MFA in writing from the University of Oregon, has taught for many years in Poets-in-the-Schools programs throughout Oregon, and also at Lane Community College in Eugene. She has been the poetry editor of *Northwest Review* and a MacDowell Colony Fellow. Scates's poems have appeared in *Prairie Schooner, American Poetry Review, Crazy Horse, Ironweed*, and *Northwest Review*. Her first book, *Toluca Street* (1989), won an Agnes Lynch Starrett Poetry Prize and was co-winner of the 1990 Hazel Hall Award for poetry from the Oregon Institute of Literary Arts.

Salem: Two Windows

I'm sitting at a friend's table
watching a young woman
hold on to the railing
as she climbs the front steps to her house.
Her small daughter follows behind

carrying a bag of groceries too big for her.
Now the woman turns,
many months pregnant,
and closes the door
leaving me to think about silence,
the line of tension pulling at me,
its denial.

Driving here
I wanted to name everything
as if naming would say it was not part of me—
the giant paper mill
and its constant yellow flame,
the smell of pulp that spills
over the collars of children in schools
called Sunrise and Mountain View,
Spring blurred by mud and sleet
in the milltowns that I passed.

I teach. I tell the kids
don't censor, let the self out you didn't
know you had. There's a boy in class
who remembers how light flickers through trees
when he stands knee deep in stream water fishing,
who says *I don't know if you'll understand*
but there are voices coming through me;
and born in 1968,
a child who listened around the kitchen table,
he speaks his uncle's tongues
on some airstrip in Vietnam.

The girl is on the street again tossing a ball—
it lands in her hands,
that's the simple law of gravity.
To my right a window facing a wall of bricks,
winter sunlight staining the glass
though I can't see its source,
and the bare branches of a bush
ready to blossom.

Perfume

I know the perfume
of a woman who held me as a child.
Tonight it blurs my hands,
the cloth of my blouse.

On occasion
she wore silk, pearls
trailing into a world
other than our blank street.
She was lonely on hot afternoons
lifting her fingers through my hair,
my head pillowed against
her generous flesh.

She's dead. And dying
waited to outlive what had gone wrong
her body breaking down,
air pressing in
the way wind tears clouds apart
flaying them like a whip to tissue.

I wrote to tell her
that I was seven, crying
the day their Buick pulled away
to a new neighborhood, to ask
if she remembered the red clown,
the cardboard squares of her son's
circus ring. I didn't say
I remembered her touch.
I'd return it now, hold her
through that scent of soap, camphor
clinging from the trees out in the yard.
We are temporal,
our bodies the sum of all we'll know.
But something happens
outside of ourselves.
That fragrance,
the layerings of air
I sank closer to her through,
yields now
like the door to her familiar house.

☙

Sandra Scofield

Sandra Scofield was born in Wichita Falls, Texas. She has lived in Ashland, Oregon, for twenty years. Ms. Scofield is the author of three novels: *Gringa* (1989), *Walking Dunes* (1992), and *Beyond Deserving*, which was a finalist for the 1991 National Book Award, and won a 1992 American Book Award.

Shallows

The girl in the water with her father. A fish.
The current is on the salmon's side. The father says
he could lose it in on the rocks. He talks on,
of red roe and sinkers, the uncertainty of success.

The girl sees the fish churning at the surface,
a flash of spray. She knows about whiskered fish and
guppies. She knows about eels and whales,
dolphins and the shark. Like the capitals of countries,
fish can be named. But this is her father's river,
cold on her ankles, and she, her father's daughter,
does not know fish. And if hooking a salmon,
and landing one, are not the same thing,
let this part go on.

In the steep canyon of the river, the sun
has already set. The fish sulks. The man
moves like a stalker, holding tension in the line,
and winds. The fish is there again, green and silvery,
alive, alive. The girl sees its eye.

The fish could get away, her father says,
could snap the line, could still win.
But they know how it will end. The fish
is only a fish. Her father swings it bankward
until its belly touches gravel. The girl moves
from behind her father, through the shallow water.
She sees the slick stones, the water, the sudden panic
of the fish. She hears the line pop. In her chest
fins flutter and slap against her love, the ribbed
frame of it. It is the fish.

The fish bucks in the instant of her motion.
Water gushes cold around her thighs. Suddenly,
she is astride. She finds a gill with her hand,
grasps purchase, and rides. Her father will reach them,

girl and fish, and it will be as if this never was.
But now she knows
The glisten of the bait cluster, the bounce of a weight
on the bottom. The play of light and shadow
on the canyon wall. The haplessness of prey.

A fish eats its own and struggles for the current.
A father knows shallow water from deep.
A girl knows a fish and cannot speak.
She wishes for a net, but not too much.

Peter Sears

Peter Sears was born in New York City and grew up in Westchester County and Long Island. He was an English major at Yale, a German linguist in Army intelligence, and a high school English teacher and coach. He has taught creative writing at Reed College and has been dean of students at Bard College. Peter Sears's poems have appeared in the *New York Times, Saturday Review, Atlantic Monthly,* and *Poetry Northwest.* He is the author of four chapbooks and *Tour: New & Selected Poems* (1987), a full collection. He is also the author of *Secret Writing* (1986), a poetry writing text for high school students.

Halloween of the Sudden Hand

We wait for dark, then, dressed commando,
move as one, like cilia. We work backyards
and sheds, hanging heads we made from junk
and painted loony in my cellar.
Once little kids scarf the candy,
and front porch lights go out, we stalk
the shadow side of the pointed-turret house,
where crazy lady lives with her retarded son.
We creep the long pole up to a lit window
on the second floor and tap our brown-paper
head with green marbles for eyes.
No luck. Gently we lift it over to
the next window, a dark window. A hand comes out,
pats our head and takes out one eye.
After that, anyone messing with the old lady
and her son answered to us.

The Lady Who Got Me to Say Solong Mom

Somewhere along the lettuce I nudge a lady who says
Amazing how you resemble my daughter! At the yogurt
we meet again. Would you say Solong Mom for an old
woman who misses her daughter? . . . Why not, for a lady,
daffy in loneliness, Solong Mom. I end up behind her
at the checkout line. The guy rings up my lettuce,
yogurt and yam and says $43.16 . . . What! You're nuts!
. . . Your mother says the checkbook's in your purse.

My mother! She's not my mother. Out the door I shoot,
scan the parking lot. She's loading up the backseat,
the frontseat. Hey, get back in and pay! She hips me,
we grapple. She's strong, then she's sad and weak,
standing there, staring around. The cart rolls off,
a bag dumps. We grab at each other. This is crazy.
She tilts her head, I tilt mine. Smack! She gets me
one good. I clout her. Get back in there and pay!

Whoopee! she yelps and gallops around me whoopeeing,
swinging her purse, and pops me on the nose. I tackle
her, grab a skinny leg, drag her across the lot like
an old hose, through the whooshing door, squiggling,
kicking. The manager hollers, What's going on? . . .
This lady just tried to rob me by pretending she's
my mother. That's right. Ask the checkout guy. $43.16
for my lettuce, yogurt and yam. . . . Is that true, ma'am?

I don't have a daughter, I don't have a son. Cats
and a parakeet named Oswald who's deaf. He loves
the three-way lightbulbs I lift from Woolworth's.
My old kook roommate babbles about being a princess.
It's enough to make you want to flush your head. This
girl is the daughter I really want. I want to ask her
back for dinner. I feel a lot better now. Thanks.

❦

Karyl Severson

Karyl Severson was born in Vancouver, Washington, and lives in Portland, Oregon. She has attended Lewis & Clark College, and holds a master's degree in English from Portland State University. Severson is a technical writer who has worked for a number of local corporations. She has been writing poetry intermitttently since high school.

Tejon Pass

Chased down I-5 toward Bakersfield
by the putrid stench of acre upon acre
of beef cattle stock yards, we wind up the small
desert mountains before Los Angeles.
If you look quickly you see the green and ivory
flash of cliff swallows patching their mud domes
impacted in crevices of interstate overpasses.
A thin pink film of heat and dust, hazed with
humidity and petrochemicals, colors everything
before us with the same mist of the photographer's lens
in a Doris Day movie.

Rounding the last long curve of highway at this
elevation blurred by eighty miles an hour, Tejon Pass
bursts on us like technicolor.
Brake lights jam as drivers seek the nearest
exit, wanting to see what they believe, caught in
the once-every-spring miracle of Tejon wild
flowers: long sweeps of indomitable orange
California poppies stitched onto yard after yard
of mountain lupine, purple like royalty against the
common white of yellow-eyed daisies and modest
blue flax.

This is the scene that lasts five minutes:
the long panoramic sweep of the camera
focuses and enlarges the destination
before us, where Tejon Pass breaks open on the
overheating fog of the Simi Valley below,
poppies blazing floral fire at our backs.

Floyd Skloot

Floyd Skloot was born in Brooklyn, New York, and has lived in Portland, Oregon, since 1984. His poetry, essays, and fiction have appeared in *Harper's, Shenandoah, Northwest Review,* the *American Scholar,* and *Gettysburg Review.* He is the author of a novel, *Pilgrim's Harbor,* and two collections of poems, *Kaleidoscope* (1986) and *Wild Light* (1989). "I see myself as an Oregon poet because this is the first place where I have truly felt at home."

You Asked for It

Show me film clips of William McKinley.
Show me Charles Atlas pulling six autos
down two miles of road. I would like to see
the vault at Fort Knox, chimps with hammertoes,
a man boning chickens while blindfolded.

Show me Ebeye Atoll, near Kwajalein,
worst slum in the Pacific. Show me red
squill being made into rat poison, pain
free surgery as performed in Shansi,
old friends playing poker underwater.

Then show me love as it was meant to be.
Show me an old man and his grown daughter
walking alone near a cranberry bog,
not the Robot Man and his Robot Dog.

Susan Spady

Susan Spady was born in Eugene and grew up in Bandon. Except for two years in Chicago and seven in Alaska, she has lived her life thus far in Oregon. Spady has worked sporadically as a teacher, tutor, cook, researcher, and more consistently as a writer and organic gardener. She earned an MFA from the University of Oregon and has published poems in *Poetry Northwest, CALYX, Northwest Review,* and *Calapooya Collage.* "I write out of a fascination with weather and growing things, and often out of the isolation of growing up in a small town, my house surrounded by overgrowth and swamp."

Underpants

showed when girls climbed the monkey
bars, so some girls didn't. Some who did
would kick a boy in the mouth if he got smart.
Others showed off their pink and lace,

wiggled high overhead to boys yelling
London, France. Earthbound, I sucked in
my pot belly and tried to stand in some regal way
so a book on my head, when I walked,

wouldn't fall—Daddy said. Mine
were never panties, were plain
as Oxfords correcting my feet. By junior high

those fancy-pants climbers were cheerleaders
flirting from under their minis, tossing
smiles at the crowd through pearled lips.
They did splits: hello,

from between our legs! And my book
slid off frontways now, sweaters revealing
bras I made only a dent in
and slouched to hide. I didn't think much

about underpants. I was sealed shut,
spoke sarcastic nothings to boys, prayed
every night for God to make me
sinless and new. While pompoms exploded

like fireworks from cheerleaders' fingers, I sat
in the bleachers distorting my face
on my saxophone, wearing the Pep Band's sickly
gold, my disdain for those high-kickers—

but it's all right. Because first
I stopped going to Sunday School
and then wearing underpants—opened my stride
to winds that long full skirts

gathered in. I visited London and France,
climbed stairways with risers of blue sky
over men always looking
but never upward.

Primus St. John

Primus St. John was born in New York City. He teaches creative writing and African, Caribbean, and African-American literature at Portland State University. His poems have appeared in magazines and anthologies, and he is the author of three collections of poetry: *Skins on the Earth* (1976), *Love Is Not a Consolation: It Is a Light* (1982), and *Dreamer* (1990). St. John has won a Discovery Award and two National Endowment for the Arts fellowships, and was a co-winner of the Oregon Book Award for poetry in 1990. He also edited a poetry anthology for schools, *Zero Makes Me Hungry* (1976).

Pearle's Poem

She sits in the marketplace
Issuing, like a bright star.
The origin of this beauty
Is her print dress,
So wild and deeply moving
It is a fable
By which to live,
To blend into
As if it were a mosaic of water
Coursing through Guyana
To the unreadable sea.
It has the lightning of her heart,
The thundering battles
Of her guilt and pain,
The dense jungles of her unrequited sorrow
Where the bright birds of her hope
Calypso into their ectasy.

In front of her
Is her biblical bondage
Of yams, breadfruit,
Mangoes and pears,
Each stacked like a separate prayer,
A redeeming angel,
And the triumphant disposition
Of a true saint.
Women like her
Do not cry or laugh in public,
They condense
The antithetical flaws of the world

Into an awakened responsibility of color.
They are not imperialist
With an urgent knowledge;
They are people who doze in impudent hats
Who have remained
The intricately unravelled villagers
Of the themes of rain and sun
And draught
Part earth, part wind
And like my dying mother,
Part fire.

Kim Stafford

Kim Stafford grew up in Oregon, Iowa, Indiana, California, and Alaska. He teaches at Lewis & Clark College and is director of the Northwest Writing Institute. He has received fellowships from the National Endowment for the Arts and his book, *Having Everything Right,* won a Western States Citation for Excellence. He is the author of the poetry collections *A Gypsy's History of the World* (1976), *The Granary* (1982), and *Places and Stories* (1987). He has co-authored *Braided Apart* (1976) with his father, William Stafford. Kim Stafford holds a PhD in medieval literature from the University of Oregon. His most recent book is *Lochsa Road* (1992).

A Sermon on Eve

"You know Eve's mother was a man,"
he said, "and she one bone too many
in his side when he lay numb
and lazy in the summer grass alone?
Down fell the sun on that only
naked man, and stirred within him
then; he slept, and she rose
lovely from the bone, parted
from him for a bride, fair,
full-grown, filled with bewilderment
to be conceived and shaped and so
delivered into flesh. And there
old Adam lay still dreaming on,
stretched foolish, awkward at her feet,

helpless in sleep and solitude, bare
as stone but warm and breathing
like a wave. Sisters and brothers,
when his eyes bloomed wide, and he
looked up for her dark form
against the sun, the plain radiance
of light and shape, of hair
where it glimmered, caused
his mouth to open as he lay
bound within her swaying shadow
of the grass. She looked upon him,
saw the careless sprawl of his limbs
gather, afraid and separate, chilled
by her departure from within
his body's chamber. Her heart was
clenched against returning there—
the air was warm; she stirred, no
longer rooted to him, turned away
yet lingered by. My children, this
is the beginning—how each created thing
knows itself, a single spinning in delight
that then is woven to the world again
and dwells within the garden. Wind
embraced the willow there, and Eve's hair
billowed, and her arms were lifted
in a flame of praise. Old Adam, husk
from which she came, lay stilled
by wonder in the grass, withered
like us all when God the midwife's
sudden hands draw forth and shape
for other purposes the kindled spirit
from our frame that labors at its loss
but then lies quiet and content. Good
people, Eve bowed and gave him breath
again. Peace to you all. Amen."

The Rocking Chair

In the earthquake the rocking chair,
patient so long, begins to move.

In the earthquake, people have no time
for the rocking chair, their shadows
scuttling across the floor, while
the rocking chair takes it easy,
leans back, lets it happen:

the comb thrown down, the dishes
chattering, the mirror flickering
through the air, and birds
leaving the world for good.
But the rocking chair stays
in touch, thoughtful calm—
a little squeak at the joints
like every afternoon.

When the yard yawns wide, the house
lurching from its crumbling foundation,
and everyone like moles stumbling
suddenly into the daylight, no one
notices the sun crossing the floor
faster than most days,
except the rocking chair
on its smiling feet
dancing alone
in a corner.

Clem Starck

Clemens Starck says, ". . . place, or locality, is as important to me as a poet as accurate physical dimensions are to a carpenter. Where the narrator of a poem is located seems to me of essential interest." Starck was born in Rochester, New York. Since dropping out of Princeton, he has been a ranch hand in eastern Oregon, a merchant seaman, and a student of Chinese. For twenty years he has worked as a journeyman carpenter. His poems have appeared in many magazines and anthologies, and a collection of his work, *Journeyman's Wages*, will be published by Story Line Press in 1994.

Slab on Grade

At dawn the concrete trucks
are already there: revving their engines,
rumbling and throbbing, one by one
maneuvering into position.
Enormous insects,
on command
they ooze from their huge revolving abdomens
a thick gray slime.

Insects attending to insects,
the crew fusses over them, nursing wet concrete
into the forms.

Someone to handle the chute,
a couple laborers mucking, one pulling mesh, and two
finishers working the screed rod—
this is called "pouring
slab on grade."

What could be flatter or more nondescript
than a concrete slab?
For years people will walk on it,
hardly considering that it was put there
on purpose,
on a Thursday in August
by men on their knees.

Me and Maloney

Job's nearly over,
me and Maloney all that's left of the crew.
Sunk in the hillside,
hundreds of tons of reinforced concrete
formed in the shape of a drum
ninety-two feet in diameter, eighteen feet deep—
it could be a kiva, or a hat box, or look from the air
like a missile silo.

It could be a storage tank for toxic waste.
It could be a vault to house
the national treasure.

In any case, it's finished,
ready for backfill. Now it's the earth's.

And I'm left with Maloney,
who likes to drink beer after work
and tell stories.
Construction stories. Ex-wife stories. Stories
like how he clubs possums to death with a two-by-four
when he finds them
prowling in back of his warehouse at night.

He laughs, telling the stories.

Maloney quit drinking once.
After a year and nine months he decided he'd rather
die of alcohol
than boredom.

I know what he means. I work
for Maloney Construction.
When it rains we work in the rain. When it snows
we work in the snow.
I am Maloney's right-hand man:
when he laughs I laugh too.

❧

Lisa M. Steinman

Lisa Steinman was born in Connecticut, and has taught at Reed College for the past seventeen years. She is the author of three books of poetry, *Lost Poems* (1976), *All That Comes to Light* (1984), and *A Book of Other Days* (1993), and a book of literary scholarship, *Made in America*. She has been a fellow of the National Endowment for the Arts, Oregon Arts Commission, National Endowment for the Humanities, and the Rockefeller Foundation. Her poems have appeared in many magazines. "I am trying to write a poetry that is inclusive of everything from people's speech to the kitchen sink."

A Pigeon Poem

We kept
carrier pigeons
(passenger pigeons
being extinct)
and so that they
would not fly
away
forever
their wings were clipped.
When,
occasionally,
we would have or want
to send a message
to those who
from over the hill
could not see our house,
we would strap a note
to the bird's side
and push it off
down the road
pudgy feet
walking the miles
to town and friends.
Sometimes,
growing impatient for a sign
we would drive
the route ourselves,
often passing the pigeon
trudging faithfully
clasping its message
as we sped
by.

Kaz Sussman

Kaz Sussman is a carpenter by trade, an anarchist by nature, and an expatriate New Yorker by circumstance. He got into poetry, he says, "like everyone else, because that's where the big bucks are!! My interests, in particular, are in poetry that is unfiltered by the pale gauze of overintellectualization. My work, as a writer and artist, has seen some small success in a variety of formats."

El Conjunto Fabuloso

for Tanya on her birth

If a supreme being sits
he sits not in judgment
but in jam:
congas steady, timbales tight,
blind angels blowin' blues harps,
and strumpets sizzlin' on trumpets.
Sweet beat, upbeat, heartbeat, drumbeat,
marimba, jimbay, kalimba, clave,
The roll of their rhythm is the pulse
of life, of movement and matter,
beating in a newborn heart.

And if a supreme being sits
he sits in session
stretching time on skins:
shaping space with dance.
Tumba, conga, quinto, salsa, samba.
The beat carries the breeze
and stirs the seasons forward.
Tim timtim bale,
bongos, bass, and casaba.
Horns, like young hawks,
hungering for solo flight.
O molimo howling in the night.

And if a supreme being sits
he sits in,
as just another member of the band
with a beat day gig.

But when they play, oh ja,
this fabulous band, este conjuncto fabuloso,
with their hands of lava and ice,

of time recalled, of coral and light.
Skin to skin to skin me quinto
alive again, conga, tumba.
Keyboards, like ivory mauls,
cutting chords to afro-cuban cantos,
fingering covens of song
into cauldrons of syncopation.
Traps set and snares strung
beneath a river of sticks..
The beat calling all to bear witness
to the primal dance of secret dreams.

And if a supreme being sits
surely he sits tapping time between tunes.
Looking down at new arrivals
he smiles and croons
"hey baby,
        let's wail."
                ❦

William Sweet

William T. Sweet was born south of the Columbia River, east of Astoria and west of
Portland. His growing up years were spent following the timber as it was logged from
various parts of western Oregon. He received a BA and an MFA in creative writing from
the University of Oregon; and in the past was managing editor of the *Northwest Review*,
editor of the defunct *Pacific Quarterly,* and an instructor at Linn Benton Community
College. Sweet's poems have been published in the U.S., Australia, and the Philippines
in magazines such as *Northwest Review, Tweed, Human Voice Quarterly,* and *Alkahest*.
He currently teaches at Lane Community College in Eugene.

Field Burning
> *I think our story should not end—*
> *or go on in the dark with nobody listening.*
> —William Stafford

The furrow rolled black from the plow
and when it was safely rimmed
men in white T-shirts and blue jeans
touched it off with torches
to burn the blight.

At noon
I cried through billows

of rye smoke
and watched while the house melted
into waves of heat.

Yet, it was there at supper
with whole spuds,
corn on the cob,
butter melting along the edge
of a blue willow plate.

That night I got out of bed,
walked to the center of the field
and watched a star fall
for hours until it was eclipsed by the dawn.

Mark Thalman

Mark Thalman was born in Eugene, Oregon, and received his MFA in creative writing from the University of Oregon. He has been a teacher for Chemeketa Community College's Prison Program in Salem, Oregon, and is currently a language arts teacher for a Hillsboro junior high school. Some of his poems have appeared in *Greenfield Review, Spectrum, Poetry Now, Rocky Mountain Review,* and *Pearl.* "While many poets are from out of state and have adopted Oregon as their home, I am one of a few native born poets . . . . I write about a landscape and attitudes of a people I have known all my life."

Catching the Limit

I troll along the south shore,
where other fishermen say
the angling is no good: too shallow,
too many weeds. With their fish finders,
they cluster off Princess Creek,
but I don't see them catching anything.

The lake lies flat mirroring sky.
An osprey rides the currents,
until he spies a trout,
folds his wings and drops
like a swift mountain stream
falling over the edge of a cliff,
plunging talons first
into his own reflection . . .

Emerging in a fury of spray,
wings widespread, using them as oars,
the bird strokes against the surface,
flapping steadily to reach the air again,
nosing his wriggling prey into the wind.

I point the bow at the spot
where the osprey caught the rainbow.
More times than not, that is the place
my pole starts to bend.

Gail Tremblay

Gail Tremblay (Onondaga, MicMac, and French Canadian) was born in Buffalo, New York, in 1945. She holds a BA from the University of New Hampshire and an MFA from the University of Oregon. Besides writing poetry, she is also a fiber mixed media sculptor who works with weaving, metal, and wood. Tremblay's work has appeared in *CALYX, Denver Quarterly, Maize,* and *Northwest Review.* She is also the author of three collections of poetry, most recently *Indian Singing in 20th Century America* (1990). Gail Tremblay is on the faculty at Evergreen State College in Olympia, Washington.

Strategies to Survive Living in White Towns

During those days when sorrow is so deep
it takes too much energy to cry, one rocks
silence inside a body cavity where nothing
seems empty of grief. In a world where kindness
seems powerless against cruelty, torturers
can inhabit any home on your block, and the lives
of children can be disfigured by adults who forget
that love is not about bending others to do
unspeakable tasks to feed an unbearable need
to know power. On days when friends, knocking
on the door, shiver in terror, clothes torn
because someone has jumped out of the alley
and grabbed and grabbed and grabbed with greedy
hands at a body that is not theirs, it becomes
an endless struggle to find the words to comfort
where nothing is comfortable. One wonders

how sunrises and flowers usher in new days
and seasons gracing experience again while men
plot to exploit this graceful planet that makes
life possible. The contradictions overwhelm
the sense of what is natural, what is familiar
inside the sacred circle where magic is a way
of finding harmony and balance, and power
is the will to give and serve, to support life
in all its mystery. It is true, that even
among the people, confusion and selfishness
were always a possibility: tragedy could always
make someone envy those that did not suffer as much
until the beaten longed to take things they did not
have. But a whole culture that sings about scarcity,
embraces hunger, and grows so insatiable thousands
forget to share the wild fruits that the dirt
in its profound fertility provides to feed
the multitudes, and instead destroy these things
that make survival real, such confusion maims
and replicates the dulling anguish that kills
feeling. In such a world tears are worth
the struggle to keep care alive, and giving
is the only way to establish new patterns that will
tell the heart that hurt is not inevitable.

＊

George Venn

Born in Tacoma, Washington, in 1943 into a family of Protestant fundamentalists, George Venn was taught early to love words, sweat, fishing, and song. At Spirit Lake High School in Idaho, he was a four-year letterman, student body president, and a member of the National Honor Society. He holds BA and MFA degrees from the College of Idaho and the University of Montana, and has lived, studied, and taught in Ecuador, Spain, England, and China. In 1970, Venn was appointed director of the creative writing program at Eastern Oregon State College, La Grande. From 1970 to 1987, he served as advisory editor to *Oregon East*, one of the few nationally recognized student literary magazines in the Northwest. Poet, scholar, essayist, teacher, folklorist, translator, editor, conservationist, and critic, his writing has appeared in many of the leading publications in the region—where the particular forever reveals the universal. Author of three books, most recently *Marking the Magic Circle* (1987), Venn's work has been recognized with an Oregon Book Award and a Pushcart Prize for Poetry.

Forgive Us . . .

Fifty years of your butchering art
are here, Grandfather. I hear the crash
of your falling ax into alder, the whisk
of your keen knife on the blue steel
while lambs and wethers bleat in the barn.

They knew your one quick stroke across
their throats would make their ends
the best you could create. I still don't
like the blood, Grandfather, but I know
now the need for meat.

"Nothing should suffer," you said,
and sought out old dying queens in hives
and pinched their heads. Mensik's calf—
you told us not to watch; bad dreams
would come, you said, so we walked out

and watched you anyway through a crack
in the wall. One deadly swing—no more—
from the spiking maul buckled the steer
instantly to its knees on the hay.
We knew your power then, and ran away.

And now this God, Grandfather, this God
whose songs you sang, whose church
your worship built, whose book you read,
whose name you never said in vain—
He's got you here in His shepherd's barn.

Oh, he's a shoddy butcher, Grandfather.
He's making you suffer his rusty dull
deathknife for years, crippling your legs,
then cutting off your speech to tremble,
then tying you up in a manured bed.

He won't bring you down with any grace
or skill or swift humane strike of steel.
Day after day, you sit in His hallway
in your wheelchair and nurses walk by
like angels and shout half your name.

Ah, this God of yours, Grandfather, this
God has not learned even the most simple
lesson from the country of your hands.

You should have taught Him how to hone
His knife, that the slaughtering of rams
is the work of those brave enough to love
a fast deft end.

Conjuring a Basque Ghost

for Jean Ospital

You died as I could—
snag on the mind. I've fallen enough
timber to know how easy it is not to hear
that slight deadly crack in the top.
I know you didn't look up. The chainsaw roared
in your ears as you stood waiting like
a lamb while the widowmaker fell.

Three white horses graze your pasture now,
Jean Ospital. Your gates are locked, wife gone
to town, boys back in school two weeks after
the funeral. All your sheep are gone in steel
trucks. At your auction, everything sold high.
The realtor is out there now nailing up *For Sale*.

Do you want me to show how you loved your dogs
or drank the brown goat's milk? Should I say we
spoke in Espanol that day going down to buy
those five black fleeces still waiting here?
Should I say the ache in your eyes as you saw
the pasture dying in the heat, your ewes

grown thin? Should I put here your jeans
reeked with lanolin and sweat? Should I buy
your farm? I had no such money when the empty
trucks rolled in. What do you want from me?

Watching my wife spin the wool your dead hands
sheared, I make the little I know into this prayer
for you, Jean Ospital: *Pyrenees, receive
this man. I send him home. Inside the mountain
that watched him being born, cover him
with wool and let him dream.*

This is all I can say for you. *Adios, pastor.*
Leave me now. I have wood to cut today.

D.M. Wallace

D.M. Wallace was born in Twin Falls, Idaho, and moved to Oregon when she was twenty to attend the University of Oregon, where she received a BA in film. Her father's family, the Wallaces, were original settlers of the Tillamook area in Oregon. She is married to Rodger Moody, editor of *Silverfish Review*. Some of her poems have appeared in *Pointed Circle, Sow's Ear,* the *Northwest Magazine* section of the *Sunday Oregonian,* and *Slackwater Review*.

The Jewel

for Julian

As silent as a fire
just beginning, soft brown
moles come to my skin,
scatter themselves over
my belly, my arms, my neck.
One arose close to my navel,
small and starlike in the
crown of my first pregnancy.
And the second time, another,
lighter, but close beside
like the next bead
on a string.

As silent as the house where
children sleep in their own beds
I sit at the kitchen table
counting my blessings, making
fun of my coupon box, making
eyes at my husband who touches
my new mole with his fingertip
and talks about the brightness,
the spring moon waxing.

As silent as conception itself
my soul grew open to children,
my own willingness to change
and become the mother light,
the full moon rising slowly
and balloonlike from the horizon
of myself, my own needs falling
away to reveal whole, new planets
of desire like the new moles that
bejewel my belly, my children
with their mark on me forever.

Doyle Wesley Walls

Doyle Wesley Walls teaches creative writing and literature at Pacific University in Forest Grove, Oregon. He came here from Texas. Walls has written criticism for *Modern Drama, American Literature,* and *Contemporary Literary Criticism* and produced cartoons for *Studies in Literary Humor, Sands, Thalia,* and the *Chaouteau Review.* His poems have appeared in *Poet and Critic, Puerto Del Sol, New York Quarterly, Abraxas,* and the *Minnesota Review.* He has been nominated three times for a Pushcart Prize and once for a General Electric Foundation Award for Younger Writers.

Clean Dirt

Shoveling mud tarp after tarp,
running past thirty rows of cotton
against the West Texas wind,
clutching a shovel and a bent iron bar
from which a wet tarp flaps
like a farmer's flag,
leaving a trail of dark round mudballs
in the dusty road and a few tiny frogs
who squirt to the nearest bar ditch.

The new tarp secured I look
back up the ditch to see my father
bending to pick up even more tubes
and then adding them to the bulk
in his outstretched arms.
He strides out of the wide ditch
like Poseidon rising from the sea,
water, mud, and moss dripping from
his irrigation boots and the tubes.
"If these were all the tubes I could carry,"
 he says to me, "could I carry one more?"
"I think you could," I say, although
I know the catch. He laughs
and slings the tubes across the ditch
two at a time into their proper rows,
spinning on the last one to return
and pull last night's final tarp.
The water obeys his command.

Pump, set; cross row; pump, set; cross row—
until thirty silver streams are set in motion.
Scooping handfuls of dark-green moss
and faded floating stalks from the water,

ripping careless weeds and volunteer maize
from the darkening ditch,
then baptizing the dried mud from our arms
over the side of the last tarp.
Listening to the earth drink water
while the dry leaves of the cotton plants
rattle in the breeze,
while the sun and the moon both hover
 in the same sky.
"Clean dirt," my father says
as he turns and smiles.
Then I notice the whiteness of his teeth
and how white are the whites of his eyes.

Homework

We ask, "Where's Central America?"
Our son says, "It's in my room,"
and continues to cut his meat.
He's right: Central America is hanging
on his wall. It's his map. He worked on it
all last week in his kindergarten class.

We don't press him on the particulars—
Where is Honduras? Where is El Salvador?
Where is Nicaragua?—because
we're normal Americans, that is to say,
stupid about geography, well not
absolutely stupid, though perhaps
dangerously stupid, but stupid enough anyway
for our stupidity to make a big difference.
We are sure that Central America is
in our backyard.

We're having a fourth for dinner, President
Reagan, who's almost at the table
with us via televison. Mr. Reagan
is saying that Central America should be located
in our back pocket.

We ask our son to eat more potatoes, carrots,
and bread, more body-building foods.
We ask, "Where's Central America?"
Our son repeats, "It's in my room."
Our son will be eighteen in thirteen years.

Ingrid Wendt

Born in Aurora, Illinois, Ingrid Wendt came to Oregon in 1966 to attend graduate school. She has taught for twenty years at colleges and universities as well as in Poet-in-the-Schools residencies in hundreds of elementary, middle, and secondary school classrooms. Her book, *Starting with Little Things: A Guide to Teaching Poetry in the Classroom* (1983), has been adopted by teachers and school districts nationwide, and is now in its second printing. Widely published in periodicals and anthologies, Wendt was the 1982 winner of the D.H. Lawrence Award. Her second book of poems, *Singing the Mozart Requiem* (1987), received the 1988 Oregon Book Award for poetry from the Oregon Institute of Literary Arts. She has co-edited the anthology/textbook *In Her Own Image: Women Working in the Arts* (1980), and serves as an associate editor of *CALYX*.

Mushroom Picking, I Talk with a Bear

"Whenever I feel afraid, I hold my head erect,
and whistle a happy tune, and no one will suspect
I'm afraid."
      The King and I, Oscar Hammerstein

I could of course moralize, say forgetting to sing
was what did it. Or haste, one last chance:
chanterelles blunt tongues dissolving luminous
into the too-early dusk, unrecognizable
constellations ready to wink and go out. Oh,

I knew what I was after, climbing alone on the overgrown
logging road, wading the inarticulate grass
snarled brown. And maybe the bear did, too: that
unmistakable scat I stepped around
fresh with the orchard just that morning I'd been

told was raided, telling me if I wanted to keep
going I'd have to belt out a human announcement,
keep it up through clouds closing darker than moss
around me, thick glisten of needles, the edges
of leaves and air between blurring. And yes,

the bear would have been there anyway, I might
never have known; focusing not on the words
I was singing, no Anna lost in Siam, and I wasn't
afraid, though maybe I should have been,

thinking instead of someone I should have

long before this forgotten, last words
that never were spoken: hidden
months, years at a time, deep as mycelium
feeding on decay this possbile danger I couldn't
identify. No field guide for it. Nothing to see.

No excuse, that day in the Coast Range forgetting
to sing, at last the mushrooms I hunted for opening
out of the gloom: golden
wings, victory
marking the edge of the road. No

mistaking that low unambiguous roar,
my surprise at how close
anything big as that could not be heard coming
"Bear," I said, loud as I could. "I hear you.
Don't worry. I'm here. You're there. That's fine."

Bear language I made up on the spot,
trusting what mattered was not
what I said but that I was saying it, no
question at all of running away from it,
silent as humus my fingers

picking double time more than I'd come for:
chanterelles, fir needles, soil
still in the making; wordless
resolve I took with the dinner
down the hill. The basis for

moral decision a moment's experience shifts.
Behind me, a bear
too real to be a metaphor,
somewhere ahead, the letter
I didn't yet know I would write.

❦

Miles Wilson

Miles Wilson was born in South Dakota. In the years he lived in Oregon before moving to San Marcos, Texas, he lived in a number of towns and taught at Central Oregon Community College, worked in fire management, and was a partner in a small logging company. He has won the University of Iowa's John Simmons Short Fiction Award. His first collection of poetry was *Going the Distance* (1990). He was a 1991 National Endowment for the Arts fellow.

For San Dwayne Francisco
Missing in Action, North Vietnam

You must have looked as big as America, looming
beneath your chute above their fields,
enlarging in the fertile air
coming down, the land blooming with craters, colors
as though your whole life had been
black and white.

I heard years later from a high school friend:
your wingman saw the chute seed;
he had ground contact.
Then the decay of silence.

In the end the names:
American, pilot, criminal.
Drought, flood, plague.
Names that twisted their lives,
blackened their tongues.
How could they believe your own—
blind dates, bartenders, colonels never did—
detect in bland, professional hands
seasons of nail and knuckle,
a farmer's knowing how
grace and grief come
from the sky?

How could they know you
unintentional as frost? A pilot by accident
of reflex, harrowing with rocket pods and cannon,
the only tools in all those acres of air.

May crops grow where you are
in that extravagant country, lavish
as Benton County wheat is plain,
your right life
leaching shrapnel from the earth.

John Witte

John Witte was born in Albany, New York, and attended Colby College as an undergraduate, and the University of Oregon's MFA program. His poems have appeared in the *New Yorker*, the *Paris Review*, *American Poetry Review*, and *Antaeus*. His collection, *Loving the Days* (1978), was published by Wesleyan University Press. Witte has received fellowships from the National Endowment for the Arts, the Oregon Arts Commission, and the Provincetown Fine Arts Work Center. He has also been the editor of *Northwest Review* in Eugene for fourteen years.

Breast Poem

Hungry, your mother gone
for the afternoon, you point to my chest,
the breast recognizable under the hair, the nipple
asleep. This is how you strain toward her, and she lifts
her blouse, and you woozily
open your lips.

We read a book.
You understand from my voice
that there is sadness. Someone is lost in the story,
but it will be ok.

During the labor I felt you
letting go at last, slipping through the bone gates into time.

You cry, and I open my shirt. I hold you
nuzzling asleep, your lips moving in willing self-deception
beside this rough chest, this poor
parody of a breast.

❧

Blue School

A child might have dreamed this
blue school on its hill overlooking the river,
its doors open, waiting for him to get dressed, and eat breakfast,
the bittersweet certainty it is there,
and he is going.

Home is a bend in the river, a place to stretch
a boom across and catch the timber
felled upstream, sluiced down flumes and chuted into the current
at spring freshet.

But the mill is down.
Stacked raw lumber walls the road. A skeleton crew
oils the machinery, revolving the huge, toothed wheel. The tavern
is full, but quiet.

If this were antiquity,
it might have seemed that a goddess,
a spirit in the river or woods, in love with
someone there, had blessed and protected the town. Then angered,
betrayed, she turned her face, like the sun
away from them.

The school gleams spiritual blue,
the children drowsy in the steam heat,
reading at their carved desks, or singing
to the piano, or sprinting over the playground, glad to be away
from the rotting house, the shouting and tears.
Maybe their parents wanted them to go
to school in the sky.

The eye is most sensitive to blue and green,
and our memory cherishes anything
blue with the clarity
of a dream. I climbed, a baby,
out of my crib, over the dresser to the casement window,
and looked out: a nest in the tree, and four blue eggs I leaned
against the glass and fell
into the warm air.

I was not in the room
when my mother came for me. I was not
dead where they found me in the bushes below, but asleep,
and dreaming, itself a weightlessness,
a kind of flight.

Vincent Wixon

Vincent Wixon was born and raised on a dairy and grain farm in southwestern Minnesota. He has lived in Ashland and taught English at Crater High School since 1975. In 1988, he was Oregon Teacher of the Year. Wixon has published poetry in a number of magazines and journals, including *Portland Review, Northwest Magazine, Poetry Now, Oregon English Journal, Fireweed,* and *Calapooya Collage,* and is co-producer of two video documentary portraits of the late Oregon poet William Stafford.

Rain

1.

Finally
as I lay reading
the drops began to sound
on the roof
slowly then steadily
The porch light showed
the deck wet
the drops almost white
like snow

2.

This morning
the drops hanging on branches
an inch of water
in the overturned lid of the garbage can
a puddle waiting at the drain by the garage
a robin hunch-shouldered in the leafless birch

3.

Farther up the rain
becomes half snow half water
and at one precise point
completely flakes
piling up deeper
around the trees

4.

In late spring the snow
melts feeding the roots
trickling through the soil
moving down slopes
joining with other water .
running rivulets, streams,
ending in a reservoir
to water a parched town below

5.

When the water doesn't come
when the heavens stay clear
when the ground is dry and hard in December
and the maple leaves still blow
along the drive
people begin to fear—
not the panic they feel in September
when there's been no rain since May
and the hills are brown
when smoke drifts into the valley
huge, old prop planes fly over
orange retardant stains
on their bellies—
but a fear that at last
after years of predictions
and articles in the papers
there truly will not be enough water
not just to wash the cars
and water the lawns
but not enough to drink
and they begin to think
maybe, after all, the world
really does change
there really was an ice age
then maybe a desert age
may come to this valley
what happened to the Anasazi
may happen to them
their grain may be perfectly
preserved and found by some
hiker six-hundred years from now

🌾

Elizabeth Woody

Elizabeth Woody (Wasco/Navajo) majored in creative writing at the Institute of American Indian Arts in Santa Fe, New Mexico. Some of her poems have appeared in *Greenfield Review*, *Fireweed*, the *Portland Review*, *Tyuoni*, *Akwewon*, *Songs from This Earth on Turtle's Back*, and *The Clouds Threw This Light*. Her first collection of poetry, *Hand into Stone* (1988), won an American Book Award.

A Warrior and the Glass Prisoners
I. *The Glass Girl—a Dream*

I like what the soldiers give
if it shines or I see my face in it.

> *Hiding in the grass.*
> *I haven't a name. My family is dead.*
> *Saddened, I have forgotten it is from this.*
> *Encircled, the soldier calls me.*
> *He named me Mona Glass, "Mona Glass,*
> *you and the women come back!*
> *We won't shoot. It will be better*
> *to come back, than running."*

He is a good man. He has many nice things.
He doesn't think of some far away woman
when he touches me.
Maybe I am his wife.
He told me all the men
are put in cages,
somewhere, singing of death.

> *The women say if we can get away we can find*
> *another land. Nothing can be done if we stay.*
> *Waiting for gifts and food from these Blue Men.*
> *Hearing the children cry and be sent off.*
> *Digging in the dirt.*
> *Dead is dead, without the spirit.*
> *I know this is against me. I do not dig in the dirt.*
> *I have spirit and my beauty and my presents.*
> *I think nothing can be done without the men.*

I stand and wave my arms toward him.
The women run and the grass flattens from our fall.
I hold together the front of my dress
and all the mirrors I have sewn on,
sparkle and break.

II. *Don't Touch Me When I Sleep*

I called her "Woman" in Cheyenne.
She was Vietnamese and young, very young.
She kept my hooch clean and cooked for me.
She rubbed my shoulders.
My name is John Hawk.
I drank and talked to her in my language.
> *She looked so familiar*
> *In the sweaty night.*

She made my hooch out of nothing, it seemed.
She made it look like a sweatlodge.
I sweated enough, but I am not clean yet.
I have killed so many people.
I killed a Grandmother because my C.O. said to,

"Kill her! Shoot or get shot in the back, Hawk!"
She could have a bomb in her bundle.
I shot her. I trembled so much, I hoped to miss.
She had little army tins in her sack,
cans she begged from good soldier boys,
like me. My woman didn't cry.
> *What is the battle, anyway? Am I in it now?*
> *It's dark. Her legs are smooth and feel good.*

I think about the Indian girls back home
who are afraid of me.
In their bones I know they remember.
One time I came back and she was gone.
Every girl I turned around looked like my younger sister.
I got drunk and shot up the little hooch.
I left it for good, all tore up.
> *I talk Vietnamese to the women.*
> *I am sure they remember 'Nam*
> *and that I killed their Grandmothers.*

I wear fatigues when I Traditional Dance
at the Veteran's Pow Wow.
My duffle bag is packed with everything I own.
I am waiting for someone to stop
and tell me to go home.

Victoria Wyttenberg

Victoria Wyttenberg was born in Grants Pass, Oregon. She holds an MFA from the University of Washington. Wyttenberg has taught at Grants Pass High School, and since 1970 at Sunset High School in Beaverton. Her poems have appeared in *Poetry Northwest, Seattle Review,* the *Portland Review, Hubbub, Mississippi Mud,* and the *Northwest Magazine* of the *Sunday Oregonian.*

The School Photographer

The photographer had a room like a box where he controlled
the light, kept prints all shades of grey
like father's hair. In the morning he could make twilight,
in mid-day, midnight, shuttering stars,
reflectors, metal moons. He knew how to airbrush scars.

His wife sat under a blanket
in a wheelchair he pushed to football games,
wheels spindled silver.
I pictured lovemaking, saw him lift her
gently into bed where she lay calm, nude, immobile.

Did her soul glow
in the dark like an alarm clock?
My father walked past me to get to mother.
Once she locked the door and he broke it
to splinters. One night he pushed her downstairs.

Maybe he wanted her wheelchair-bound
but she lay in a heap, cried, then walked away.
One morning the photographer called me from class
for yearbook pictures. He said light following
his hand would be lovely on my hair.

I thought of my body passing through the lens
like a ghost, becoming one-dimensional,
kept forever on paper in the pose he shaped.
Then he asked me to lift my pleated skirt
from my saddle shoes so he could see
the angle of my legs.

Higher, he said, lift it higher
as he arranged the shadows.
He wasn't handsome and I didn't like him
but thought of his wife in her wheelchair,
of father when he broke down the door
and I stood, letting him change the light.

Bibliography

Suggested Further Reading
See Copyright Acknowledgments on page 316 for authors or works not listed below.

Part I. Native Singing: Oregon Tribal Lyrics
Curtis, Edward S. *The North American Indian*. New York: Johnson Reprint Corporation, 1911.

Frachtenberg, Leo J. *Alsea Tales and Myths*. U.S. Bureau of American Ethnology, Bulletin No. 67, 1920.

———, A.S. Gatschet, and Melville Jacobs. *Kalapuya Texts*. Seattle: University of Washington Publications in Anthropology, Vol. 11, June 1945.

Gatschet, Albert Samuel. *The Klamath Indians of Southwestern Oregon*. Washington, DC: Government Printing Office, Department of the Interior, 1890.

———. "Songs of the Modoc Indians." *American Anthropologist*, Vol. VII (January 1894).

Gogol, John M. *Native American Words*. Portland, OR: Takmahnawis Publishers, 1973.

Hymes, Dell, trans. "When It Storms in Winter." *Calapooya Collage* 16.

———. "A Tualatin Shaman Named Shimxin." Unpublished.

———. "When the New Moon Appears." *Calapooya Collage* 15 (August 1991).

Jacobs, Elizabeth D. *Nehalem Tillamook Tales*, ed. Melville Jacobs. Corvallis: Oregon State University Press, 1990.

Jacobs, Melville. "Clackamas Chinook Myths and Tales." In *The Content and Style of an Oral Literature*. New York: Wenner-Gren Foundation, 1959.

———. *Coos Myth Texts*. Seattle: University of Washington Publications in Anthropology, Vol. 8, No. 2, 1940.

———. "A Recent Study of the Dreams of the Coos, with Some Examples." In Alfred Powers, *History of Oregon Literature*. Portland, OR: Metropolitan Press, 1935, 12-17.

———. *Santiam Kalapuya Ethnologic Texts*. Seattle: University of Washington Publications in Anthropology, Vol. 11, 1945.

———. *Texts in Chinook Jargon*. Seattle: University of Washington Publications in Anthropology, Vol. 7, No. 1, 1936.

Judson, Katherine Berry. *Myths and Legends of the Pacific Northwest*. Chicago: A.C. McClurg, 1910.

Kelly, Isabel. "Northern Paiute Tales." *Journal of American Folklore*, 51 (1938).

Marsden, W.L. "The Northern Paiute Language of Oregon." *University of California Publications in American Archaeology and Ethnology*, Vol. 20 (1923).

Ramsey, Jarold, editor and compiler. *Coyote Was Going There*. Seattle: University of Washington Press, 1977.

———. *Love in an Earthquake*. Seattle: University of Washington Press, 1973.

Rothenberg, Jerome, ed. *Shaking the Pumpkin: Traditional Poetry of the Indian North Americas*. New York: Doubleday, 1972. Revised ed. New York: Alfred van der Marck Editions, 1986.

Sapir, Edward. *Takelma Texts*. Philadelphia: Anthropological Publications of the University of Pennsylvania Museum, Vol. 2, No. 1, 1909.

———. "Religious Ideas of the Takelma Indians of Southwest Oregon." *Journal of American Folklore*, 20 (1907).

———. "Wishram Ethnography." University of Washington Publications in Anthropology, 3 (1930). Reprinted in *The Collected Works of Edward Sapir*, Vol VII. Berlin and New York: Mouton de Gruyter, 1990.

Spier, Leslie. "The Ghost Dance of 1870 among the Klamath of Oregon." Seattle: University of Washington Publications in Anthropology, Vol. 2, No. 2 (November 1927).

Spinden, Herbert J. *Songs of the Tewa.* New York: The Exposition of Indian Tribal Arts, 1933.

———. "Nez Perce Tales." In *Folk Tales of Salish and Sahaptin Tribes,* ed. Franz Boas. Memoirs of the American Folklore Association, 1917.

Swann, Brian. *Song of the Sky: Versions of Native American Songs and Poems.* Ashuelot, New Hampshire: Four Zoas Night House Ltd., 1985.

Part II. Tales Half Told: Nineteenth-Century Oregon Poems

Anonymous ("Drunk for a Week").

For poems on similar themes, see: "Ruby Wine," Isola Worth. *The New Northwest* (July 4 , 1871); "Pitiless Night, " Belle W. Cooke. *The New Northwest* (Nov. 3, 1871) .

Anonymous ("To the Oregon Emigrants of 1846") .

Similar poems can be found in Powers, A. *History of Oregon Literature*, pages 162-165. Portland, OR: Metropolitan Press, 1935.

See also "Oregon," by Major T.J. Eckerson, 1st U.S. Artillery. *Oregon Spectator* (May 16 , 1850), reprinted in *Oregon Native Son*, Vol. 1, No. 6 (October 1899).

Anonymous ("The Bachelor's Decision").

The opposite kind of poem—in *praise* of woman—is by another anonymous poet "E": "To Miss Susan," in the *Oregon Spectator* (July 23, 1846).

Bailey, Margaret Jewett. *The Grains, Or Passages in the Life of Ruth Rover, With Occasional Pictures of Oregon, Natural and Moral* (Portland, OR: Carter & Austin, 1854.) Reprinted, with a foreword by Edwin Bingham. Corvallis: Oregon State University Press, 1986.

———. "May Morning in Oregon," a poem in *Oregon Spectator* (May 28, 1846).

"*Ruth Rover*, 1854, by Mrs. Margaret J. Bailey of French Prairie," in Powers, A. *History,* 211-214.

"Margaret Jewett Bailey," by Evelyn Leasher and Robert J. Frank, in *The Grains. . .* Corvallis: Oregon State University Press, 1986.

Baldwin, Henry H.

See his diary account of the wreck in Dodge, Orvile. *Pioneer History of Coos and Curry Counties, Or.* Bandon, OR: Western World Publishers-Printers, 1969, 114-120.

For other shipwreck and ocean poems see: "She Sailed One Day," Sam Simpson. *Oregon Native Son*, Vol. 1, No. 5 (September 1899); "A Message from the Sea" and "The Sailor's Grave," Samuel A. Clarke. *Sounds by the Western Sea and Other Poems.* Salem, Oregon: Clarke & Craig, Willamette Farmer Office, 1872; "To a Wave," Col. E.D. Baker, in *Poetry of the Pacific*, May Wentworth, editor. San Francisco: Pacific Publishing Company, 1867; "Lost at Sea," Frances Fuller Victor. *The New Penelope and Other Stories and Poems.* San Francisco: A.L. Bancroft & Co., 1877; *The Light Station on Tillamook Rock,* Madeline DeFrees. Corvallis, OR: Arrowood Books, 1991.

Clarke, Samuel A. *Sounds by the Western Sea and Other Poems.* Salem, OR: Clarke & Craig, Willamette Farmer Office, 1872.

———. "Legend of the Cascades," *Harper's New Monthly Magazine* , Vol XLVII, No. CCLXXXV (February 1874).

———. *Pioneer Days of Oregon History.* New York: J.K. Gill Company, 1905.

"Samuel A. Clarke." Powers, A. *History,* 344-349.　　　.

For prose versions of this same legend, see: Balch, Frederick Homer. *The Bridge of the Gods: A Romance of Indian Oregon.* Chicago: A.C. McClurg, 1890; Judson, Katharine Berry. *Myths and Legends of the Pacific Northwest.* Chicago: A.C. McClurg, 1910; Love, Glen, ed. *The World Begins Here. Oregon Literature Series,* short fiction volume. Corvallis: Oregon State University Press, 1993.

For poems on other Indian legends, see "Multnomah Falls" and "Memaloose Island," Valentine Brown. *Tales and Other Verse*. Portland, OR: published by the author, 1900. "Memaloose Island" reprinted in Powers, A. *History*.

Cooke, Belle W. *Tears & Victory*. Salem, OR: E.M. Waite, 1871.
"Belle W. Cooke." Powers, A. *History*. 278-288. Contains her poem "Crossing the Plains."

Lee, Anna Maria Pittman.
Oregon Historical Quarterly, XXXVI:75; T. Bay, *Life and Letters of Mrs. Jason Lee*.
"The First Oregon Poem" in Powers, A. *History*, 67-68.
Gay, Theressa. *Life and Letters of Mrs. Jason Lee*. Portland, OR: Metropolitan Press, 1936.

Markham, Elizabeth. *Poems*. Portland, OR: The J.K. Gill Company, 1921.
———— . "Sorrowful tidings to us have come." *Oregon Specator*, Vol. 3, No. 9 (June 1, 1848). This poem, not in her book, is in response to the Whitman "massacre" of 1847.
See sections of the diary of Elizabeth Dixon Smith in *Covered Wagon Women*, Kenneth L. Holmes, ed. Volume I. Glendale, CA: The Arthur H. Clark Co., 1983.
"Elizabeth Markham" in Powers, A. *History*, 456-458.

Miller, Joaquin. *Joaquin Miller's Poems*. 6 vols. San Francisco: Whitaker and Ray, 1909-10.
———— . *Selected Writings of Joaquin Miller*. Ed. Alan Rosenus. Eugene, OR: Urion Press, 1977.
Lawson, Benjamin S. *Joaquin Miller*. Western Writers Series number 43. Boise: Boise State University, 1980.
Horner, John. "The Miller Family in Literature." *Oregon Native Son*. Vol. 1, No. 4 (August 1899).
For other wagon train poems see Powers, Alfred. *Poems of the Covered Wagons*. See also Belle Cooke's "Crossing the Plains" in Powers, A. *History*, 287-88; "After Twenty Years," Abigail Scott Duniway, in *David and Anna Matson*. Portland, OR: Duniway Publishing Co., 1881; "My Native Home," Elizabeth Markham, *Oregon Spectator* (November 29, 1849).
Among many poems written in honor of Miller, see: "Joaquin Miller," Lorenzo Sosso. *Pacific Monthly*, Vol. XV, No. 4 (April 1906); "To the Poet of the West—Joaquin Miller," Mary Carolyn Davies, and "Joaquin Miller Crosses the Mountains," Howard McKinley Corning, in Powers, A. *History*.

Miller, Minnie Myrtle. Eleven poems and a biography in "Minnie Myrtle Miller." Powers, A. *History*. 247-277.
Horner, John. "The Miller Family in Literature." *Oregon Native Son*. Vol. 1, No. 4 (August 1899).
"The Poetess of the Coquille," a poem by Barbara Drake, in *What We Say to Strangers*. Portland, OR: Breitenbush Books, 1986.
"Lines to Minnie Myrtle," a poem by Robert Starkey, *Sparks of Poetic Fire*. Marshfield, OrR: Coos Bay News Printing House, 1880.

Minto, John. *Rhymes of Early Life in Oregon and Historical and Biographical Facts*. Salem, OR: Statesman Publishing Co., circa 1910.
"John Minto of Salem," in Powers, A. *History*, 458-460. Contains poem "The Oregon Cow-Boy's Song."

Simpson, Sam. *The Gold-Gated West*. Philadelphia: J.B. Lippincott Company, 1910.
For other poems on Oregon places see: "The Klamath," O.C. Applegate. *Oregon Native Son*, Vol. 1, No. 11 (April 1900); "Mount Jefferson," Rob Roy Parrish, *Echoes from the Valley*. Portland, Oregon: George H. Hymes, 1884; "To Johnson Mountain," Henry H. Woodward, in Powers, R. "Literature," 264; "An Address to Mount Hood," James Clyman, in Powers, A. *History*, 55; "Ode to Mount Hood," Valentine Brown. *Poems*. Portland, OR: published by the author, 1900, 82-84.

Starkey, Robert. *Sparks of Poetic Fire, A Collection of Poems.* Marshfield, OR: Coos Bay News Printing House, 1880.

Victor, Frances Fuller. *The New Penelope and Other Stories and Poems.* San Francisco: A.L. Bancroft, 1877.

———. *Poems.* Portland, OR: Howe, Davis & Kilham, 1900.

———. *History of Oregon,* Hubert Howe Bancroft. San Francisco: The History Company, 1888. Reprinted New York: Arno Press, 1967.

———. *The Early Indian Wars of Oregon.* Salem, OR: F.C. Baker, 1894.

"Frances Fuller Victor" in Powers, A. *History,* 305-316.

Caughey, John Walton. *Hubert Howe Bancroft, Historian of the West.* New York: Russell & Russell, 1946.

American Women Writers: A Critical Reference Guide from Colonial Times to the Present. Vol. 2. Lagdon Lynne Faust, editor. New York: Frederick Ungar Publishing Co., 1983.

White, Willis.

For other tall tales in poetry, see: "Adventures of a Columbia Salmon," by Henry N. Peers (Piscator). *Oregon Spectator,* Vol. 1, No. 24. (Sept. 2, 1847).

Another example of humorous verse is a long poem by George H. Chance, D.D.S., *The Dental Chair. Poems of Lights and Shadows.* Portland, OR: A.G. Walling, 1875.

Woodward, Henry H. *Lyrics of the Umpqua.* New York: John B. Alden, Publisher, 1889.

"Poet of the Oregon Backwoods," Alice Bay Maloney, *Oregon Historical Quarterly,* Vol L., No. 2 (June 1949), 122-133.

"H.H. Woodward." Powers, Ruth McBride. "Literature," in *A Century of Coos and Curry.* Emil R. Peterson and Alfred Power, eds. Portland, OR: Binfords & Mort, Publishers, 1952. Pages 259-297.

Part III. Leaving the Myths: Poems in Transition

Brown, Valentine. *Tales and Other Verse.* Portland, OR: published by the author, 1904.

———. *Poems.* Portland: published by the author, 1900.

"The Chinook Wind." (article) *Oregon Historical Quarterly,* Vol. 41. 103-106.

"The Chinook Wind." (poem) Ella Higginson. *The Voice of April Land.* New York: Macmillan, 1903.

"The Oregon Chinook." (poem) Sam Simpson. *The Gold-Gated West.* Philadelphia: J.B. Lippincott Co., 1910.

"The Chinook Wind." (poem) Bert Huffman. *Pacific Monthly,* Vol. XV, No. 4 (April 1906). 418-419.

Davies, Mary Carolyn. *The Drums in Our Street: A Book of Poems.* New York: Macmillan Company, 1918.

———. *Youth Riding.* New York: Macmillan Company, 1919.

———. *Marriage Songs.* Boston: Harold Vinal, 1923.

———. *The Golden West in Story and Verse.* New York: Harper & Brothers, 1932.

"Mary Carolyn Davies" in Powers, A. *History.* 644-645.

Hall, Hazel. *Curtains.* New York: John Lane Company, 1921.

———. *Walkers.* New York: Dodd, Mead and Company, 1923.

———. *Cry of Time.* New York: E.P. Dutton & Co., 1928.

———. *Selected Poems.* Beth Bentley, ed. Boise, ID: Ahsahta Press, 1980.

"Hazel Hall," Eleanor H. Matthews. *Anthology of Northwest Writing: 1900-1950.* Strelow, Michael, and *Northwest Review* staff. Eugene, OR: Northwest Review Books, 1979 .

"Hazel Hall," in Powers, A. *History.* 650-651.

A Tribute to Hazel Hall, Viola Price Franklin, ed. Caldwell, ID: Caxton Printers, Ltd., 1939.

Hartless, William. "Mary's River Reminiscences," in Jacobs, Melville (ed.). *Kalapuya Texts.* Seattle: University of Washington Publications in Anthropology, Vol. 11 (1945). 336-350. See this same volume for other Kalapuya lyrics.

Hedges, Ada Hastings. *Desert Poems.* Portland, OR: Metropolitan Press, 1930.

———. Poems in Harrison, Henry. *Oregon Poets: An Anthology of 50 Contemporaries.* New York: Henry Harrison, Poetry Publisher, 1935.

"Ada Hastings Hedges," Powers, A. *History.*

Higginson, Ella. *A Bunch of Western Clover.* Poems. New Whatcomb, WA: Edson & Irish, Printers, 1874.

———. *The Flower That Grew in the Sand and Other Stories.* Seattle: The Calvert Co., 1896.

———. *A Forest Orchid. Stories.* New York: Macmillan, 1897.

———. *When the Birds Go North Again.* Poems. New York: Macmillan, 1898.

———. *The Voice of April Land.* Poems. New York: Macmillan, 1903.

"Ella Higginson," in Powers, A. *History.*

"Ella Higginson, Poet Laureate of Washington," by Lelah Jackson Edson, in *The Fourth Corner: Highlights from the Early Northwest.* Bellingham, WA: Cox Bros., 1951.

Holmstrom, Frances. *Western Windows.* Portland, OR: Metropolitan Press, 1937.

———. *Rich Lady.* Portland, OR: Binfords & Mort, 1941.

———. *Oregon Mist.* Portland, OR: Binfords & Mort, 1951.

"Frances Holmstrom," in "Literature," Powers, R.

Huffman, Bert. *Song of the Oregon Pine and Other Poems.* Pendleton, OR: Press of East Oregonian, 1907.

———. *Echoes of the Grande Ronde.* La Grande, OR: La Grande Printing Company, 1934.

Lockley, Fred. "Observations and Impressions of the Journal Man," *Oregon Journal* (November 17, 1914).

"Bert Huffman," in Powers, A. *History.*

Hunt, Joe. See Jacobs, Melville. *Northwest Sahaptin Texts.* Seattle: University of Washington Publications in Anthropology, 1929, I.

Katsuko. In *Issei*, by Kazuo Ito. Translated by Shinichiro Nakamura and Jean S. Gerard. Seattle: Executive Committee for Publication of *Issei: A History of Japanese Immigrants in North America*, c/o Japanese Community Service, 1973.

Lampman, Ben Hur. *How Could I Be Forgetting?* Portland, OR: Metropolitan Press, 1933.

———. *The Tramp Printer.* Portland, OR: Metropolitan Press,1934.

———. *At the End of the Car Line.* Portland, OR: Binfords & Mort, 1942.

———. *The Wild Swan, and Other Sketches.* New York: T.Y. Crowell Co., 1947.

———. *The Coming of the Pond Fishes.* Portland, OR: Binfords & Mort, 1946.

Markham, Edwin. *The Man with the Hoe and Other Poems.* New York: Doubleday &McClure, 1899.

———. *The Gates of Paradise and Other Poems.* Garden City, NY: Doubleday, Page & Co., 1920.

Slade, Joseph W. "Edwin Markham." *Dictionary of Literary Biography.* Vol 54: American Poets, 1880-1945. Third Series, Part 1, A-M. Detroit: Gale Research Co., 1987. 284-293. Markam's poem "The Valley" has been set to music and recorded on the 33 1/3 record album "Seven Songs by Howard Swanson." American Recording Society. 100 Sixth Avenue, New York, NY.

Morgan, Carrie Blake. *The Path of Gold.* New Whatcomb, WA: Edson & Irish, 1900.

Olsen, Charles Oluf. Poems in Harrison, Henry. *Oregon Poets.*

Reed, John. *Collected Poems.* Westport, CT: Lawrence Hill & Company, 1985.

———. *Ten Days That Shook the World.* Foreword by V.I. Lenin. New York: The Modern Library, 1935.

Tamu. See Katsuko, above.

Wata, Sam. See Kelly, Isabel, "Northern Paiute Tales." *Journal of American Folklore,* 51 (1938), 363-437.

Wood, C.E.S. *Collected Poems.* New York: The Vanguard Press, Inc., 1949.

———— . *The Mill Race Sonnets.* Eugene, OR: private printing, 1911.

———— . *A Book of Indian Tales.* New York: Vanguard, 1929.

———— . *Heavenly Discourse.* New York: Vanguard, 1927.

    Barnes, Tim. "C.E.S. Wood: Vision and Versatility." *Oregon English Journal* 13:1 (Spring 1991), 28-31.

    Bingham, Edwin R. *Charles Erskine Scott Wood.* Western Writers Series number 94. Boise, ID: Boise State University, 1991.

    ———— . "Charles Erskine Scott Wood and the *Pacific Monthly.*" *Oregon English Journal* 13:1 (Spring 1991), 32-34.

Part IV. Pioneers on Aesthetics: Poems by Early Oregon Modernists

Barnard, Mary. *Cool Country.* In *Five Young American Poets.* Norfolk, CT: New Directions, 1940.

———— . *Sappho: A New Translation.* Berkeley: University of California Press, 1958.

———— . *The Mythmakers.* Athens: Ohio University Press, 1966.

———— . *Time and the White Tigress.* Portland, OR: Breitenbush Books, 1986.

———— . *Collected Poems.* Portland, OR: Breitenbush Books, 1979.

    Hardt, Ulrich H. "An Interview with Four Poets." *Oregon English Journal* Vol. XI: 23 (Spring 1989), 69-80.

    Helle, Anita. "The Odysseys of Mary Barnard." *An Anthology of Northwest Writing,* Michael Strelow and the *Northwest Review* staff, eds. Eugene, OR: Northwest Review Books, 1979. 227-232.

Bright, Verne. *Mountain Man.* Caldwell, ID: Caxton Printers, 1948.

    See Harrison, Henry. *Oregon Poets.*

    See Powers, A. *Oregon Literature.* 639-340.

Coffield, Glen. *Northwest Poems.* Portland, OR: Rose City Publishers, 1954.

———— . *Selected Poems: 1943-1950.* Eagle Creek, OR: The Grundtvig Press, 1951.

———— . *Remember Now Thy Creator.* Waldport, OR: Civilian Public Service Camp for Conscientious Objectors, 1944.

    Eshelman, William R. *Materials on the Untide Press 1944-1948.* In University of Oregon Special Collection box #34—"Camp Waldport Collection."

Corning, Howard McKinley. *The Mountain in the Sky: A Book of Oregon Poems.* Portland, OR: Metropolitan Press, 1930.

———— . *This Earth and Another Country: New and Selected Poems.* Portland, OR: Tall Pine Imprints, 1969.

———— . *Willamette Landings: Ghost Towns of the River.* Portland: Oregon Historical Society, 1947 and 1973.

Davis, H.L. *Collected Essays and Short Stories.* Moscow: University of Idaho Press, 1986. Includes "Status Rerum," co-authored with James Stevens, the notorious 1927 essay blasting the quality of Northwest literature of the time.

———— . *Proud Riders and Other Poems.* New York: Harper and Brothers, 1942.

———— . *The Selected Poems of H.L. Davis.* Boise, ID: Ahsahta Press, 1978.

———— . *Honey in the Horn.* New York: Harper and Brothers, 1935.

———— . *Team Bells Woke Me, and Other Stories.* New York: William Morrow, 1953.

    Bain, Robert. *H.L. Davis.* Boise State University Western Writers Series, Number 11. Boise, ID: Boise State University, 1974.

Corning, Howard McKinley. "All the Words on the Pages, I: H.L. Davis," *Oregon Historical Quarterly*, Vol. LXXIII, No. 4 (December 1972), 292-331.

DeFrees, Madeline. *From the Darkroom*. (under the name Sister Mary Gilbert). Indianapolis: Bobbs-Merrill, 1964.

———. *When Sky Lets Go*. New York: Braziller, 1978.

———. *Imaginary Ancestors*. Seattle: Broken Moon Press, 1990.

———. *The Light Station on Tillamook Rock*. Corvallis, OR: Arrowood Books, 1990.

Eberman, Willis. *The Pioneers*. Portland, OR: Binfords & Mort, 1959.

———. *Chant for the Shades of Animals*. Portland, OR: Dunham Printing Co.,   1967.

———. *Lines to Be Left in the Earth*. Portland, OR: Binfords & Mort, 1951.

———. *I, Too, Am a Traveler*. Seaside, OR: Eberman, 1972.

Emerson, Helen. *Paris without Hemingway and Other Places*. Portland, OR: private edition.

Everson, William. *Eastward the Armies: Selected Poems 1935-1942*. Torrance, CA: Labyrinth Editions, 1980.

———. *The Residual Years: Poems 1934-1948*. New York: New Directions, 1968.

———. *The Veritable Years: Poems 1949-1966*. Santa Barbara, CA: Black Sparrow Press, 1978.

———. *A Canticle to the Waterbirds*. Berkeley, CA: Eizo, 1968.

———. *The Masks of Drought*. Santa Barbara, CA: Black Sparrow Press, 1980.

Marecki, Joan. "William Everson." *Contemporary Authors*. New Revision Series, Volume 20. Detroit: Gale Research Co., 1981-.

Stafford, William. *The Achievement of Brother Antoninus*. Glenview, IL: Scott Foresman, 1967.

Gale, Vi. *Odd Flowers & Short-Eared Owls*. Portland, OR: Prescott Street Press, 1984.

———. *Love, Always*. Denver, CO: Alan Swallow, 1965.

———. *Clearwater*. Denver, CO: Alan Swallow, 1974.

———. *Nineteen Ing Poems*. Portland, OR: Press 22, 1970.

See Brown, ed. *Oregon Signatures*.

Guthrie, Woody. *Bound for Glory* (autobiography). New York: E.P. Dutton, 1943.

———. Introduction to *Ten of Woody Guthrie's Songs, Book One,* dated April 3, 1945. In *An Anthology of Northwest Writing*. Michael Strelow and *Northwest Review* staff, eds. Eugene, OR: Northwest Review Books, 1979.

Haislip, John. *Not Every Year*. Seattle: University of Washington Press, 1971.

———. *Seal Rock*. Daleville, IN: Barnwood Press, 1986.

See Brown, ed. *Oregon Signatures*.

Hall, James B. *Bereavements* (poems). Brownsville, OR/Williams, OR: Story Line Press/Castle Peak Editions, 1991.

———. *The Hunt Within* (poems). Baton Rouge: Louisiana State University Press, 1973.

———. *Stopping on the Edge* (novel). Middletown, CT: Wesleyan University Press, 1988.

———. *I Like It Better Now* (stories). Fayetteville: The University of Arkansas Press, 1992.

———. "James B. Hall." *Contemporary Authors Autobiography Series*, Volume 12. Detroit: Gale Research Co., 1990.

See Brown, ed. *Oregon Signatures*.

Hanson, Kenneth O. *The Distance Anywhere*. Seattle: University of Washington Press, 1967.

———. *The Uncorrected World*. Middletown, CT: Wesleyan University Press, 1973.

———. (translator) *Growing Old Alive*. Port Townsend, WA: Copper Canyon Press, 1978.

———. *Lighting the Night Sky*. Portland, OR: Breitenbush, 1983.

See Brown, ed. *Oregon Signatures*.

Hitchcock, George. *The Piano beneath the Skin*. Port Townsend, WA: Copper Canyon Press, 1978.

———— . *The Wounded Alphabet: Poems Collected and New, 1953-1983.* Santa Cruz, CA: Jazz Press, 1983.

———— . *My Travels in Remote America* (novel). Brownsville, OR: Story Line Press, 1992.

———— . "Some Sketches from a Life." *Contemporary Authors Autobiography Series,* Volume 12. Detroit: Gale Research Co., 1990.

Hoff, Clara. See Verseweavers Poetry Society. *Fabric of Song, Volume II.* Mill Valley, CA: The Wings Press, 1955.

Iwatsuki, Shizue.

Ota, Alan. "Poet Vocalizes Historical Awareness." Portland *Oregonian.* February 16, 1979.

Turning Shadows into Light: Art and Culture of the Northwest's Early Asian/Pacific Community. Mayumi Tsutakawa and Alan Chong Lau, eds. Seattle: Young Pine Press, 1982.

The Japanese-American Historical Plaza in Portland contains a "story wall" which depicts in verse the history of Japanese-Americans in the Northwest. See *Sunset* article, "Echoes of Japan on Portland's Waterfront," in the November 1990 issue.

Kambouris, Haralambos.

Applegate, Shannon. "Unexpected Texts and Contexts: Oregon's Ethnic Diaries and Letters." *Oregon English Journal,* Vol. 14, No. 1 (Spring 1992).

————, and Terence O'Donnell, eds. *Talking on Paper. Oregon Literature Series,* Letters and diaries volume. Corvallis: Oregon State University Press, 1994.

Le Guin, Ursula. *The Left Hand of Darkness* (novel). New York: Ace Books, 1969.

———— . *The Lathe of Heaven* (novel). New York: Charles Scribner's Sons, 1971.

———— . *Always Coming Home* (novel). New York: Harper and Row, 1985.

———— . *Wild Angels* (poems). Santa Barbara, CA: Capra Press, 1975.

———— . *Hard Words* (poems). New York: Harper & Row, 1981.

———— . *Wild Oats and Fireweed* (poems). New York: Harper & Row, 1988.

Bucknall, Barbara. *Ursula Le Guin.* New York: Ungar, 1981.

Cummins, Elizabeth. *Understanding Ursula Le Guin.* Columbia: University of South Carolina Press, 1990.

Spivak, Charlotte. *Ursula Le Guin.* Boston: Twayne Publishers, 1984.

Matthews, Courtland. *After Many Winds.* Portland, OR: privately published, 1974.

———— . *Aleutian Interval.* Seattle: F. McCaffrey, 1949.

See Powers, A. *Oregon Literature.*

See Harrison, Henry. *Oregon Poets.*

Matthews, Eleanor. *Ever the Sunrise.* Mill Valley, CA: Wings Press, 1954.

———— . *The Unseen Wing.* Portland, OR: Matthews, 1973.

McGahey, Jeanne. *Oregon Winter.* Andes, NY: Woolmer/Brotherson, 1973.

———— . *Homecoming with Reflections: Collected Poems.* Princeton, NJ: *Quarterly Review of Literature,* 1989.

McGinley, Phyllis. *Times Three: Selected Verse from Three Decades.* New York: The Viking Press, 1961.

———— . *Husbands Are Difficult.* New York: Duell, Sloan and Pearce, 1941.

———— . *Stones in a Glass House.* New York: The Viking Press, 1946.

Wagner, Linda Welshimer. *Phyllis McGinley.* New York: Twayne Publishers, Inc., 1971.

Wiloch, Thomas. "Phyllis McGinley." *Contemporary Authors.* New Revision Series, Volume 19. Detroit: Gale Research Co., 1987. 325-327.

Moll, Ernest G. *Sedge Fire.* New York: H. Vinal, 1927.

———— . *Campus Sonnets.* Portland, OR: Metropolitan Press, 1934.

———— . *Blue Interval,* poems on Crater Lake. Portland, OR: Metropolitan Press, 1935.

———. *Beware the Cuckoo and Other Poems.* Sydney, Australia: Australian Pub., 1947.

———. *Below These Hills.* Melbourne, Australia: Melbourne University Press, 1957.

———. *The Road to Cactus Land.* Sydney, Australia: Edwards & Shaw, 1971.

See Brown, ed. *Oregon Signatures.*

Morden, Phyllis. See Harrison, Henry. *Oregon Poets.*

Ostroff, Anthony. *Imperatives.* New York: Harcourt, Brace, and World, 1962.

———. *A Fall in Mexico.* New York: Doubleday, 1977.

———. (editor) *The Contemporary Poet as Artist and Critic.* Boston: Little, Brown, 1964.

Pratt, Laurence. *A Saga of a Paper Mill.* Caldwell, ID: The Caxton Printers, Ltd., 1935.

———. *April Out of Stone.* Caldwell, ID: The Caxton Printers, Ltd., 1946.

———. *Black Fire, White Fire.* Mill Valley, CA: Wings Press, 1953.

———. *Lowbrow Limericks.* Portland, OR: privately printed), 1958.

Salisbury, Ralph. *Ghost Grapefruit.* Ithaca, New York: Ithaca House, 1972.

———. *Pointing at the Rainbow: Poems from a Cherokee Heritage.* Marvin, SD: Blue Cloud Quarterly, 1980.

———. *Going to the Water: Poems of a Cherokee Heritage.* Eugene, OR: Pacific House Books, 1983.

———. (editor) *A Nation within: Contemporary Native American Writing.* Hamilton, New Zealand: Outrigger Publishers, 1983.

(all the above books available through Greenfield Review Press)

———. *One Indian and Two Chiefs* (stories). Tsaile, AZ: Navaho Community College Press, 1993.

———. "The Quiet between Lightning and Thunder." *I Tell You Now: Autobiographical Essays by Native American Writers.* Brian Swann and Arnold Krupat, eds. Lincoln: University of Nebraska Press, 1987.

Shannon, Ellen. *Memory's Children.* Astoria, OR: Wayfaring Tree Press, 1985.

———. *On the Way to Easter.* Astoria, OR: Wayfaring Tree Press, 1992.

Snyder, Gary. *Riprap.* Ashland, MA: Orgin Press, 1959.

———. *Riprap and Cold Mountain Poems.* San Francisco: Four Seasons Foundation, 1965.

———. *Six Sections from Mountains and Rivers without End.* San Francisco: Four Seasons Foundation, 1965.

———. *The Back Country.* New York: New Directions, 1967.

———. *Myths & Texts.* New York: New Directions, 1978.

Kherdian, David. *Gary Snyder.* Berkeley, CA: Oyez, 1965.

Leary, Paris, and Robert Kelly, eds. *A Controversy of Poets.* New York: Doubleday Anchor, 1965.

Steuding, Bob. *Gary Snyder.* Boston: Twayne Publishers, 1976.

Videotape: "Philip Whalen and Gary Snyder." (Poetry USA Series) Bloomington, IN: NEW, 1966. Contains Snyder reading "Hay for the Horses."

Stafford, William. *Down in My Heart* (prose, about the conscientous objector years). Elgin, IL: Bretheren Press, 1947. Reprinted 1971.

———. *Traveling Through the Dark.* New York: Harper & Row, 1962.

———. *Stories That Could Be True.* New York: Harper & Row, 1977.

———. *Passwords.* New York: Harper & Row, 1991.

———. *The Animal That Drank Up Sound* (a picture book made from the poem of the same title). San Diego, CA: Harcourt, Brace, Jovanovich, 1992.

See Brown, ed. *Oregon Signatures.*

Stafford's Way, poems about and for William Stafford. Tom Ferté, editor. Monmouth, OR: Adrienne Lee Press, 1991 .

Love, Glen. "William Stafford." *Fifty Western Writers,* F. Erisman and R. Etulain, eds. Westport, CT: Greenwood Press, 1982.

Two half-hour videos: 1) "William Stafford: What the River Says"; 2) "William Stafford: The Life of the Poem." Both directed by Vincent Wixon and Michael Markee. Ashland, OR: TTTD Productions, 1989 and 1992. Available from 126 Church Street, Ashland, OR 97520.

Stevens, James. *Big Jim Turner*. Garden City, NY: Doubleday, 1948. Reprint: Albuquerque: University of New Mexico Press, 1975.

———. *Homer in the Sagebrush*. New York: Alfred A. Knopf, 1928.

———. *Status Rerum: A Manifesto. Upon the Present Condition of Northwestern Literature Containing Several Near-Libelous Utterances Upon Persons in the Public Eye*. With H.L. Davis. The Dalles, OR; Privately Printed, 1927. Reprinted in *H.L. Davis: Collected Essays and Short Stories*. Moscow, ID: University of Idaho Press, 1986.

Claire, Warren L. "Introduction." *Big Jim Turner*. Albuquerque: University of New Mexico Press, 1975.

Tracy, Paul. *Horsemeat and Other Lines*. Caldwell, ID: self-published, 1967.

———. *Owyhee Horizons*. Caldwell, ID: Caxton Printers, 1968.

Harrison, Henry. *Oregon Poets*.

Part V. Arriving and Leaving Here

Allen, Paula Gunn. *Skins and Bones: Poems 1979-1987*. Albuquerque, NM: West End Press, 1988.

Averill, Diane. *Branches Doubled Over with Fruit*. Orlando: University of Central Florida Press, 1991.

———. *The Ella Featherstone Poems: A Sellwood Sequence*. Portland, OR: Howlet Press, 1990.

Axelrod, David. *The Jerusalem of Grass*. Boise, ID: Ahsahta Press, 1992.

———. *The Kingdom at Hand*. La Grande, OR: Ice River, 1993.

Barnes, Jim. *A Season of Loss*. West Lafayette, IN: Purdue University Press, 1985.

———. *La Plata Cantata*. West Lafayette, IN: Purdue University Press, 1989.

———. *Summons and Signs: Poems by Dagmar Nick*. Kirksville, MO: Chariton Review Press, 1980.

———. *The American Book of the Dead*. Champaign: University of Illinois Press, 1982.

Barnes, Tim. *Mother and the Mangos*. Portland, OR: Charles Seluzicki Fine Books, 1991.

Barrington, Judith. *History and Geography*. Portland, OR: Eighth Mountain Press, 1989.

———. *Trying to Be an Honest Woman*. Portland, OR: Eighth Mountain Press, 1985.

Bird, Gloria. *Full Moon on the Reservation*. Greenfield Center, NY: Greenfield Review Press, 1993.

Broumas, Olga. *Beginning with O*. New Haven, CT: Yale University Press, 1977.

———. *Black Holes, Black Stockings*. Middletown, CT: Wesleyan University Press, 1985.

———. *Pastoral Jazz*. Port Townsend, WA: Copper Canyon Press, 1983.

———. *Perpetua*. Port Townsend, WA: Copper Canyon Press, 1989.

Carlile, Henry. *Running Lights*. Port Townsend, WA: Dragon Gate, 1981.

———. *Rain*. Pittsburgh, PA: Carnegie Mellon University Press, 1993.

———. *The Rough-Hewn Table*. Columbia: University of Missouri Press, 1971.

Carver, Ray. *Fires: Essays, Poems, Stories*. New York: Random House, 1989.

———. *New Path to the Waterfall: Poems*. New York: Atlantic Monthly, 1990.

———. *Ultramarine*. New York: Random House, 1987.

———. *Where Water Comes Together with Other Water*. New York: Random House, 1989.

Chin, Marilyn. *Dwarf Bamboo*. Greenfield Center, NY: Greenfield Review Press, 1987.

Costanzo, Gerald. *In the Aviary*. Columbus: University of Missouri Press, 1975.

———. *The Lap of the Bridesmaids*. Cleveland, OH: Bits Press, 1991 .

———. *Nobody Lives on Arthur Godfrey Boulevard Anymore*. Brockport, NY: BOA Editions, 1992.

———. *Poems*. Reno, NV: West Coast, 1973.

Crawford, Tom. *If It Weren't for Trees*. Amherst, KS: Lynx House Press, 1986.

———. *I Want to Say Listen*. Tucson, AZ: Ironwood Press, 1979.

Curtis, Walt. *Peckerneck Country*. Forest Grove, OR: Mr. Cogito Press, 1978.

———. *Rhymes for Alice Blue Light*. Amherst, KS: Lynx House, 1984.

Daniel, John. *Common Ground*. Lewiston, ID: Confluence Press, 1988.

DePreist, James. *The Distant Siren*. Salem, OR: Willamette University Press, 1989.

———. *This Precipice Garden*. Salem, OR: Willamette University Press, 1986.

Diaz-Horna, Efrain. *The Many Faces of Love*. Mt. Angel, OR: Abby Press, 1983.

Doubiago, Sharon. *Hard Country*. Albuquerque, NM: West End Press, 1982.

———. *Oedipus Drowned*. Albion, CA: Pigmy Forest Press, 1988.

———. *Psyche Drives the Coast: Poems 1975-1987*. Port Townsend, WA: Empty Bowl Press, 1990.

Drake, Albert. *Homesick*. Traverse City, MI: Canoe Press, 1988.

———. *Returning to Oregon*. Cincinnati, OH: Cider Press, 1975.

———. *Riding Bike in the Fifties*. Okemos, MI: Stone Press, 1973.

Drake, Barbara. *Love at the Egyptian Theatre*. East Lansing, MI: Red Cedar, 1978.

———. *What We Say to Strangers*. Portland, OR: Breitenbush Books, 1987.

Driscoll, Jeremy. *The Night of St. John*. Scio, OR: Taucross Farms Press, 1989.

———. *Some Morning*. Brownsville, OR: Story Line, 1992.

Edmo, Ed. *These Few Words of Mine*. Marvin, SD: Blue Cloud Quarterly Press, 1985.

George, Phil. *Kautsas (Grandmothers)*. Spalding, ID: Pacific Northwest National Park Forest Association, 1985.

Goldburg, Ellen. *Naming*. Portland, OR: Olive Press, 1976.

———. *Rocking the Boat*. Portland, OR: Gobble Gobble Press, 1973.

Harper, Michael S. *Dear John, Dear Coltrane*. Urbana: University of Illinois Press, 1985.

———. *Healing Song for the Inner Ear*. Urbana: University of Illinois Press, 1985.

———. *History Is Your Own Heartbeat*. Urbana: University of Illinois Press, 1971.

———. *Images of Kin*. Urbana: University of Illinois Press, 1977.

———. *Nightmare Begins Responsibility*. Urbana: University of Illinois Press, 1975.

———. *Photographs: Negatives: History as Apple Tree*. Orinda, CA: Scarab Press, 1972.

———. *Rhode Island: Eight Poems*. Roslindale, MA: Pym-Rand Press, 1981.

Heynen, Jim. *A Suitable Church*. Port Townsend, WA: Copper Canyon, 1982.

———. *How the Sow Became a Goddess*. Lewiston, ID: Confluence Press, 1977.

———. *Maedra Poems*. Orangeburg, SC: Peaceweed Press, 1974.

———. *Notes from Custer*. Ann Arbor, MI: Bear Claw Press 1975.

———. *The Funeral Parlor*. Port Townsend, WA: Graywolf, 1976.

Hongo, Garrett. *River of Heaven*. New York: Knopf, 1988.

———. *Yellow Light: Poems*. Middletown, CT: Wesleyan University Press, 1982.

Howell, Christopher. *The Crime of Luck*. Sunderland, CA: Panache Books, 1977.

———. *Sea Change*. Seattle: L'Epervier Press, 1985.

———. *Sweet Afton*. San Francisco: True Directions, 1991 .

———. *Though Silence: The Ling Wei Texts*. Seattle: L'Epervier Press, 1981.

———. *Why Shouldn't I*. Seattle: L'Epervier Press, 1978.

Inada, Lawson. *Before the War: Poems as They Happened*. New York: Morrow, 1971.

———. *Legends from Camp*. Minneapolis: Coffee House, 1992.

———. *Three Northwest Poets: Albert Drake, Lawson Inada, Douglas Lawder*. Madison, WI: Quixote Press, 1970.

Jensen, Peter, et al. *Confluence: Selected Poems*. Eugene, OR: Walking Bird Press, 1992.

Johnson, David. *Butch beneath the Stars*. Eugene, OR: Champion Canyon Press, 1978.

———. *Eleven Poems for Julie Ellen*. Eugene, OR: Champion Canyon Press, 1975.

Johnson, Harold. *Dry Boats*. Portland, OR: First Press, 1984.

Kelly, Brigit. *To the Place of Trumpets*. New Haven: Yale University Press, 1988.

Killeen, Ger. *A Wren*. Emporia, KS: Bluestem Press, 1989.

Krysl, Marilyn. *Dian Lucifera*. Berkeley, CA: Shameless Hussy Press, 1983.

———. *Midwife*. New York: The National League for Nursing, 1989.

———. *More Palomino, Please, More Fuschia*. Cleveland, OH: Cleveland State University Poetry Center, 1980.

———. *Saying Things*. Omaha, NB: Abattoir Editions, 1975.

———. *What We Have to Live with*. Santa Fe, NM: Teal Press, 1989.

Le Guin, Ursula. *Hard Words*. New York: Harper & Row, 1981.

———. *No Boats*. Seattle: Ygor & Buntho Press, 1991.

———. *Wild Angels*. Santa Barbara, CA: Capra Press, 1975.

———. *Wild Oats and Firewood*. New York: Harper & Row, 1988.

McPherson, Sandra. *Elegies for the Hot Season*. New York: Ecco Press, 1982.

———. *The God of Indeterminacy: Poems*. Chicago: University of Chicago Press, 1993.

———. *Patron Happiness*. New York: Ecco Press, 1984.

———. *Radiation*. New York: Ecco Press, 1973.

———. *Streamers*. New York: Ecco Press, 1989.

———. *The Year of Our Birth*. New York: Ecco Press, 1978.

Miranda, Gary. *Grace Period*. Princeton: Princeton University Press, 1983 .

———. *Listeners at the Breathing Place*. Princeton: Princeton University Press, 1979.

Muller, Erik, Peter Jensen, and David Johnson. *Confluence: Selected Poems*. Eugene, OR: Walking Bird Press, 1992.

Orr, Verlena. *I Dance Naked in a Dream*. Portland, OR: Howlett, 1989.

Ortiz, Simon. *Woven Stone*. Tucson: University of Arizona Press, 1992.

Pavlich, Walter. *The Lost Comedy*. Portland, OR: Howlett Press, 1991.

———. *Of Things Odd and Therefore Beautiful*. Ft. Collins, CO: Leaping Mountain Press, 1987.

———. *Ongoing Portraits*. Daleville, IN: Banwood Press, 1985.

———. *Running near the End of the World*. Iowa City: University of Iowa Press, 1992.

———. *Theories of Birds & Water*. Seattle: Owl Creek Press, 1990 .

Peterson, Paulann. *Under the Sign of a Neon Wolf*. Lewiston, ID: Confluence Press, 1989.

Poupeney, Mollie. *My Neckline and the Collapse of Western Civilization*. Kensington, CA: Smartweed Press, 1987.

Quinn, John. *Easy Pie*. Omaha, NB: Buttonmaker Press, 1987.

———. *The Wolf Last Seen*. Eugene, OR: Pacific House Books, 1987.

Ramsey, Jarold. *Dermographia*. Iowa City: Cornstalk Press, 1983.

———. *Love in an Earthquake*. Seattle: University of Washington Press, 1973.

———. *The Space between Us*. London: Adams Books, 1970.

Root, Judith. *Weaving the Sheets*. Pittsburgh: Carnegie Mellon University Press, 1988.

Root, William Pitt. *Faultdancing*. Pittsburgh: University of Pittsburgh Press, 1986.

Runciman, Lex. *The Admirations*. Amherst, KS: Lynx House, 1989.

———. *Luck*. Seattle: Owl Creek Press, 1981.

Rutsala, Vern. *Backtracking*. Brownsville, OR: Story Line, 1985.

———. *The Journey Begins*. Athens: University of Georgia Press, 1976.

———. *Laments*. Minneapolis: New Rivers Press, 1975.

———. *Paragraphs*. Middletown, CT: Wesleyan University Press, 1978.

———. *Ruined Cities*. Pittsburgh: Carnegie Mellon University Press, 1987.

———. *Selected Poems of Vern Rutsala*. Brownsville, OR: Story Line, 1991.

———. *Walking Home from the Icehouse*. Pittsburgh, PA: Carnegie Mellon University Press, 1980.

————. *The Window*. Middletown, CT: Wesleyan University Press, 1964.

Scates, Maxine. *Toluca Street*. Pittsburgh, PA: University of Pittsburgh Press, 1989.

Sears, Peter. *New and Selected Poems*. Portland, OR: Breitenbush Books, 1987.

Skloot, Floyd. *Kaleidoscope*. Eugene, OR: Silverfish Review Press, 1986.

————. *Wild Light*. Eugene, OR: Silverfish Review Press, 1989.

St. John, Primus. *Dreamer*. Pittsburgh, PA: Carnegie Mellon University Press, 1990.

————. *Love Is Not a Consolation; It Is a Light*. Pittsburgh, PA: Carnegie Mellon University Press, 1982.

————. *Skins on the Earth*. Port Townsend, WA: Copper Canyon Press, 1976.

Stafford, Kim. *The Granary*. Pittsburgh, PA: Carnegie Mellon University Press, 1982.

————. *A Gypsy's History of the World*. Port Townsend, WA: Copper Canyon Press, 1976.

————. *Having Everything Right*. Lewiston, ID: Confluence Press,1986.

————. *Places & Stories*. Pittsburgh, PA: Carnegie Mellon University Press, 1987.

Starck, Clem. *Journeyman's Wages*. Brownsville, OR: Storyline, 1994.

Steinman, Lisa. *All That Comes to Light*. Corvallis, OR: Arrowood Books, 1989.

————. *A Book of Other Days*. Corvallis, OR: Arrowood Books, 1993.

————. *Lost Poems*. Ithaca, MA: Ithaca House, 1976.

Thi, Song. *dattam dung*. Beaverton, OR: Nam Trung, 1989.

Tremblay, Gail. *Indian Singing in 20th Century America*. Corvallis, OR: Calyx Press, 1990.

————. *Night Give Woman the Word*. Omaha, NB: F-Limited, 1980.

————. *Talking to the Grandfathers*. Omaha: University of Nebraska, Omaha Press, 1981.

Venn, George. *Marking the Magic Circle*. Corvallis: Oregon State University Press, 1987.

————. *Off the Main Road*. Portland, OR: Prescott Street Press, 1978.

————. *Sunday Afternoon: Grand Ronde*. Portland, OR: Prescott Street Press, 1976.

Wendt, Ingrid. *Moving the House*. Brockport, NY: BOA Editions, 1980.

————. *Singing the Mozart Requiem*. Portland, OR: Breitenbush Books, 1987.

Witte, John. *Loving the Days*. Middletown, CT: Wesleyan University Press, 1978.

Woody, Elizabeth. *Hand into Stone*. New York: Contact Two, 1988.

Supplementary Bibliography, Parts I-IV
Newspapers and Periodicals Founded Before 1960

The following publications contain work by Oregon writers in many issues. Notice special issues devoted to Oregon poets.

American Mercury. Founded January 1924 by H.L. Mencken and G.J. Nathan, published in New York. Ceased publication in 1980. Oregon poets represented mainly in the 1920s and '30s. Special Oregon poets section in June 1926.

Frontier. Missoula, Montana, 1919 (under the name *The Montanan* for a year). Edited and published by H. G. Merriam. In 1933 it absorbed the *Muse and Mirror* of Seattle and the *Midland* of Iowa City, and became *Frontier and Midland*. Ceased publication in Summer 1939.

The Lariat. Salem, Oregon, 1922-1929. Edited by Colonel E. Hofer. See April 1924 for winners of "The Circuit Rider" contest.

The Literary Monthly, later the *Literary Magazine*. Portland, Oregon, 1933-1934. Originally the *Outlander*.

New Northwest. Published by Abigail Scott Duniway. Weekly newspaper from May 5, 1871-February 24, 1887.

Northwest Review. Eugene, Oregon, 1957-present. Special Oregon Poets issue. Vol. XIV, No. 3 (Spring 1975).

Oregon Democrat. Albany, Oregon, 1859-1925. Newspaper. The Sunday magazine regularly published Oregon writers.

The Oregonian. Portland, Oregon, 1850-present. The Sunday magazine regularly published Oregon writers.

Oregon Magazine. Salem, Oregon, 1918-1931.

Oregon Spectator. Oregon City, February 5, 1846-March, 1855. Weekly newspaper. Poems in nearly every issue.

The Outlander. A Quarterly Literary Review. Portland, Oregon. Edited by Albert Richard Wetjen, Roderick Lull, James Stevens, Borghild Lee. Only two issues published, 1933.

Overland Monthly. San Francisco, First Series, 1868-1875. Edited by Bret Harte. Continued until May, 1923, when it combined with *Out West Magazine*. Special Oregon poets issue November 1924.

Oregon East. La Grande. Eastern Oregon State College. 1950-present. Published annually.

Oregon Native Son. Portland, Oreton, 1899-1901. (United with *Pacific Monthly* in May, 1901.) Published monthly.

Oregon State Review: Spindrift. Corvallis. 1959-1968. Student publication.

Pacific Monthly. Seattle, 1891-1899. Became *Sunset Magazine* in 1899.

West Shore. Portland, Oregon, 1875-1891. Monthly. Published by L. Samuel.

Articles

Allen, Eleanor. "Oregon Becomes an Active Center for Writers," *The Oregonian* (March 29, 1936), Mag. p.6.

Botkin, B.A. "We Talk about Regionalism—North, East, South, and West." *The Frontier* (May 1933).

Corning, Howard McKinley. "A.R. Wetjen: British Seaman in the Western Sunrise." *Oregon Historical Quarterly*, Vol. LXXIV, No. 2 (June 1973), 145-178.

———. "All the Words on the Pages, I: H.L. Davis." *Oregon Historical Quarterly*, Vol. LXXIII, No. 4 (December 1972), 293-331.

———. "Charles Alexander: Youth of the Oregon Mood." *Oregon Historical Quarterly*, Vol. LXXIV, No. 2 (March 1973), 34-70.

———. "The Prose and the Poetry of It." *Oregon Historical Quarterly*, Vol. XXIV, No. 3 (September 1973), 244-267.

Fuller, Ethel Romig. "Who and How Good Are the Poets." *Oregonian* (November 19, 1933), Mag. p. 3.

Hardt, Ulrich H. "An Interview with Four Poets," *Oregon English Journal*, Vol. XI, No. 2B (Fall 1989), 69-80.

Hymes, Dell. "Discovering Oral Performance and Measured Verse in American Indian Narrative." *New Literary History*, 8 (Spring 1977), 431-437.

Jacobs, Melville. "The Fate of Indian Oral Literatures in Oregon." *Northwest Review*, 3 (Summer 1962), 90.

Powers, Ruth McBride. "Literature," in *A Century of Coos and Curry*. Emil R. Peterson and Alfred Powers, eds. Portland, OR: Binfords & Mort, Publishers, 1952. Pages 259-297.

Stevens, James. "The Northwest Takes to Poesy." *The American Mercury*, 16 (January 1929).

Tedlock, Dennis. "Toward an Oral Poetics." *New Literary History*, Vol. VIII, No. 3 (Spring 1977).

Venn, George. "The Search for Sacred Space in Western American Literature." *Portland Review*, 22 (1976).

———. "Continuity in Northwest Literature." *Marking the Magic Circle*. Corvallis: Oregon State University Press, 1987.

Victor, Frances Fuller. "The Literature of Oregon." *The West Shore* (January 1876).

Books

Allen, Paula Gunn. *The Sacred Hoop: Recovering the Feminine in American Indian Traditions.* Boston: Beacon Press, 1986.

Buan, Carolyn and Richard Lewis, eds. *The First Oregonians.* Portland, OR: Oregon Council for the Humanities, 1991.

Dodge, Orvil. *Pioneer History of Coos and Curry Counties, Or.* Bandon, OR: Western World Publishers - Printers, Second Edition 1969.

Hardt, Ulrich, ed. Special Oregon Poets issue of *Oregon English*, Volume XI, Number 2B (Fall 1989).

———. Regionalism: Literature of Oregon issue of *Oregon English Journal*, Vol. XIII, No. 1 (Spring 1991).

Horner, John B. *Oregon Literature.* Corvallis, OR: Statesman Job Print (Salem, OR), 1899.

Horner, John B. *Oregon: Her History. Her Great Men. Her Literature.* Corvallis, OR: Press of the *Gazette-Times*, 1919.

McWilliams, Carey. *The New Regionalism in American Literature.* Seattle: University of Washington Book Store, 1930.

Nelson, Herbert. *The Literary Impulse in Pioneer Oregon.* Corvallis: Oregon State College Press, 1948.

Powers, Alfred. *History of Oregon Literature.* Portland, OR: Metropolitan Press, 1935.

Reyes, Karen. *Finding a New Voice: The Oregon Writing Community between the World Wars.* Portland: Portland State University Master's thesis, 1986.

Stern, Theodore. *The Klamath Tribe: A People and Their Reservation.* Seattle: University of Washington Press, 1965.

Swann, Brian, ed. *Smoothing the Ground: Essays on Native American Oral Literature.* Berkeley: University of California Press, 1983.

Waldman, Carl. *Atlas of the North American Indian.* New York: Facts on File Publications, 1985.

Individual Poets Not Included in Parts I-IV

Where books are not available, at least one magazine or anthology publication is cited.

Allen, Eleanor. *Seeds of Earth.* Portland, OR: Metropolitan Press, Publishers, 1933.

Anonymous ("O.P.Q."). "Yellow Fever," *Oregon Spectator*, 1848. (Another gold rush poem, "Gold! Gold! Gold!", by Major T.J. Eckerson (lst U.S. Artillery), can be found in the *Oregon Spectator*, May 16, 1950. *Poems of the Covered Wagons*, edited by Alfred Powers (Portland, OR: Pacific Publishing House, 1947), contains a section on "The Forty-Niners," which includes Joaquin Miller's "Men of Forty-Nine.")

Applegate, O.C. "The Klamath." *Oregon Native Son.* Volume I, No. 11 (April 1900).

Baker, E.D. "To a Wave." In *Poetry of the Pacific.* May Wentworth, ed. San Francisco: Pacific Publishing Co., 1861.

Buchanan, John A. *Sunset at the Bar.* Astoria, OR. Posthumous publication by D.J. Ferguson, Presbyterian Manse, Astoria. 1936. (Contains "The Circuit Rider"—one of many entries in the "Circuit Rider Contest" of 1924.)

Chance, George H., D.D.S. *The Dental Chair. Poems of Lights and Shadows.* Portland, OR: A.G. Walling, Pringer, 1875.

Collins, Dean. *White Crown Singing.* Portland, OR: Binfords & Mort, 1940.

Curry, George L. "Nature," a poem in *Oregon Spectator* (August 5, 1847).

———. "Trouble," a poem in *Oregon Native Son*, Vol. 1, No. 1 (May 1899).

Davies, Laura Thomas. *Laura's Poems.* Portland, OR: Laurel M. Victoria Davies, 1936.

Downey-Bartlett, Laura B. *Chinook-English Songs.* Portland, OR: Kubli-Miller Company, 1914.

Duniway, Abigail Scott. *David and Anna Matson*. Portland, OR: Duniway Publishing Co., 1881.

Eckerson, Maj. Theo. J. "Oregon." *Oregon Native Son*, Vol. 1, No. 6 (October 1899).

Euwer, Anthony. *The Friendly Firs*. Portland, OR: Binfords & Mort, 1931.

——. *The Limeratomy*..... New York: J.B. Pond, 1917.

Gatlin, George. *Some Must Wander*. Portland, OR: Metropolitan Press, 1934.

Grannatt, Harry Silleck. *The Pied Typer of Shrdlu-etaoin*. Portland, OR: Binfords & Mort, 1939.

Hammond, Eleanor. Seven poems in *The Lariat* (March 1923).

Kidd, Walter Evans. *Oregon Odyssey of Wheels* (by Conrad Pendleton [i.e. W.E. Kidd]). Fort Smith, AK: South and West, Inc., 1973.

——. "Calf Pasture Gate." *The Frontier*, Volume XIII, No. 1 (November 1932).

Land, T.C. "My First Impressions of the Coquille Valley," in Dodge, Orvile. *Pioneer History of Coos and Curry Counties, Or.* Bandon, OR: Western World Publishers-Printers, 1969, 407-412.Lee, Borghild. In *Oregon Poets*. Henry Harrison, ed. New York: Henry Harrison, 1935.

——. Six poems in *The Lariat* (January 1925).

Lister, Queene B. "Youth." In *The American Mercury*. (November 1929).

Parrish, Rob Roy. *Echoes from the Valley*. Portland, OR: George H. Hymes, Printer and Publisher, 1884.

Parsons, Mabel Holmes. *Listener's Room*. Portland, OR: Binfords & Mort, 1940.

Peers, Henry N. (Piscator). "Adventures of a Columbia Salmon." *Oregon Spectator*, Vol. II, No. 16 (September 2, 1847).

Powers, Ruth McBride. In *Oregon Poets*. Henry Harrison, ed. New York: Henry Harrison, 1935.

Skavlan, Margaret. In *Oregon Poets*. Henry Harrison, ed. New York: Henry Harrison, 1935.

Walking Bull, Montana. *Wo Ya-ka-pi: Telling Stories of the Past and Present by American Indians*. with Gilbert Walking Bull. Monmouth, OR: Bull, 1976.

——.See poems in *Calapooya Collage* 12. (Monmouth, OR: Western Oregon State College, 1988).

Anthologies

Brown, R.D., Thomas Kranidas, and Faith G. Norris, eds. *Oregon Signatures*. Corvallis: Oregon State College Press, 1959.

Harrison, Henry. *Oregon Poets: An Anthology of 50 Contemporaries*. New York: Henry Harrison, Poetry Publisher, 1935. Foreword by Ethel Romig Fuller.

Lerner, Andrea, ed. *Dancing on the Rim of the World: An Anthology of Northwest Native American Writing*. Tucson, AZ: Sun Tracks and The University of Arizona Press, 1990.

Lockley, Fred, ed. *The Lockley Files*. Compiled and edited by Mike Helm. Eugene, OR: Rainy Day Press, 1981.

Merriam, H.G., ed. *Northwest Verse*. Caldwell, ID: Caxton Printers, 1931.

Moore, Dallas, ed. *Sunset Trails: An Anthology of Recent Oregon Verse*. Corvallis, OR: The New University Press, 1933.

Poetry Clinic. *A Gift of Words: A Collection of Original Poetry by Douglas County and Umpqua Territory Poets*. Roseburg, OR: The Poetry Clinic, 1952.

Powers, Alfred. *Poems of the Covered Wagons*. Portland, OR: Pacific Publishing House, 1947.

Ramsey, Jarold. *Coyote Was Going There: Indian Literature of the Oregon Country*. Seattle: University of Washington Press, 1977.

Strelow, Michael, and *Northwest Review* staff. *An Anthology of Northwest Writing: 1900-1950*. Eugene, OR: Northwest Review Books, University of Oregon, 1979.

Swann, Brian. *Song of the Sky: Versions of Native American Songs and Poems.* Ashuelot, NH: Four Zoas Night House, Ltd., 1985.

Trusky, A. Thomas, ed. *Women Poets of the West: An Anthology, 1850-1950.* Boise, ID: Ahsahta Press, 1978. (Contains poems by Ella Higginson and Hazel Hall.)

Verseweavers. *Fabric of Song.* Portland, OR: Loomis Printing Company, 1945.

———. *Fabric of Song, Volume II.* Mill Valley, CA: The Wings Press, 1955.

Wentworth, May, ed. *Poetry of the Pacific.* San Francisco: Pacific Publishing Company, 1867.

Supplementary Bibliography, Part V

Selected Regional Periodicals Publishing Oregon Poets

Bellingham Review
Calapooya Collage
Calyx
Cutbank
Denali
The Eugene Magazine
Field
Fine Madness
Fireweed
High Plains Literary Review
The Hispanic
Hubbub
Mississippi Mud
Mr. Cogito
Northwest Review
Oregon English Journal
Oregon Times
Poet and Critic
Poetry Northwest
Poetry Now
The Pointed Circle
Portland Review
Silverfish Review
Three Rivers Poetry Journal
The University of Portland Review

Sources and Copyright Acknowledgments

Every effort has been made to find the legal copyright holders of the material reproduced herein. If for some reason we have overlooked a copyright holder who should be acknowledged, we have done so inadvertently or because our best efforts to do so failed. Thus all of these works are reprinted in good faith. If anyone can bring to our attention copyrighted material the holders of which we have not acknowledged, we shall be happy to do so in a subsequent edition.

Part I. Native Singing: Oregon Tribal Lyrics

"Moon Eclipse Exorcism." Schwerner, Armand. *Shaking the Pumpkin: Traditional Poetry of the Indian North Americas*, ed. Jerome Rothenberg. New York: Doubleday, 1972. Source: Frachtenberg, Leo J. *Alsea Tales and Myths.* U.S. Bureau of American Ethnology, Bulletin No. 67, 1920.

"Thunderstorm Exorcism." Ramsey, Jarold, editor and compiler. *Coyote Was Going There.* Seattle: University of Washington Press, 1977. Reprinted by permission of University of Washington Press. Source: Frachtenberg, Leo J. *Alsea Tales and Myths.* U.S. Bureau of American Ethnology, Bulletin No. 67, 1920.

"Morning Song." Ramsey, Jarold. *Love in an Earthquake.* Seattle: University of Washington Press, 1973. Source: Herbert Spinden, "Nez Perce Tales." In *Folk Tales of Salish and Sahaptin Tribes*, ed. Franz Boas. Memoirs of the American Folklore Association, 1917.

"Three Guardian Spirit Songs of Mad Coyote." Spinden, Herbert J. *Songs of the Tewa.* New York: The Exposition of Indian Tribal Arts, 1933.

"Spirit-Power Songs." Jacobs, Elizabeth D. *Nehalem Tillamook Tales*, ed. Melville Jacobs. Corvallis, Oregon: Oregon State University Press, 1990.

"Clackmas Lyrics." Jacobs, Melville. "Clackamas Chinook Myths and Tales." In *The Content and Style of an Oral Literature.* New York: Wenner-Gren Foundation, 1959.

"When It Storms in Winter." Hymes, Dell, trans. *Calapooya Collage* 16. Source: Sapir, Edward. *Takelma Texts.* Philadelphia: Anthropologocial Publications of the University of Pennsylvania Museum, Vol. 2, No. 1, 1909.

"When the New Moon Appears." Hymes, Dell, trans. *Calapooya Collage* 16. Source: Sapir, Edward. *Takelma Texts.* Philadelphia: Anthropologocial Publications of the University of Pennsylvania Museum, Vol. 2, No. 1, 1909.

"A Tualatin Shaman Named Shimxin." Unpublished. By permission of the author. Source: Jacobs, Melville. *Santiam Kalapuya Ethnologic Texts.* Seattle: University of Washington Publications in Anthropology, Vol. 11, 1945.

"The Shaman Cimxin of the Tualatins." Gogol, John M. *Native American Words.* Portland, Oregon: Takmahnawis Publishers, 1973. Source: Jacobs, Melville. *Santiam Kalapuya Ethnologic Texts.* Seattle: University of Washington Publications in Anthropology, Vol. 11, 1945.

"Incantations." Gatschet, Albert Samuel. *The Klamath Indians of Southwestern Oregon.* Washington: Government Printing Office, Department of the Interior, 1890.

"Songs of Satire and Social Criticism." Gatschet, Albert Samuel. *The Klamath Indians of Southwestern Oregon.* Washington: Government Printing Office, Department of the Interior, 1890.

"Cooing and Wooing Songs." Gatschet, Albert Samuel. *The Klamath Indians of Southwestern Oregon.* Washington: Government Printing Office, Department of the Interior, 1890.

"The Walkers (Animals) and Winged Things (Birds) Fought." Jacobs, Melville. *Coos Myth Texts.* Seattle: University of Washington Publications in Anthropology, Vol. 8, No. 2, 1940. Reprinted by permission of the University of Washington Press.

"My Sweetheart." Jacobs, Melville. "A Recent Study of the Dreams of the Coos, With Some Examples." In Alfred Powers, *History of Oregon Literature*. Portland, Oregon: Metropolitan Press, 1935, pp. 12-17.

"Cradle Song." Gatschet, Albert Samuel. "Songs of the Modoc Indians." *American Anthropologist,* Vol. VII (January 1894) and Judson, Katherine Berry. *Myths and Legends of the Pacific Northwest.* Chicago: A.C. McClurg, 1910.

"How the Animals Found Their Places." Ramsey, Jarold. *Love in an Earthquake.* Seattle: University of Washington Press, 1973. Source: Kelly, Isabel. "Northern Paiute Tales." *Journal of American Folklore,* 51 (1938).

"The Thunder Badger." Ramsey, Jarold. *Love in an Earthquake.* Seattle: University of Washington Press, 1973. Source: Marsden, W.L. "The Northern Paiute Language of Oregon." *University of California Publications in American Archaeology and Ethnology,* Vol. 20 (1923).

"Girls' Game." Ramsey, Jarold. *Love in an Earthquake.* Seattle: University of Washington Press, 1973. Source: Jacobs, Melville. *Texts in Chinook Jargon.* Seattle: University of Washington Publications in Anthropology, Vol. 7, No. 1, 1936.

"A Kalapuya Prophecy." Ramsey Jarold. In Rothenberg, Jerome, ed. *Shaking the Pumpkin: Traditional Poetry of the Indian North Americas.* Revised ed. New York: Alfred van der Marck Editions, 1986. Source: Jacobs, Melville. *Santiam Kalapuya Ethnologic Texts.* Seattle: University of Washington Publications in Anthropology, Vol. 11, 1945.

Parts II-IV

Anonymous. "Drunk for a Week." *The New Northwest* (October 27, 1871).

Anonymous. "To the Oregon Emigrants of 1846." *Oregon Spectator*, Vol 1, No. 17 (September 17, 1846).

Anonymous ("T"). "The Bachelor's Decision." *Oregon Spectator*, Vol. 1,No. 25 (January 21, 1847).

Bailey, Margaret Jewett. "We Call Them Savage." *The Grains. Or, Passages in the Life of Ruth Rover, With Occasional Pictures of Oregon, Natural and Moral.* Portland, Oregon: Carter & Austin, Printers, 1854. Reprinted with a foreword by Edwin Bingham. Corvallis, Oregon: Oregon State University Press, 1986.

Baldwin, Henry H. "The Wreck" from *Pioneer History of Coos and Curry Counties, Oregon* by Orvil Dodge. Bandon, OR: Western World Publishers-Printers, 1969. Reprinted by permission of Western World.

Barnard, Mary. "Roots" and "Logging Trestle" from *Collected Poems.* Copyright © 1979 by Mary Barnard. Reprinted by permission of the author.

Bright, Verne. "Stone Breaker." *The Frontier and Midland*, Vol. XVI (1935-36). "Strange Fruit." *The Frontier*, Vol. XII, No. 3 (March 1932).

Brown, Valentine. "The Chinook Wind." *Tales and Other Verse.* Portland, Oregon: published by the author, 1904.

Clarke, Samuel A. "Legend of the Cascades." *Harper's New Monthly Magazine*, Vol. XLVII, No. CCLXXXV (February 1874).

Coffield, Glen. "Crossing Hawthorne Bridge." *Northwest Poems.* Portland, Oregon: Rose City Publishers, 1954.

Cooke, Belle W. "Snow Birds." *Tears & Victory.* Salem, Oregon: E.M. Waite, 1871.

Corning, Howard McKinley. "Pruning Vines." *This Earth and Another Country.* Portland, Oregon: Tall Pine Imprints, 1969.

Davies, Mary Carolyn. "War." *The Drums in Our Street.* New York: The Macmillan Company, 1918. "Traps." *Youth Riding.* New York: The Macmillan Company, 1919.

"Appreciations II," "The Circuit Rider." *The Skyline Trail*. Indianapolis, Indiana: The Bobbs-Merrill Company, 1924.

Davis, H. L. "Proud Riders" and "The Rain Crow." From *The Selected Poems of H. L. Davis* by H. L. Davis. Boise State University, Boise, ID: Ahsahta Press, 1978. Reprinted by permission of Ahsahta Press.

DeFrees, Madeline. "Horatio Alger (1834-1899)," from *Imaginary Ancestors*. Seattle: Broken Moon Press, 1990. Copyright © 1990 by Madeline DeFrees. "What the Coastwise Know" from *The Light Station on Tillamook Rock*. Lewisburg, PA: The Press of Appletry Alley, Collectors' Limited Edition, 1989. Trade Edition, Corvallis: Arrowwood Books, Inc., 1990. Copyright © by Madeline DeFrees. Reprinted by permission of the author.

Eberman, Willis. "The Others" and "The Journey." *The Pioneers and Other Poems*. Portland, Oregon: Binfords & Mort, 1959. Copyright © 1959 Binford & Mort Publishers. Reprinted by permission. "Elk." *Chants for the Shades of Animals and Other Poems*. Portland, Oregon: Dunham Printing Co., 1967.

Emerson, Helen. "Forgive Me, Grandma" first appeared in *Forum*, vol. XXXVI (4), Autumn 1985. Muncie Indiana: Ball State University. Reprinted by permission of the author.

Everson, William. "The Raid." *Eastward the Armies: Selected Poems 1935-1942*. Torrance, California: Labyrinth Editions, 1980.

Fuller, Ethel Romig. "Fireweed" and "These Are the Strong." *White Peaks and Green*. Chicago: Willett, Clark and Colby, 1928.

Gale, Vi. "Cape Foulweather" and "At That, the Day Ended Well." *Odd Flowers and Short Eared Owls*. Portland, Oregon: Prescott Street Press, 1984. Copyright © 1964, 1970, 1974, 1984 by Vi Gale. Reprinted by permission of the author.

Haislip, John. "At Grandmothers" from *Not Every Year*. Seattle: University of Washington Press, 1971. "The Visit" from *Seal Rock*. Daleville, IN: The Barnwood Press, 1986. Reprinted by permission of the author.

Hall, Hazel. "Measurements," "Monograms." *Curtains*. New York: John Lane Company, 1921. "Inheritance." *Cry of Time*. New York: E.P. Dutton & Co., Inc., 1928.

Hall, James B. "Memorial Day: 1959" from *Bereavements: Selected and Collected Poems*, Story Line Press, 1991. Reprinted by permission of the author.

Hanson, Kenneth O. "Eels at the Dalles" and "First of All" copyright © by Kenneth Hanson. Reprinted by permission of the author.

Hartless, William. "I Am the Only One Now" retranslation by Dell Hymes. Reprinted by permission of Mr. Hymes.

Hedges, Ada Hastings. "Neighbor," "The Desert Wife: III, X, XII," and "Silent Juniper" from *Desert Poems* by Ada Hastings Hedges. Portland: Metropolitan Press, 1930. Reprinted by permission of Binford & Mort Publishing Co.

Higginson, Ella. "Hate" and "God's Creed." *When the Birds Go North Again*. New York: Macmillan, 1903.

Hitchcock, George. "May All Earth Be Clothed in Light" from *The Wounded Alphabet*, Jazz Press, 1984. Reprinted by permission of the author.

Hoff, Clara S. "Plow-Woman in Time of War." *Fabric of Song*. Vol. II, by Verseweavers Poetry Society. Mill Valley, California: The Wings Press, 1955.

Holmstrom, Frances. "The High Lead Tree," "The Shearers," and "Values" from *Western Windows* by Frances Holmstrom. Portland: Metropolitan Press, 1937. Reprinted by permission of Binford & Mort Publishing Co.

Huffman, Burt. "Umatilla County Statistics" from *Echoes of the Grande Ronde*. La Grande, OR: La Grande Printing Co., 1934. Copyright ©1934 by Eldridge Huffman. Reprinted by permission of Joyce Huffman.

Hunt, Joe. "I Leave the Myths," retranslation by Dell H. and Virginia Hymes. *Calapooya Collage* 13 (August 1989). Original dictation first collected by Melville Jacobs, *Northwest Sahaptin Texts* (Seattle: University of Washington Publications in Anthropology, 1929), I, 181-82. Reprinted by permission of Mr. Hymes.

Issei Poets of Hood River: Katsuko, "Two Haiku;" Tamu, "Haiku." *Issei: A History of Japanese Immigrants in North America.* Kazuo Ito, editor. Translated by Shinichiro Nakamura and Jean S. Gerard. Seattle: Executive Committee for Publication of *Issei: A History of Japanese Immigrants in North America*, 1973. Pp. 494, and 497. Made and printed in Japan by Japan Publications, Inc.

Iwatsuki, Shique. "At Tule Lake Camp" and "Returning Home." Translated by Stephen W. Kohl. *Turning Shadows Into Light: Art and Culture of the Northwest's Early Asian/Pacific Community.* Seattle Young Pine Press, 1982. Reprinted by permission of Mr. Kohl.

Kambouris, Haralambos. "Peripetias." *Pages of my Life.* Manuscript Diary. Demotic Greek and English Trans. Manuscripts Division of the Marriott Library, Greek Archives, Ms. 530. Salt Lake City, UT: University of Utah.

Lampman, Ben Hur. "How Could I Be Forgetting?" from *How Could I Be Forgetting?* by Ben Hur Lampman. Portland: Metropolitan Press, 1933. Reprinted by permission of Binford & Mort Publishing Co.

Lee, Anna Maria Pittman. "Must My Dear Companion Leave Me?" *History of Oregon Literature,* by Alfred Powers. Portland, Oregon: Metropolitan Press, 1935.

Le Guin, Ursula K. "The Grey Quaker" © 1988 by Ursula K. Le Guin from *Wild Oats and Fireweed* by Ursula K. Le Guin, Harper & Row, 1988. "To Walk In Here" © 1983 by Ursula K. Le Guin from *In the Red Zone* by Ursula K. Le Guin, Lord John Press, 1983. Reprinted by permission of the author. "An April Fools Day Present for my Daughter Elisabeth." Unpublished. Printed by permission of the author.

Markham, Edwin. "The Man with the Hoe." *The Man with the Hoe and Other Poems.* New York: Doubleday & McClure Company, 1899.

Markham, Elizabeth. "A Contrast on Matrimony" from *Poems* by Elizabeth Markham. Portland: J.K. Gill Co., 1921. Reprinted by permission of Brodart Co.

Matthews, Eleanor. "The Foragers." *Fabric of Song. Vol. II,* by Verseweavers Poetry Society. Mill Valley, California: The Wings Press, 1955.

McGahey, Jeanne. "Oregon Winter." *Homecoming With Reflections: Collected Poems.* Princeton, New Jersey: Quarterly Review of Literature, 1989.

McGinley, Phyllis. "Carol with Variations, 1936" copyright © 1932-1960 by Phyllis McGinley; Copyright 1938-42, 1944, 1958, 1959 by the Curtis Publishing Co. Used by permission of Viking Penguin, a division of Penguin Books USA Inc.

Miller, Joaquin. "Exodus for Oregon." *Joaquin Miller's Poems. Volume Two: Songs of the Sierras.* San Francisco: The Whitaker & Ray Company, 1909. (Reprinted in *The Complete Poetical Works of Joaquin Miller.* New York: Arno Press, 1972. "Pace Implora." *The West Shore* (October 1878).

Miller, Minnie Myrtle. "Have Mercy." *The New Northwest* (August 16, 1871).

Minto, John. "The Oregon Farmer's Song." *Rhymes of Early Life in Oregon and Historical and Biographical Facts.* Salem, Oregon: Statesman Publishing Co. (circa 1880).

Moll, Ernest G. "Sheep-Killer" from *Poems 1940-1955.* Sydney: Angus and Robertson, 1957. Reprinted by permission of the author.

Morden, Phyllis. "City Vignettes" appeared in *The Frontier.*

Morgan, Carrie Blake. "The Old Emigrant Road," "Faith." *The Path of Gold.* New Whatcom, Washington: Edson & Irish, 1900.

Olsen, Charles Oluf. "Zero Hour in the Factory." *May Days: An Anthology of Verse from Masses and The Liberator.* New York: Boni & Liveright, 1973.

Ostroff, Anthony. "Winter Salmon." *Northwest Review,* Vol. XIV., No. 3 (Spring 1975).

Partridge, Beverly. "January Lambing" from *Fireweed,* vol. 2 (2), January 1991; *Chadalsoin Review,* Summer 1990. Reprinted by permission of the author.

Pratt, Laurence. "Head Logger," "Chinese Laborers." *A Saga of a Paper Mill.* Caldwell, Idaho: The Caxton Printers, Ltd., 1935.

Reed, John. "America 1918" (excerpt Part I). *Collected Poems.* Westport, Connecticut: Lawrence Hill, 1985.

Salisbury, Ralph. "Come Near the Western Edge, I Try a Last Myth for the Childhood of My Sons." *Ghost Grapefruit and Other Poems.* Ithaca, NY: Ithaca House, 1972. "My Brother's Poem: Vietnamese War 1969." *Going to the Water: Poems of a Cherokee Heritage.* Eugene, Oregon: Pacific House Books, 1983.

Shannon, Ellen. "Daughter I." *Memory's Children.* Astoria, Oregon: Wayfaring Tree Press, 1985. Reprinted by permission of the author.

Simpson, Samuel L. "Beautiful Willamette." *The Gold-Gated West.* Philadelphia: J.B. Lippincott Company, 1910.

Snyder, Gary. "Bear" from *Left Out in the Rain: New Poems 1947-1985* by Gary Snyder. Copyright © 1986 by Gary Snyder. Reprinted by permission of North Point Press, a division of Farrar, Strous & Giroux, Inc. "Hay for the Horses" from *Riprap and Cold Mountain Poems* by Gary Snyder. Copyright © 1958, 1959, 1965 by Gary Snyder. Reprinted by permission of North Point Press, a division of Farrar, Strous, & Giroux, Inc.

Stafford, William. "Traveling Through the Dark" and "Fifteen" from *Stories That Could Be True* by William Stafford. New York: Harper & Row, 1977. Copyright © 1977 by William Stafford. Reprinted by permission of the author. "Assurance" appeared in *Smokes Way,* Graywolf Press, 1978.

Starkey, Robert. "A Specimen." *Sparks of Poetic Fire. A Collection of Poems.* Marshfield, Oregon: Coos Bay News Printing House, 1880.

Stevens, James. "Forest Sunrise," "Sunup Hangover." *Big Jim Turner.* Garden City, NY: Doubleday & Co., 1948.

Tracy, Paul. "Herder," "The Plumber," and "Pioneer on Aesthetics." From *Owyhee Horizons* by Paul Tracy. Caldwell, ID: the Caxton Printers Ltd., 1968. Reprinted by permission of the Caxton Printers, Ltd. "Horsemeat" appeared in *The Frontier.* Reprinted by permission.

Usada, Yoko. "Poem" from *North American Post,* Spring 1990. Translated by Keiko Tamizawa. Reprinted by permission.

Victor, Frances Fuller. "Do You Hear the Women Praying?" *The New Penelope and Other Stories and Poems.* San Francisco: A.L. Bancroft & Co., Printers, 1877.

Wata, Sam. "The Beginning of the Earth," arranged by Dell Hymes, from Isabel Kelly, "Northern Paiute Tales." *Journal of American Folklore,* 51 (1938): 437-438. Reprinted in *Coyote Was Going There,* edited by Jarold Ramsey. Seattle: University of Washington Press 1977. Reprinted by permission of Mr. Hymes.

White, Willis. "Ace Carey and the Bear." *A Century of Coos and Curry History of Southwest Oregon,* by Emil K. Peterson and Alfred Powers. Portland, Oregon: Binfords & Mort, Publishers, 1952. Reprinted by permission of Coos County Historical Society.

Wood, Charles Erskine Scott (C.E.S.). "First Snow" and "Poet in the Desert: XLII, LI (excerpt)." *Collected Poems.* New York: The Vanguard Press, Inc., 1949.

Woodward, Henry H. "The Homeless Girl." *Lyrics of the Umpqua.* New York: John B. Alden, Publisher, 1889.

Part V

Allen, Paula Gunn. "What the Moon Said" and "Dear World" from *Skins and Bones,* West End Press, 1988. Copyright © 1988 by Paula Gunn Allen. Reprinted by permission of the author.

Appel, Dori. "A Double Life" from *Yankee* magazine, 1989, reprinted by permission of the author.

Axelrod, David. "Skill of the Heart" from *Jerusalem of Grass*, Ahsahta Press. Copyright © 1992 by David Axelrod. Reprinted by permission of the author.

Baker, Alison. "Flying" first appeared as "Hunting" in *Interim*. Reprinted by permission of the author.

Barnes, Jim. "A Choctaw Chief Helps Plan a Festival in Memory of Pushmataha's Birthday" f om *The Fish on Poteau Mountain* by Jim Barnes. Copyright © 1980 by Cedar Creek Press. Reprinted by permission of the author.

Barnes, Timothy L. "Winter Fog Along the Willamette" from *CutBank 12* reprinted by permission of the author.

Barrington, Judith. "Beating the Dog" was published in *And a Deer's Ear, Eagle's Song and Bear's Grace*, ed. Theresa Corrigan and Stephanie Hoppe, Cleis Press, 1988. Reprinted by permission of the author.

Bird, Gloria. "The Women Fell Like Beautiful Horses" appeared in *CALYX*, Vol. 12, no. 3. "My Digging Stick" and "The Women Fell Like Beautiful Horses" reprinted by permission of the author.

Broumas, Olga. "Cinderella" appeared in *Beginning With O*, Yale University Press, 1977. "Sweeping the Garden" appeared in *Soie Sauvage*, Copper Canyon Press, 1980. Reprinted by permission of the author.

Bush, John. "Puller on the *Ann*" won an honorable mention in the *Atlantic* competition, 1974 and appeared in *Underpass*, 1974. It was also included in the anthology *Oregon East 1950-1985*, 1985. Reprinted by permission of the author.

Carlile, Henry. "Train Whistles in the Wind and Rain" from *Shenandoah*, 1991; *The Pushcart Prize*, XVII: *Best of the Small Presses*, 1992; *Rain*, Carnegie Mellon University Press, 1993. Reprinted by permission of the author.

Carver, Raymond. "Still Looking Out for Number One" and "Where Water Comes Together with Other Water" reprinted by permission of Tess Gallagher.

Castañares, Tina. "Three Deer" and "In Eastern Oregon" [for Pablo]. Reprinted by permission of the author.

Chin, Marilyn. "The Floral Apron" and "Gruel" were first published in *Ploughshares*. Both poems are included in *The Phoenix Gone, The Terrace Empty* to be published by Milkweed Editions, Spring 1994. Reprinted by permission of the author.

Christensen, Linda. "He Looks for Worms," which originally appeared in *Oregon English Journal,* and "How to Act Male at My Mother's House Over the Holidays" reprinted by permission of the author.

Costanzo, Gerald P. "Dinosaurs of the Hollywood Delta" from *Kansas Quarterly, The Pushcart Prize* X, 1985-86. New York: Pushcart/Penguin Books. Reprinted by permission of the author.

Crawford, Tom. "Otis Cafe" printed by permission of the author.

Culligan, Kathleen. "Something Learned about Fish" first appeared in *Chimes 93*, St. Mary's College, Notre Dame, Indiana. Reprinted by permission of the author.

Curtis, Walt. "Cabbages in the Garden" from *Rhymes For Alice Blue Light*, Lynx House Press, was chosen for a Prescott Street Press postcard series. Reprinted by permission of the author.

Daniel, John. "Dependence Day" first appeared in *Poetry*. Copyright © 1990 by the Modern Poetry Association. Reprinted by permission.

Diaz-Horna. Efrain. "For John Sinclair" reprinted by permission of the author.

Drake, Albert. "Garage" appeared in *Garage*. Santa Barbara: Mudborn Press. Reprinted by permission of the author.

Drake, Barbara. "Shy Child" from *What We Say to Strangers*, Breitenbush Publications, 1987, and "Stink Ant" reprinted by permission of the author.

Driscoll, Jeremy. "Praying" was first published in the author's collection *Some Morning*, Two Rivers Press, 1980; and again in *Some Other Morning*. Story Line Press, 1992. Reprinted by permission of the author.

Durbin, Libby. "Between Jobs" from *California Quarterly*, Spring 1990, No. 32/33. Reprinted by permission of the author.

Eberman, Alice Ann. "Finding" originally appeared in *CALYX, A Journal of Art and Literature by Women*, vol. 12 (1), Summer 1989. Reprinted by permission of the author.

Edmo, Ed. "Indian Education Blues" printed by permission of the author.

Epple, Juan. "The Oregon Trail" in Spanish and English. English translation by Steven White. Reprinted by permission of the author.

Ferrell, Wm. "The Ground War" appeared in *Mr. Cogito*. Used by permission of the author.

Gogol, John. "Boy in a Cherry Tree" from *Mr. Cogito*, vol. IX (3), 1990. Reprinted by permission of the author.

Hagen, Cecelia. "My Children Are the Bright Flowers" originally appeared in *Exquisite Corpse*. Reprinted by permission of the author.

Harper, Michael S. "We Assume: On the Death of Our Son, Reuben Masai Harper" copyright © 1970, 1985 by Michael S. Harper. Originally appeared in *Dear John, Dear Coltrane*, University of Pittsburgh Press; reprinted by University of Illinois Press, 1985. Reprinted by permission of the author.

Heynen, Jim. "During the First Three Minutes of Life" from *Out of This World: Poems for the Hawkeye State*, Iowa State University Press. Reprinted by permission of the author.

Howell, Christopher. "Bird Love" from *Poetry Northwest*, 1991. Reprinted by permisison of the author.

Imani, Carol. "like a wandering jew" reprinted by permission of the author.

Inada, Lawson F. "The Shovel People" originally appeared in *Legends from Camp* by Lawson Inada, Coffee House Press, 1993. Reprinted by permission of publisher and author. Copyright © 1993 by Lawson Inada.

Jensen, Peter. "Barracuda" was published in *Confluence* in 1992. Reprinted by permission of the author.

Johnson, David. "Li's Poem" and "Vaudeville In the Garden" from *Confluence*. Walking Bird Press, 1992. Reprinted by permission of the author.

Johnson, Harold. "The Names of Summer: A War Memory" was published in *Fireweed*, October, 1991. Reprinted by permission of the author.

Kelly, Brigit. "Those Who Wrestle with the Angel for Us" from *To the Place of Trumpets*, Yale University Press, 1988. Reprinted by permission.

Killeen, Ger. "The Sowing Fiddle" from *Hubbub* and "A Full Bucket" reprinted by permission of the author.

Kirk, Lee Crawley. "With Stars in My Forehead" from *Calapooya Collage* 14. Reprinted by permission of the author.

Klauke, Amy. "Recognizable Terrors" and "As You Pass" reprinted by permission of the author.

Krysl, Marilyn. "Feet" from *Midwife*. New York: National League for Nursing, 1989. Reprinted by permission of the author.

La Morticella, Barbara. "Valentines" reprinted by permission of the author.

Ladd-Bruni, Nela. "Enemy and Friend." Grateful acknowledgment is made to the editors and publishers of the folowing publications in which this poem first appeared: Timberline, *Women's Struggles, Women's Visions.*

Leong, Wing K. "Ripe Autumn Grapes" reprinted by permission of the author.

May, Kerry Paul. "The Gift" first appeared in *Pacifica Literary Awards Magazine* sponsored by the Lane Literary Guild and Lane Regional Arts Council, 1987. Reproduced by permission of the author.

McPherson, Sandra. "Lament, with Flesh and Blood" © 1988 by Sandra McPherson. From "Streamers" by Sandra McPherson, published by the Ecco Press. Reprinted by permission.

Mestas, Juan. "Ephesus 91" originally appeared in *The Portlander*, vol. II, 1993-94. Reprinted by permission.

Miranda, Gary. "Horse Chestnut" and "Love Poem" are from *Listeners at the Breathing Place* (1979) and *Grace Period*(1983), respectively, both from Princeton University Press. Reprinted by permission of the author.

Moody, Rodger. "Night Shift" first appeared in *Permafrost*; copyright © 1980 by *Permafrost.* Reprinted by permission of *Permafrost* and Rodger Moody.

Muller, Erik. "Mare" from *Confluence: Selected Poems* by Peter Jensen, Erik Muller, and David Johnson. Eugene: Walking Bird Press, 1992.

Niflis, Michael. "Old Movie Monsters" appeared in *Harper's Magazine.* "Thunderstorm" appeared in the *Nation.* Reprinted by permission of the author.

Orr, Verlena. "Learning the Language From Dad" first appeared in *Northwest Magazine.* Reprinted by permission of the author.

Pavlich, Walter. "Three Hearts of the Octopus" is reprinted from *Running Near the End of the World* by Walter Pavlich. Iowa City, Iowa: University of Iowa Press, 1992. Copyright © 1992 by Walter Pavlich. Reprinted by permission of the author.

Peña-Reyes, Myrna. "No More War, 1945" from *Solidarity,* May-June 1988, Manila, Phillipines. Reprinted by permission of the author.

Petersen, Paulann. "Moles" from *Blue Unicorn* and "The Moon Recounts the Birth of the Sun" from *Sequoia* reprinted by permission of the author.

Powell, Amanda. "Square Dance at the Fairgrounds" reprinted by permission of the author.

Quinn, John. "The Trough at Rockwall Spring" first appeared in *Oregon Historical Quarterly,* vol. LXXVI (2), and was reprinted in *Cold Drill,* 1993. "In Oregon" first appeared in *Northwest Review*, vol. XIV (3), and was included in *The Wolf Last Seen,* Abattoir Editions, 1980, and Pacific House Books, 1987. Reprinted by permission of the author.

Ramsey, Jarold W. "The Kit" from *Hand Shadows*, copyright © 1989 by the *Quarterly Review of Literature.* Reprinted by permission of the author. "

Root, Judith. "Free Will and the River." First appeared in the *Nation.* Copyright © 1988 by Judith Root. Reprinted by permission of the author.

Runciman, Lex. "Fathers and Infants" copyright © 1989 by Lex Runciman, from *The Admirations* (Lynx House Press). Reprinted by permission of the author.

Rutsala, Vern. "The World" and "Lela and Others" from *Selected Poems* by Vern Rutsala, Story Line Press, 1991. Copyright © 1991 by Vern Rutsala. Reprinted by permission of the author.

Scates, Maxine. "Perfume" and "Salem: Two Windows" are reprinted from *Toluca Street* by Maxine Scates, by permission of the University of Pittsburgh Press. Copyright © 1989 by Maxine Scates.

Scofield, Sandra. "Shallows" reprinted by permission of the author.

Sears, Peter. "The Lady Who Got Me to Say Solong Mom" from *Portland Review* and "Halloween of the Sudden Hand" reprinted by permission of the author.

Severson, Karyl. "Tejon Pass" reprinted by permission of the author.

Skloot, Floyd. "You Asked for It" previously appeared in *Harper's*, January, 1988, and in the *New England Review*. Reprinted by permission of the author.

Spady, Susan. "Underpants" originally published by *CALYX, A Journal of Art and Literature by Women*, vol. 13:2, Summer, 1991. Reprinted by permission of the author.

St. John, Primus. "Pearle's Poem" reprinted by permission of the author.

Stafford, Kim. "The Rocking Chair" and "Sermon on Eve" copyright © 1982 by Kim R. Stafford. Reprinted by permission of the author from The Granary, Carnegie-Mellon University Press.

Starck, Clem. "Slab On Grade" and "Me and Maloney" appear in *Journeyman's Wages*, to be published by StoryLine Press in 1993. Reprinted by permission of the author.

Steinman, Lisa M. "A Pigeon Poem" first appeared in *Café Solo* (number 4) and in *Lost Poems* (Ithaca House, 1976). Reprinted by permission of the author.

Sussman, Kaz. "El Conjuncto Fabuloso" previously published in *Denali*. Reprinted by permission of the author.

Sweet, William. "Field Burning" first appeared in *Stone City I*, Ron Talney, ed., 1977. Reprinted by permission of the author.

Thalman, Mark. "Catching the Limit" first appeared in *Calussa Review*, 1989. Reprinted by permission of the author.

Tremblay, Gail. "Strategies to Survive Living in White Towns" reprinted by permission of the author.

Venn, George. "Forgive Us . . ." appeared in *Off the Main Road*, Prescott Street Press, 1978. "Conjuring a Basque Ghost" appeared in *Marking the Magic Circle*, Oregon State University Press, 1987. Reprinted by permission.

Wallace, D. M. "The Jewel" first appeared in *Lactuca*; copyright © 1989 by *Lactuca*. Reprinted by permission of *Lactuca* and D. M. Wallace.

Walls, Doyle Wesley. "Clean Dirt" from *The Texas Anthology*, Sam Houston State University Press, 1979. "Homework" from *Pax: A Journal for Peace Through Culture*, vol. 4 (1), Spring 1987. Reprinted by permission.

Wendt, Ingrid. "Mushroom Picking, I Talk with a Bear" from *Singing the Mozart Requiem*, Breitenbush Publications, 1987. Copyright © 1987 by Ingrid Wendt. Reprinted by permission.

Wilson, Miles. "For San Dwayne Francisco Missing in Action, North Vietnam" appeared in *New Mexico Humanities Review*. Reprinted by permission of the author.

Witte, John. "Breast Poem" first appeared in the *New England Review*. "Blue School" first appeared in the *Ohio Review*. Used by permission.

Wixon, Vincent. "Rain" reprinted by permission of the author.

Wyttenberg, Victoria. "The School Photographer" was first published in *Poetry Northwest*, 1990. Reprinted by permission of the author.

ART

Cover of paperback edition: Detail from "Southern Exposure" by Jennifer Joyce. Watercolor. From the Art about Agriculture collection, Oregon State University.

Part I, page 9: Indian stone sculpture of owl, originally found on Sauvie Island. Date unknown. Courtesy of the Oregon Historical Society, order number OrHi37752.

Part II, page 31: "Oregon—A Mail Carrier in the Forest" by "W.H.B." Cover illustration from *West Shore*, "an illustrated journal published every Saturday" for Portland, Oregon, and Spokane Falls, Washington. August 23, 1890.

Part III, page 61: "Men in the Park" by Arthur Runquist, 1945-46. Casein on paper. Reproduced courtesy of the Portland Art Museum, Vivian and Gordon Gilkey Collection.

Part IV, page 95: "Head" by Amanda Snyder. Ink and crayon. Reproduced courtesy of the Portland Art Museum, Vivian and Gordon Gilkey Collection.

Part V, page 153: "Platter" by Baba Wague Diakite, 1991. Ceramic. Courtesy of Jamison Thomas Gallery.

AUTHOR PHOTOGRAPHS

The Oregon Council of Teachers of English and the Oregon State University Press would like to thank the following for providing photographs of authors and for permission to reproduce them: John B. Hudson, courtesy of the Smithsonian Institution; Annie Miner Peterson, from the Beckham Collection, courtesy Stephen Dow Beckham; Frances Holmstrom, courtesy of Anna Smith; Mary Barnard, photograph © Mary Randlett 1983; Madeline DeFrees, photograph by Jean Swift; Anthony Ostroff, courtesy of Miriam Ostroff; Ursula K. Le Guin, photograph by Marian Wood Kolisch © 1990; Tim Barnes, photograph by Ilka Kuzrik; Judith Barrington, photograph by Barbara Gundle 1989; Olga Broumas, photograph © by Ariel Jones; Henry Carlile, photograph by Kim Fortuny; Raymond Carver, photograph by Marion Ettlinger, courtesy of Tess Gallagher; Marilyn Chin, Department of English and Comparative Literature, San Diego State University; Gerald Costanzo, photograph by Gregg Wareham; Kathleen Culligan, photograph by Gary Poush; John Daniel, photograph by Marilyn Daniel; Juan Epple, photograph by Ted Polumbaum; Christopher Howell, photograph by Denny Miles; Lawson Fusao Inada, photograph by Helga Motley, 1992; Peter Jensen, courtesy of Walking Bird Press; Harold L. Johnson, courtesy of PSU Poetry Committee; Sandra McPherson, photograph by Walter Pavlich; Walter Pavlich, photograph by Sandra McPherson; John Quinn, photograph by Linda Quinn; Jarold Ramsey, courtesy of Photography Unit, University of Rochester; Judith Root, photograph by Kent Anderson; Maxine Scates, photograph by Bill Cadbury; Sandra Scofield, photograph by Christopher Briscoe; Kim Stafford, photograph by W.E. Stafford; Doyle Wesley Walls, photograph by Laurie G. Hill; Elizabeth Woody, photograph by Mel Buffington; Victoria Wyttenberg, photograph by Photo Art Commercial Studios.

The following photographs were provided courtesy of the late William Stafford: Howard McKinley Corning; William Stafford age 8; Vi Gale; Kenneth O. Hanson.

The following photographs of authors were provided courtesy of the Oregon Historical Society: Anna Maria Pittman Lee, negative number OrHi486; Henry H. Woodward, negative number OrHi89089; Samuel A. Clarke, negative number OrHi89087; Belle W. Cooke, negative number OrHi89088; Willis White, negative number OrHi89307; C.E.S. Wood, negative number OrHi56266; Ella Higginson, negative number OrHi25807; Ella Higginson age 10, negative number OrHi89313; Ethel Romig Fuller, negative number CN011155, photograph by Al Monner; Ada Hastings Hedges, negative number CN011423, photograph by Bushnell Studio; Ben Hur Lampman, negative number CN008900; Laurence Pratt, negative number OrHi89306; James Stevens, negative number OrHi27739; H.L.Davis, negative number OrHi27399; H.L. Davis age 3, negative number OrHi37616, collection of Quentin Davis at Douglas County Museum; Eleanor Matthews, negative number CN012756; Courtland Matthews .

The following photographs were provided by the authors: Helen Emerson; self-portrait by George Hitchcock; Beverly Partridge; John Haislip; Ralph Salisbury; Ernest G. Moll; William Stafford; Gary Snyder; Dori Appel; Jim Barnes; Gloria Bird; John Bush; Tina Castañares; Linda Christensen; Tom Crawford; Walt Curtis; Efrain Diaz-Horna; Albert Drake; Barbara Drake; Jeremy Driscoll; Libby A. Durbin; Alice Ann Eberman; Ed Edmo; William Ferrell; John M. Gogol; Cecelia Hagen; Jim Heynen; Carol Imani; David Johnson; Brigit Pegeen Kelly; Ger Killeen; Lee Crawley Kirk; Amy Klauke; Marilyn Krysl; Nela Ladd-Bruni; Wing K. Leong; Kerry Paul May; Juan Mestas; Gary Miranda; Rodger Moody; Erik Muller; Michael Niflis; Verlena Orr; Paulann Petersen; Amanda Powell; Lex Runciman; Vern Rutsala; Peter Sears; Karyl Severson; Floyd Skloot; Primus St. John; Clem Starck; Lisa M. Steinman; Kaz Sussman; Gail Tremblay; George Venn; Ingrid Wendt; Miles Wilson; John Witte; Vincent Wixon.

Photographs by Ron Finne: Lottle Evanoff; Elizabeth Markham; John Minto; Frances Fuller Victor; Joaquin Miller; Minnie Myrtle Miller; Samuel L. Simpson; Edwin Markham; William Hartless; Burt Huffman; Hazel Hall; John Reed; Mary Carolyn Davies; Mary Carolyn Davies as a baby; Paul Tracy; Clara Hoff; Phyllis McGinley; Phyllis McGinley age 6; Glen Coffield; James B. Hall.

Photographs by Susan Seubert: Shizue Iwatsuki (from *Turning Shadows into Light*, Young Pine Press, 1982); Jeanne McGahey (from *Quarterly Review of Literature*); Willis Eberman (from *The Pioneers and Other Poems*, Binford & Mort Publishers, 1959).

Index

Index of Titles

Index of Authors